WITHDRAW

UTSA LIBRARIES

D0403266

Six Justices on Civil Rights

DAVID C. BAUM
1934-73

DAVID C. BAUM MEMORIAL LECTURES

Six Justices
on Civil Rights

Edited and with an Introduction by
RONALD D. ROTUNDA

OCEANA PUBLICATIONS, INC.
London   Rome   New York

LIBRARY
The University of Texas
At San Antonio

© 1983 by Oceana Publications, Inc.

Frank and Kurland lecture reprinted from the University of Illinois *Law Forum,* Volume 1977, number 2; Coleman and Countryman lectures reprinted from the University of Illinois *Law Forum,* Volume 1978, number 2; Nathanson and Pollak lectures reprinted from the University of Illinois *Law Forum,* Volume 1979, number 2. All of these lectures are reprinted with the permission of the Board of Trustees of the University of Illinois.

LC82-62327
ISBN 0-379-20044-9

LIBRARY
The University of Texas
At San Antonio

Preface

Professor David C. Baum taught at the University of Illinois College of Law from 1963 until his death in early 1973, when he was less than forty years old. His family and friends endowed this lecture series — The David C. Baum Memorial Lectures on Civil Liberties and Civil Rights — not only in his memory but at his express request. Deep concern for the dignity and rights of all men was central to Professor Baum's character and activities.

After receiving his undergraduate and legal education at Harvard University, Professor Baum served as law clerk for Justice Walter V. Schaefer of the Illinois Supreme Court from 1959 to 1960. He then practiced law with the Chicago firm of Ross, McGowan, Hardies and O'Keefe until he joined the faculty of the University of Illinois College of Law in 1963.

Professor Baum was an inspiration to his students and colleagues not only because of the excellence of his teaching, scholarship, and public service, but because of his remarkable human qualities. Conscientious and judicious, blending passion for justice with dispassionate objectivity, he inspired the highest level of discourse and endeavor in all who had the privilege of knowing and working with him.

Former Solicitor General Erwin N. Griswold delivered the first Baum lecture on November 8, 1973, while he was visiting George A. Miller Professor at the University of Illinois College of Law. That lecture was published in the *University of Illinois Law Forum* and later republished in a separate monograph. A series of lectures delivered in 1974, 1975, and 1976, also first published in the *University of Illinois Law Forum,* were republished in 1977 by the University of Illinois Press in a separate volume with an introduction by Professor Victor J. Stone.

This book, focusing on judicial biography, marks the second volume in what has become a series of essays by distinguished academics, jurists, and practicing lawyers. In approximately two years the College of Law plans to publish the third volume in this series, collecting the papers delivered from the fall of 1979 through the spring of 1983.* It is hoped that The David C. Baum Memorial Lectures on Civil Liberties and Civil Rights will constitute a fitting memorial to a man whose unrelenting intellectual vigor and moral commitment made his presence in the world of law invaluable.

R.D.R.

September 1982
Champaign, Illinois

---

* The death of Professor Grant Gilmore in the spring of 1982 prevents the publication of his lecture on Oliver Wendell Holmes, Jr.

Contents

The David C. Baum Memorial Lectures: The First Decade

ERWIN N. GRISWOLD
The Supreme Court's Case Load: Civil Rights and Other Problems
Delivered November 8, 1973

PAUL A. FREUND
The Judicial Process in Civil Liberties Cases
Delivered November 7, 1974

WILLIAM H. HASTIE
Affirmative Action in Vindicating Civil Rights
Delivered March 20, 1975

FRANCIS A. ALLEN
The Judicial Quest for Penal Justice:
The Warren Court and The Criminal Cases
Delivered April 10, 1975

CHARLES L. BLACK, JR.
Civil Rights in Times of Economic Stress —
Jurisprudential and Philosophic Aspects
Delivered October 29, 1975

HARRY T. EDWARDS
Racial Discrimination in Employment: What Price Equality?
Delivered October 30, 1975

JOHN P. FRANK
Hugo L. Black: Free Speech and
the Declaration of Independence
Delivered October 13, 1976

PHILIP KURLAND
Justice Robert H. Jackson — Impact on Civil Rights
and Civil Liberties
Delivered October 14, 1976

WILLIAM T. COLEMAN, JR.
Mr. Justice Felix Frankfurter: Civil Libertarian as
Lawyer and as Justice: Extent to Which Judicial
Responsibilities Affected His Pre-Court Convictions
Delivered October 12, 1977

VERN COUNTRYMAN
Justice Douglas and Freedom of Expression
Delivered October 13, 1977

NATHANIEL NATHANSON
The Philosophy of Mr. Justice Brandeis and Civil Liberties Today
Delivered November 16, 1978

LOUIS H. POLLAK
Wiley Blount Rutledge: Profile of a Judge
Delivered March 22, 1979

C. CLYDE FERGUSON, JR.
International Human Rights
Delivered October 10, 1979

GRANT GILMORE
Some Reflections on Oliver Wendell Holmes, Jr.
Delivered March 13, 1980

DANIEL J. MEADOR
Civil Courts and Civil Rights
Delivered October 21, 1980

SEAN MacBRIDE
*The Enforcement of the International Law of Human Rights
and of Humanitarian Law*
Delivered March 26, 1981

SAMUEL DASH
Preventive Detention — Imprisonment without Trial
Delivered March 10, 1982

JESSE CHOPER
Defining "Religion" in the First Amendment
Delivered April 15, 1982

ARCHIBALD COX
Freedom of the Press
Delivered October 14, 1982

JOHN KAPLAN
*Civil Liberties and the Repression of Crime —
The Other Side of the Balance*
Delivered February 21, 1983

Introduction: Judicial Biography and the Nature of Judicial Review

RONALD D. ROTUNDA*

The young (only 30 years old) and brilliant New York attorney, Alexander Hamilton, frequently absented himself from the Constitutional Convention of 1787. He played no significant role there, although at the very end he delivered an impassioned plea for unanimous ratification of the Constitution. Yet the new Constitution and the young nation owed much to Hamilton, for when he left the Convention he labored tirelessly for ratification and wrote over half of *The Federalist Papers* in support of the new Constitution.

In his *Federalist* No. 78[1] he examined the judicial department and relied on that branch to safeguard the limitations drafted into the Constitution. While the judiciary is "incontestably" and "beyond comparison the weakest of the three departments of power,"[2] he conceded, nonetheless the Constitutional limitations on legislative excess "can be preserved in practice no other way than through the medium of courts of justice, *whose duty it must be to declare all acts contrary to the manifest tenor of the Constitution void.*"[3]

The legislators cannot be the constitutional judges of their own powers, he argued to those whose support of the new Constitution he sought. "It is far more rational to suppose, that the courts were designed to be an intermediate body between the people and the legislature, in order, among other things, to keep the latter within the limits assigned to their authority. *The interpretation of the laws is the proper and peculiar province of the courts.*"[4] If there is any "irreconcilable variance" between the Constitution and a statute, "that which has the superior obligation and validity ought, of course, to be preferred; or, in other words, the Constitution ought to be preferred to the statute, the intention of the people to the intention of their agents." Thus, "whenever a particular statute contravenes the Con-

---

* Professor of Law, University of Illinois College of Law.
 1. Published under the name of *Publius,* in 1788. See A. Hamilton, J. Jay, & J. Madison, the Federalist: A Commentary on the Constitution of the United States, which collects the series, which had begun appearing in the New York press on October 27, 1787. Hamilton wrote all of *Publius* on the judiciary. See J. Goebel, Jr., 1 The Oliver Wendell Holmes Devise History of the Supreme Court of the United States: Antecedents and Beginnings to 1801 (1971) at 312.
 2. Footnote omitted, quoting de Montesquieu stating that: "Of the three powers above mentioned, the judiciary is next to nothing."
 3. Emphasis added.
 4. Emphasis added. *Cf.* Marshall, C. J., in Marbury v. Madison, 5 U.S. (1 Cranch) 137, 177 (1803) ("It is emphatically the province and duty of the judicial department to say what the law is.").

stitution, it will be the duty of the judicial tribunals to adhere to the latter and disregard the former."

Hamilton quickly anticipated — and as quickly dismissed — any concern that a doctrine granting courts the right to declare legislative acts void "would imply a superiority of the judiciary to the legislative power." The doctrine of judicial review "only supposes that the power of the people is superior to both" the legislative and judicial power because "where the will of the legislature, declared in its statutes, stands in opposition to that of the people, declared in the Constitution, the judges ought to be governed by the latter rather than the former."

To those who would argue that the courts, "on the pretense of repugnancy, may substitute their own pleasure to the constitutional intentions of the legislature," Hamilton only responded that "[t]his might as well happen in the case of two contradictory statutes; or it might as well happen in every adjudication upon any single statute. The courts must declare the sense of the law; and if they should be disposed to exercise WILL instead of JUDGMENT, the Consequence would equally be the substitution of their pleasure to that of the legislative body."[5]

While Hamilton emphasized that the Constitution controlled over ordinary legislation, and that judges, who must interpret the Constitution just as they interpret ordinary statutes, should only follow the superior law of the Constitution, he never answered the more difficult question: how carefully should the judiciary scrutinize legislation challenged as unconstitutional? What if judges exercise "will" rather than "judgment"? As Charles Evans Hughes (who was to become Chief Justice in 1930) warned in 1907: "We are under a Constitution, but the Constitution is what the judges say it is."[6]

In *Marbury v. Madison*[7] Chief Justice John Marshall, speaking for the Court, for the first time actually invalidated an Act of Congress. While he did not cite Hamilton's *Federalist Papers* No. 78, he adopted much of Hamilton's reasoning. Marshall, however, unlike Hamilton, emphasized the language of the Constitution, specifically the Supremacy Clause.[8] In *Marbury* the Court invalidated a Congressional statute which was interpreted to expand the original jurisdiction of the Supreme Court, contrary to Article III of the Constitution, as inter-

---

5. Capitalization in the original. He concluded that because judges are the "bulwarks of a limited Constitution," their need for independence argues strongly for the life tenure which the Constitution guarantees.
6. Hughes, Speech before Elmira Chamber of Commerce in 1907, Addresses and Papers, 133, 139 (1908).
7. 5 U.S. (Cranch) 137 (1803).
8. While the Supremacy Clause was central to Marshall's reasoning, Hamilton never mentioned it.

> The Supremacy Clause provides:
>
> The Constitution, and the Laws of the United States which shall be made in Pursuance thereof; and all Treaties made, or which shall be made, under the Authority of the United States, shall be the supreme Law of the Land; and the Judges in every State shall be bound thereby, any Thing in the Constitution or Laws of any State to the Contrary notwithstanding.
>
> U.S. Const., art VI, §2.

preted by the Supreme Court. In justifying judicial review, Marshall gave the example of a person convicted of treason under a statute which declares that only one witness is necessary for conviction. The Constitution clearly states that "[n]o person shall be convicted of Treason unless on the Testimony of *two* Witnesses to the same overt Act . . ."[9] In the hypothetical, the Constitution requires a precise number of witnesses and the statute under review just as clearly did not meet the precise number. Does Marshall's example mean that he thought that the Court should only invalidate legislation which is clearly in conflict with the Constitution? Should — must — the Court, in cases of doubt, defer to the legislative judgment?

Marshall, like Hamilton before him, did not focus on this question, and few of their contemporaries probably even thought about it.[10] But subsequent judges and commentators certainly have, to the present day. These later analysts of the Supreme Court, in studying its role in the American polity, have also been concerned with the conflict between democracy and judicial review. In spite of Hamilton's assurances that under judicial review the judges merely enforce the popular will as expressed in the fundamental law of the Constitution, there is no doubt that judicial review, in a very fundamental sense, is at war with democratic rule. "Popular sovereignty suggests *will;* fundamental law suggests *limit.*"[11]

These two questions — how active should the Court be; to what extent does judicial review conflict with democratic rule — are very much related. The more active the Court is, the more it conflicts with majority rule.

Judge Learned Hand, for example, believed that the judicial power to invalidate legislation was "not a lawless act" but was hardly supported by the language of the Constitution, and that therefore it should be used sparingly, only when necessary to prevent the government from violating a clear and paramount constitutional principle.[12] Hand reasoned:

> [S]ince this power is not a logical deduction from the structure of the Constitution but only a practical condition upon its successful operation, it need not be exercised whenever a court sees, or thinks that it sees, an invasion of the Constitution. It is always a preliminary question how importunately the occasion demands an answer. It may be better to leave the issue to be worked out without authoritative solution; or perhaps the only solution available is one that the court has no adequate means to enforce.[13]

---

9. U.S. Const., art. III, §3, cl. 1. (emphasis added). The clause goes on to state that in lieu of two witnesses a confession in open court is sufficient.
10. One of Hamilton's coauthors of the *Federalist Papers,* James Madison, thought that the Supreme Court would only invalidate laws that *clearly* violated the Constitution. See R. McCloskey, the American Supreme Court 9 (1960).
11. R. McCloskey, The American Supreme Court 12 (1960) (emphasis in original).
12. L. Hand, The Bill of Rights 14-29 (1958).
13. L. Hand, n. 13 supra, at 15.

Hand's argument for judicial self-restraint relies on the other branches of government to fulfill their constitutional responsibility. He was concerned that too frequent a use of judicial power atrophies the other organs of government. Judicial review is "always attended with a serious evil, namely that the correction of legislative mistakes comes from the outside, and the people thus lose the political experience, and moral education and the stimulus that comes from fighting the question out in the ordinary way and correcting their own errors." Thus judicial activism, as Professor Thayer warned, "dwarf[s] the political capacity of the people, and . . . deaden[s] its sense of moral responsibility."[14] Professor Thayer, as Hand, would therefore exercise review only in the most extreme cases. A court can only disregard a law subject to constitutional attack "when those who have the right to make laws have not merely made a mistake, but have made a very clear one, — so clear that it is not open to rational question."[15]

In contrast, Professor Herbert Wechsler was satisfied that since the framers intended to create the power of judicial review, there is a greater constitutional role for the judiciary.[16] Like Marshall, Wechsler relied on the language in the Constitution, the Supremacy Clause, to justify the judicial role. Yet to assure that judges should exercise "judgment" rather than "will," Wechsler argued that the judiciary should intervene against democratic laws only when the judges could find a "neutral principle" which was independent of the judges' view of the policies behind the law. Since judicial review is "anchored in the Constitution," specifically in the Supremacy Clause, the obligation to exercise that review cannot be attenuated.[17] Yet while Wechsler found a greater role for the judiciary than Hand, he dissented vigorously, "from those more numerous among us who, vouching no philosophy to warranty, frankly or covertly make the test of virtue in interpretation whether its result in the immediate decision seems to hinder or advance the interests or the values they support."[18] If judges are result-oriented and let their judgment turn on the immediate result before them, then courts become "naked power organ[s]," and

---

14. J. Thayer, John Marshall 106, 107 (1901). For example, in 1935 President Franklin D. Roosevelt urged a congressman to support a certain bill. His letter concluded: "I hope your committee will not permit doubts as to constitutionality, however reasonable, to block the suggested legislation." Quoted in R. Rotunda, Modern Constitutional Law 12 (1981).

15. Thayer, *The Origin and Scope of the American Doctrine of Constitutional Law,* 7 Harv. L. Rev. 129, 144 (1893). See also id. at 156:
    The checking and cutting down of legislative power, by numerous detailed prohibitions in the constitution, cannot be accomplished without making the government petty and incompetent. This process has already been carried much too far in some of our States. Under no system can the power of courts go far to save a people from ruin; our chief protection lies elsewhere.

16. Wechsler, *Toward Neutral Principles of Constitutional Law,* 73 Harv. L. Rev. 1 (1959).

17. Wechsler, n. 16 supra at 6.

18. Wechsler, n. 16 supra at 11.

different judges, with different sympathies, may properly reach different conclusions.[19] Wechsler elaborated:

> You will not charge me with exaggeration if I say that this type of *ad hoc* evaluation is, as it has always been, the deepest problem of our constitutionalism, not only with respect to judgments of the courts but also in the wider realm in which conflicting constitutional positions have played a part in our politics.
>
> Did not New England challenge the embargo that the South supported on the very ground on which the South was to resist New England's demand for a protective tariff? Was not Jefferson in the Louisiana Purchase forced to rest on an expansive reading of the clauses granting national authority of the very kind that he had steadfastly opposed in his attacks upon the Bank?
>
> [W]hether you are tolerant, perhaps more tolerant than I, of the *ad hoc* in politics, with principle reduced to a manipulative tool, are you not also ready to agree that something else is called for from the courts? I put it to you that the main constituent of the judicial process is precisely that it must be genuinely principled, resting with respect to every step that is involved in reaching judgment on analysis and reasons quite transcending the immediate result that is achieved. To be sure, the courts decide, or should decide, only the case they have before them. But must they not decide on grounds of adequate neutrality and generality, tested not only by the instant application but by others that the principles imply? Is it not the very essence of judicial method to insist upon attending to such other cases, preferably those involving an opposing interest, in evaluating any principle avowed?"[20]

Just as Wechsler went further than Hand, so others go much further than Wechsler and argue that judges should not at all be unhesitant to invalidate laws because judges have a unique role to play as guardians of the Constitution.[21] Some contend that this very active form of review is justified only to protect individual rights and liberties, rather than property and economic rights. Thus the late Justice Douglas had long objected to the "school of thought here that the less the judiciary does the better."[22] Douglas' view, he said, was well expressed by the late Edmond Cahn who had said that "we are entitled to reproach the majoritarian justices of the Supreme Court ... with straining to be reasonable when they ought to be adamant."[23] Douglas believed the "judiciary was an indispensable part of the operation of our federal system" designed to play an important role "in guarding basic rights against majoritarian control."[24]

---

19. Id. at 12.
20. Id. at 12, 15. See generally, J. Nowak, R. Rotunda, and J. Young, Constitutional Law 14-15 (1978).
21. Cf. Cooper V. Aaron, 358 U.S. 1 (1958).
22. Flast v. Cohen, 392 U.S. 83, 110 (1968) (Douglas, J., concurring). See also, W. Douglas, The Right of the People (1958).
23. Douglas, J., concurring in Flast v. Cohen, 392 U.S. 83, 110, quoting E. Cahn, *Can the Supreme Court Defend Civil Liberties?,* in Samuel, ed., Toward a Better America 132, 144 (1968).
24. Flast v. Cohen, 392 U.S. at 111, 110 (Douglas, J., concurring).

Other justices have actively used their judicial power but, unlike Douglas, have not limited that activism to matters dealing with individual rights. Thus the conservative Justice McReynolds, who supported the efforts of the Court to strike down a variety of economic and social reform measures,[25] authored *Meyer v. Nebraska*[26] and *Pierce v. Society of Sisters*,[27] two of the seminal decisions in the area of civil liberties. *Meyer* declared unconstitutional, under the due process clause, a state law prohibiting the teaching of any subject to any person in public or private schools in any language other than English. The invalid statute also forbade teaching foreign language in grade school. Meyer had been convicted of teaching the subject of reading in the German language. In *Pierce* a state law prohibited private and parochial schools. McReynolds held that the state unreasonably interfered with the "liberty" of the parents and the "property" of the schools.

McReynolds could impose his views regarding the unconstitutionality of a minimum wage or a law prohibiting parochial schools with consistency because, in his own words, "plainly, I think this Court must have regard to the wisdom of enactment."[28] Those who have argued for judicial self-restraint are quick to point out that the danger of an activism of a Douglas is that it can lead to, and be used to justify, the activism of a McReynolds.

The two-century-old debate on the nature and extent of judicial review is vividly illustrated by the judicial philosophies of the six justices discussed in this volume of The David C. Baum Memorial Lectures on Civil Liberties and Civil Rights. The essays on the six justices are not merely biographical; they also probe the judicial philosophies of each of these justices, discuss their contributions to the world of ideas, and analyze their unique roles and influences on the Court. Each of the justices, in his own way, offers a solution to the questions created by *The Federalist Papers* No. 78: how active should the Court be; to what extent does judicial review conflict with democratic rule? Each of these justices stands at a different point on a continuum that ranges from the apostles of self-restraint to the crusaders for judicial activism.

---

25. See, e.g., Hammer v. Dagenhart, 247 U.S. 251 (1918) (Congressional law prohibiting the transportation in interstate commerce of the products of child labor invalidated); Bailey v. Drexel Furniture Co., 259 U.S. 20 (1922) (Tax on products of child labor invalidated as penalty); Tyson & Bro. v. Banton, 273 U.S. 418 (1927) (theatre ticket sales regulation invalidated); Ribnek v. McBride, 277 U.S. 350 (1928) (employment agency practice and rate regulation invalidated); Railroad Retirement Bd. v. Alton R.R. Co., 295 U.S. 330 (1935) (Railroad Retirement of 1934 held to exceed Congressional Power); United States v. Butler, 297 U.S. 1 (1936) (Agricultural Adjustment Act of 1933 held to violate Tenth Amendment); Carter v. Carter Coal Co., 298 U.S. 238 (1936) (Bituminous Coal Conservation Act of 1935 held to be outside of federal commerce power).
26. 262 U.S. 390 (1923).
27. 268 U.S. 510 (1925).
28. Separate opinion of McReynolds, J., dissenting in Nebbia v. New York, 291 U.S. 502, 557 (1934).

John P. Frank, a distinguished practicing attorney, legal scholar, and former law clerk to Justice Hugo Black delivered the first lecture in this series. He presents a comprehensive, graceful, and intimate portrait of Justice Black and his influential jurisprudence. Frank illuminates Black's eighteenth century contractarian philosophy and applies this learning to a careful analysis of Black's First Amendment decisions. The essay is a masterful evaluation of Justice Black and his contributions to judicial theory.

Professor Philip Kurland delivered the second paper, a portrait of Justice Robert H. Jackson. Kurland places Jackson in the camp of judicial self-restraint, led by Justice Frankfurter — himself the subject of a later Baum lecture. But Jackson is no mere follower of Frankfurter, as Kurland well demonstrates with reference to the flag salute case,[29] where Jackson wrote the opinion reversing a Frankfurter decision that was only three years old.[30] Kurland also analyzes Jackson's contributions to the rights of aliens and discusses the Steel Seizure Case[31] from a civil liberties perspective. Throughout the essay Kurland's lengthy quotations from Jackson's opinions prove that legal writing need not compromise the King's English.

William T. Coleman, Jr., a distinguished practicing attorney, former cabinet official, and former law clerk to Justice Frankfurter delivered the third essay, on Justice Frankfurter, one of the most influential advocates of judicial self-restraint. Mr. Coleman explains how Frankfurter's understanding of his judicial role affected his pre-Court opinions. Coleman strongly disagrees with the conventional wisdom that Frankfurter was insensitive to civil rights. Rather, Frankfurter's view of judicial self-restraint, which made him eschew the judicial activism of McReynolds, also made him reject the judicial philosophy of Douglas.

Professor Vern Countryman's discussion of Justice Douglas and his free speech opinions offers an interesting contrast with Mr. Coleman's analysis of Justice Frankfurter. Countryman, who clerked for Douglas, discusses the many cases in which Douglas strongly defended and expanded the reach of the First Amendment during his more than thirty-six years on the High Court. He had a robust and vigorous view of the First Amendment, and though that view was often expressed in dissent, its influence is still with us.

Professor Nathaniel Nathanson delivered the lecture on Justice Brandeis, for whom he had clerked. Nathanson discusses two themes basic to Brandeis' jurisprudence: the right to be let alone, and the right of self-development. In discussing these themes in the context of Brandeis' life story, Nathanson speculates on how Brandeis might have voted on more recent cases in light of his philosophy and his highly developed sense of justice.

---

29. West Virginia State Board of Education v. Barnette, 319 U.S. 624 (1943).
30. Minersville School District v. Gobitis, 310 U.S. 586 (1940).
31. Youngstown Sheet & Tube Co. v. Sawyer, 343 U.S. 579 (1952).

Finally, Judge Louis Pollak, former clerk to Justice Wiley Blount Rutledge, has written a sensitive and complete portrait of a justice who spent only six short years on the High Court and who is often overlooked by scholars. When President Franklin D. Roosevelt first considered Rutledge, Frankfurter had advised the president that Rutledge was well qualified for the post; Rutledge in turn had insisted to the senator who had recommended him to the president that Frankfurter be elevated instead. Roosevelt chose Frankfurter, although eventually Rutledge joined him on the bench, where the two often disagreed. An early death for Rutledge, at age fifty-five, meant an all too brief tenure on the Supreme Court. He never had the opportunity to grow into his office and thus he never joined the ranks of a Frankfurter or a Black in the history books.

Rutledge, Pollack concedes, was rarely eloquent; he used no verbal sleight of hand, and his opinions were often too long. Yet they contained legal doctrine of great significance. It was Rutledge who authored the seminal *Thomas v. Collins*,[32] upholding the right of a union organizer to make a speech without first securing an "organizer's card" from the state authorities. *Thomas* contained the strongest language up to its time on the preferred position, the "firstness," of the First Amendment.

These six biographical and analytical essays of Rutledge, Brandeis, Douglas, Frankfurter, Jackson, and Black, discuss basic and still vital overarching themes in the history of legal ideas. They illuminate the complex variations of a sophisticated judicial philosophy. Yet these essays do more. The whole is greater than the sum of its parts because as a group these essays demonstrate that beneath these justices' competing philosophies, these six molders of modern legal theory shared a basic consensus: a belief in democratic rule, cabined by judicial review to protect minority rights and the democratic process. They often disagreed, except on fundamentals. This consensus helps explain why our society — a model of stability compared to many Latin, European, Asian, or African countries — has thus far been able to balance the tension between majority rule and control on that majority by a mechanism called judicial review, which has not been used to oppress the people but rather to confine their will to the Constitutional mandate.

---

32. 323 U.S. 516 (1945).

JOHN P. FRANK

HUGO L. BLACK: FREE SPEECH AND THE DECLARATION OF INDEPENDENCE†

*John P. Frank**

I. THE ROOTS OF FREEDOM

One mid-winter day in 1959-60, Justice Black's mind wandered from the argument before him. He dashed off a note to his secretary with meticulous instructions for dinner.[1] Dr. Alexander Meiklejohn would be at the house at 6:30 p.m., a first-time guest. She should reach Charlie Reich,[2] and Lizzie Mae, the housekeeper, should cook Charlie a New York cut steak. There were to be three tenderloins for the others; baked potato and one additional vegetable would be enough.

It was a memorable evening. The two old gentlemen—Black was seventy-four, Meiklejohn eighty-eight—could not have been of more different background. Black, almost entirely self-educated and in public life for over thirty years; Meiklejohn, a trained philosopher, former President of Amherst, and later founder of the Experimental College at the University of Wisconsin. Black, interested in a New York cut and three tenderloins; Meiklejohn, a total ascetic. Black, a great justice; Meiklejohn, universally esteemed as the foremost teacher of an era.

What brought them together was a common, yet very unusual, preoccupation with the first amendment to the Federal Constitution. By 1960, Black was the foremost judicial and Meiklejohn the foremost philosophic exponent of free speech.[3] During the damaging decade just closed, covering most of the McCarthy era, each had held embattled posts. There were others, of course, who had also borne the battle; Chief Justice Warren, Justice William O. Doug-

---

†These remarks originally were delivered at the University of Illinois College of Law, October 13, 1976 as the first of the 1976-77 David C. Baum Lectures on Civil Rights and Civil Liberties.

* Partner, Lewis & Roca, Phoenix, Arizona. B.A. 1938, M.A. 1940, LL.B. 1940, University of Wisconsin; J.S.D. 1947, Yale University, Law Clerk to Mr. Justice Black, 1942 Term.

1. Undated note, Meiklejohn file, Black Mss., Library of Congress.

2. Charles Reich is a former clerk, friend, and author, *inter alia*, of Reich, *Mr. Justice Black and the Living Constitution*, 76 HARV. L. REV. 673 (1963), from which I gain much.

3. A. MEIKLEJOHN, *Free Speech and Its Relation to Self-Government*, in POLITICAL FREEDOM 2 (1960).

las,[4] and Justice William Brennan on the judicial front, and Professor Thomas I. Emerson of Yale from academia, to name but a few.

Yet this meeting was a unique gathering of remarkable leaders, for Black and Meiklejohn were promulgating doctrines so old that they had become new again. They, the first prominent exponents of this view in two centuries, asserted that an absolute right of freedom of speech came from the underlying philosophy of the Declaration of Independence. As Professor Emerson has put it:

> Once one accepts the premise of the Declaration of Independence—that governments derive "their just powers from the consent of the governed"— it follows that the governed must, in order to exercise their right of consent, have full freedom of expression. . . .
>
> The proponents of freedom of political expression often addressed themselves to the question whether the people were competent to perform the functions entrusted to them. . . . The men of the eighteenth century, with their implicit faith in the power of reason and the perfectability of man, entertained few doubts on this score.[5]

These two, when they climbed the stairs to the Justice's study to go deep into discussion after dinner, had no doubts. In that book-lined room they were, in an important intellectual sense, two eighteenth century thinkers together in 1960.

Meiklejohn's philosophy was of the Idealist school and his free speech thinking began with Plato and developed through Kant. For him the solution of the fundamental paradox of the *Apology* and the *Crito,* superficially conflicting Socratic dialogues, was the beginning of contemporary wisdom. In the *Apology,* Socrates defies what Meiklejohn describes as the Un-Athenian Subversive Activities Committee, and he refuses to give up teaching the young those notions to which the Committee objects. Socrates will accept death rather than relinquish a free man's right to teach, think, and speak as his spirit and wisdom demand. In short, he rejects the command

---

4. This essay focuses on Justice Black. Read as a total history of free speech during Black's years on the Court, it would be utterly misleading. Theodore Roosevelt's accounts of the Spanish-American War were so self-centered that Mr. Dooley suggested he do a book, "Alone in Cuba." In the free speech wars, Black was never "alone in Cuba;" there were always others and especially Justice Douglas. For a comprehensive statement of the Douglas views, see V. COUNTRYMAN, THE JUDICIAL RECORD OF JUSTICE WILLIAM O. DOUGLAS (1974), and particularly on free speech, *id.* at 42-103. Yet the contributions of these two were very different though of equal urgency and dedication to freedom. As I have developed elsewhere, Douglas philosophically is an extension, an updating of Justice Brandeis; *see* J. Frank, *William O. Douglas,* IV THE JUSTICES OF THE SUPREME COURT 2447, 2455-59 (L. Friedman & F. Israel ed. 1969). Black's systematic application of the eighteenth century compact theory to the Bill of Rights is essentially his unique contribution.

5. T. EMERSON, TOWARD A GENERAL THEORY OF THE FIRST AMENDMENT 10 (1963).

of the State to be silent. Yet in the *Crito* Socrates refuses to escape from the unjust death penalty; his philosophy requires him to drink the hemlock. He, as a citizen, has consented all his life to accept the laws of the City of Athens. He must obey the law which governs his actions. The State may control his conduct even to ordering his death, but his beliefs and his speech no man may control but himself.[6]

Black was thinking in the same terms but, doubtless, not until Meiklejohn developed the thought did he relate it so directly to Greek philosophy. His self-schooling had grounded him well in Roman and in Greek history more than philosophy; the whole cast of his mind was historical rather than, in the technical sense, philosophical.[7] Although the room in which the two sat had well-used Greek and Roman sources, they were primarily historical sources, and there is no reason to believe that Black ever read any Kant at all.[8]

Black, son of a country storekeeper, was a product of rural Clay County, Alabama. He was admitted to the law school of the University of Alabama fundamentally because he did not have sufficient qualifications to get into its liberal arts college, and under the standards of those days it was easier to go to law school than to enter the academic program. His years as a busy county attorney and

---

6. The paradox of the two dialogues, on the resolution of which Meiklejohn based his theory of the relation of man and government, or speech and conduct, is illustrated thus:

If you say to me, Socrates, this time we will not mind Anytus, and you shall be let off, but upon one condition, that you are not to enquire and speculate in this way any more, and that if you are caught doing so again, you shall die; . . . I should reply: Men of Athens, I honour and love you; but I shall obey God rather than you, and while I have life and strength I shall never cease from the practice and teaching of philosophy, exhorting any one whom I meet. . . .

Plato, *Apology* in 7 BRITANNICA GREAT BOOKS 206 (B. Jowett trans. 1952). Socrates, considering the plea of Crito that he escape, responds in the voice of the City:

[H]e who has experience of the manner in which we order justice and administer the state, and still remains, has entered into an implied contract that he will do as we command him. And he who disobeys us is, as we maintain . . . wrong; . . . because he has made an agreement with us that he will duly obey our commands.

Id. at 217.

7. R. Newman, Hugo Black and Edmond Cahn, A Philosophical Friendship 32 (1976) (unpublished MA thesis, Univ. of Va.) [hereinafter cited as Newman], notes that Cahn gave Black Werner Jaeger's three-volume PAIDEIA: THE IDEALS OF GREEK CULTURE which the Justice found "absorbingly interesting." Black thought very highly of Edith Hamilton's THE GREEK WAY. Miss Hamilton observed that "clarity and simplicity of statement, the watchwords of the thinker, were the Greek poets' watchwords too." Black underlined those words. Newman, *supra*, at 32-33. Newman observes that Aristotle was the "favorite author" of both his subjects. *Id.* at 35. Though I have great respect for Mr. Newman's admirable work, I doubt this as to Black.

8. D. MEADOR, MR. JUSTICE BLACK AND HIS BOOKS (1974) (shows no Kant in Black's Collection). I am aware of no reference by Black to Kant.

later as a private practitioner had given him little opportunity for self-education. When he went to the Senate of the United States in the election of 1926, he was basically and fundamentally untutored in all of the farther reaches of the liberal arts and humanities.[9]

This defect Black sought to remedy. In his first two years of Senate experience he did not say much but he read a great deal. The Library of Congress had no busier or more intent student. In 1927 and 1928 Black's reading took him into classical history and he also began an immersion into seventeenth century history, the history of the courts of Star Chamber, the Glorious Revolution, the rise and fall of Stuart tyranny, all of which later was to be read so large into his Supreme Court opinions.

Before he came to the Senate, Black had encountered few occasions to be of record on freedom of speech, though his natural bent was toward civil liberties. As a county attorney as early as 1914 he had broken up the practice of abusing Negroes into forced confessions of crimes they may or may not have committed, and in a Grand Jury report he wrote some words on that subject which were later to echo in the Supreme Court Reports. His brief flirtation with the Ku Klux Klan was an expedient of 1925; it had seemed to him at the time, as he later told me, a useful expedient for a jury lawyer. He was out of it before he ran for the Senate in 1926, and the Klan supported someone else. In 1932 the Klan violently opposed his reelection because of his liberal record.

In 1929, twenty years before Meiklejohn published his first major expression on free speech, Black recorded his first utterance on the same subject; his stand made the meeting thirty years later an act of happy destiny. The subject under discussion was a bill to control the importation of what was claimed to be obscene literature; the matter was a regulation of the Customs Service. Black was against such regulation. His statement, oral and spontaneous, was unpolished; but the seeds of thought fully developed later are all there. Of free speech, he believed "that this is one of the most sacred privileges of a democracy."[10] He therefore could "not vote for any measure or any legislation which tends in the slightest degree to restrict its inestimable privilege."[11]

His illustrations he took from the history he had been reading: the monstrosity of the burning of the library at Alexandria; the

---

9. For general background, see J. Frank, Mr. Justice Black (1949).
10. 71 Cong. Rec. 4468 (1929).
11. *Id.*

persecution of Galileo, "a man who dares to peer into the sky and to decide for himself that the world in which he lived is not flat, but round."[12] He spoke of Wycliffe, translating the Bible into English and the abuse which followed; of the crucifixion of Christ for his opinions; and he expressed his scorn of those who had "feared the corruption of the youth of Greece by Socrates, that great philosopher."[13]

As for himself, he was "not afraid of any word or any expression."[14] He continued,

> If we take away from a man the right to think—or attempt to take it away, because no man and no group has ever been able to do it—we take away from him the only privilege that separates the citizen of a democracy from the citizen of a monarchy and absolute despotism.[15]

With extraordinary prophecy Black declared that he stood in the Senate and would stand in the future "against any legislation of any kind that would interfere with the sacred right of the American citizen to think as he sees fit and to be persuaded in no way except by logic and reason."[16]

Black's choice of example was catholic but his choice of authority stamped him for what he later was as a justice, an eighteenth century man. This passage I quote in some detail because it is truly vital for later understanding:

> So far as I am concerned, I prefer to follow the philosophy of Thomas Jefferson, who borrowed largely from the great English writer, John Locke. Only two days ago I read a treatise on government by John Locke which under the very amendment [under discussion] would be barred at the port of entry because John Locke maintained, as did other great philosophers, the right of the people to use force, if necessary, to overturn a government of corruption or of tyranny. Think of that! Thomas Jefferson followed Locke; Adams followed him; Hancock followed him; Hamilton followed him. They all dared to assert that there came times in the life of every people when decency demanded that the form of government theretofore holding two peoples together should be dissolved; and they dissolved that union by force and not by platitudes.[17]

For himself he accepted "the basic philosophy on which Jefferson

---

12. *Id.*
13. *Id.* at 4469.
14. *Id.*
15. *Id.*
16. *Id.*
17. *Id.*

and his friends acted."[18]

What Black said in 1929 is, essentially, what he said with greater care and polish in his written expressions on the Supreme Court. Take for example the *Barenblatt v. United States*[19] dissent in 1959, thirty years after the speech just quoted:

> The First Amendment means to me, however, that the only constitutional way our Government can preserve itself is to leave its people the fullest possible freedom to praise, criticize or discuss, as they see fit, all governmental policies and to suggest, if they desire, that even its most fundamental postulates are bad and should be changed; "Therein lies the security of the Republic, the very foundation of constitutional government." On that premise this land was created, and on that premise it has grown to greatness. Our Constitution assumes that the common sense of the people and their attachment to our country will enable them, after free discussion, to withstand ideas that are wrong. . . . Unless we can rely on these qualities—if, in short, we begin to punish speech—we cannot honestly proclaim ourselves to be a free Nation and we have lost what the Founders of this land risked their lives and their sacred honor to defend.[20]

Black and Meiklejohn took their Declaration of Independence seriously when it referred to "unalienable rights."[21] They thought of the Bill of Rights as the necessary corollary to those inalienable rights, and the written agreement essential to the establishment of the Republic. They accepted the pure Lockian compact theory of the American government on which Jefferson drew in writing the Declaration. To Meiklejohn the closing words of the Declaration of Independence, "We mutually pledge to each other our Lives, our Fortunes and our sacred Honor," represented

> a voluntary compact among political equals. We, the People, acting together, either directly or through our representatives, make and administer law [*The Apology*]. We, the People, acting in groups or

---

18. *Id.*
19. Barenblatt v. United States, 360 U.S. 109 (1959).
20. *Id.* at 145-46 (Black, J., dissenting).
21. One source analyzes the phrase thus:
The civil or legal rights that the state confers on its citizens or subjects by positive enactment or constitutional provision, it can revoke or nullify. They are alienable. To say that certain rights are inalienable is to say their possession by men does not depend upon legislation of any kind. They are inalienable because they are inherent in the nature of man. They belong to human beings in virtue of their being human. They have moral force and impose moral obligations even when they lack legal force and lack legal sanctions. They can, therefore, be called "moral rights" or "human rights" as well as "natural rights."
M. ADLER & W. GORMAN, THE AMERICAN TESTAMENT 34 (1976).

separately, are subject to the law [*The Crito*]. If we could make that double agreement effective, we would have accomplished the American Revolution.[22]

Black expressed a variant of that same compact concept when he attacked what is known as the "balancing test," popular in the 1950's, on the scope of the first amendment. Under this concept the Supreme Court balances the values of free speech in a given situation against the perils to national security and determines the validity of the legislation in the light of that result. For Black, that balance had already been struck. There is of course a possibility of menace to national security through free speech. He accepted the concept of Justice Brandeis that those who founded this nation were not cowards. They struck that balance 200 years ago.[23] They made an agreement, a decision that the value of speech outweighed the hazard to national security; in short, they chose speech. So far as Black was concerned, until the Constitution was changed by lawful process, he was prepared to enforce the eighteenth century agreement to the hilt.

What did Meiklejohn and Black talk about on the congenial evening in Black's study? Precisely what one would expect of devotees of freedom of speech, their disagreements.[24] While there were disagreements, the similarities overwhelmed the differences. They both believed that the Declaration of Independence and the Bill of Rights created an absolutely protected area of free speech. They agreed also that this protection went to the content of speech, and not to the time, place, or manner of the utterance.[25] Black, for example, had not an ounce of sympathy for tumultuous demonstrations occurring either outside of courthouses or in them.[26] Both believed that illegal conduct could and should be suppressed and punished, and each fumbled a little in attempting to draw lines among speech, incitement, and action.

Disagreements? The largest was Meiklejohn's effort to draw a line between "public" speech, which he thought completely protected, and "private" speech, which he thought not so. In his view,

---

22. A. MEIKLEJOHN, POLITICAL FREEDOM 15 (1960).

23. Konigsberg v. State Bar, 366 U.S. 36, 61 (1961).

24. Unpublished memorial statement by Black on Meiklejohn, Meiklejohn file, Black Mss., Library of Congress. As Mrs. Black recalls the evening, "we went to the study and there was a great deal of friendly banter about the difference of their views and the discussion was a lively one." Letter from Elizabeth DeM. Black to author (Sept. 13, 1976).

25. A. MEIKLEJOHN, POLITICAL FREEDOM 18-21 (1960).

26. On tumult outside courts, see text accompanying notes 164-66 *infra;* on Black's view of disorderly defendants, see Illinois v. Allen, 397 U.S. 337 (1970).

only that speech was under the protection of the first amendment which bore directly on government and its policies and its operation.[27] Black could not draw this boundary and so he included both obscenity and libel[28] within his protected area; in later life Meiklejohn joined him as to obscenity.[29] The differences are relatively insignificant as compared to the agreements.

Neither of the two significantly influenced the thinking of the other, except perhaps as to detail. These were strong men, and old, and by the time they read each other's works or, finally, talked they were not much subject to influence by anyone, if ever they were. What they gave each other was a profound sense of encouragement, apparent in later letters between the two. After Meiklejohn's death, a memorial service was held in Washington on January 15, 1965, which happened also to be a conference day of the Supreme Court. Black, speaking at the service, said: "This is the first time I have ever left one of our regular weekly conferences to go to some other meeting in the twenty-seven and one-half years I have been a member of the Supreme Court."[30] He had not known Meiklejohn personally very well he told the group; he recalled the one evening here described. "While he and I did not see eye to eye as to the exact scope of the absolute terms used in [the first amendment]," Black said, "we did fully agree that a country dedicated to freedom, as ours is, must leave political thoughts, expressions, and discussions open to the people if it hopes to maintain that freedom."[31]

II.   PRAGMATISM VS. IDEALISM: THE DECLARATION

One of the most severe critics of the Black approach to free speech was the late Alexander Bickel of Yale. In his posthumous work, *The Morality of Consent*, Bickel very fairly distinguishes be-

---

27. *See* Meiklejohn, *The First Amendment is an Absolute*, 1961 SUP. CT. REV. 245: "The revolutionary intent of the First Amendment is, then, to deny to all subordinate agencies authority to abridge the freedom of the electoral power to the people." *Id.* at 254. "The First Amendment does not protect a 'freedom to speak.' It protects the freedom of those activities of thought and communication by which we 'govern.' It is concerned, not with a private right, but with a public power, a governmental responsibility." *Id.* at 225. There are many kinds of communication which are not used as activities of governing. He mentions some others but seems to adopt for himself the statement that libel, slander, misrepresentation, obscenity, perjury, false advertising, etc. are not protected by the first amendment. *Id.* at 258. However, he also advances an argument that obscenity is covered by the first amendment. *Id.* at 262-63.

28. H. BLACK, A CONSTITUTIONAL FAITH 48 (1968).

29. Meiklejohn, *The First Amendment is an Absolute*, 1961 SUP. CT. REV. 245, 262.

30. Unpublished Black Mss., Library of Congress.

31. *Id.*

tween the views he deplores and those with which he associates himself. He describes "two diverging traditions in the main stream of western political thought—one 'liberal,' and the other 'conservative,'—[which] have competed, and still compete, for the control of the democratic process and of the American constitutional system."[32] The liberal tradition he defines as "the contractarian tradition, [which] began with the moderate common sense of John Locke."[33] The alternative tradition, "usually called conservative," can "be called Whig in the English eighteenth century sense."[34] He continues:

> The liberal contractarian model rests on a vision of individual rights that have a clearly defined, independent existence predating society and are derived from nature and from a natural, if imagined, contract. Society must bend to these rights. . . . The contractarian model . . . is committed not to law alone but to a parochial faith and a closely calibrated scale of values. It is moral, principled, legalistic, ultimately authoritarian.[35] It is weak on pragmatism, strong on theory. For it, law is not so much a process, and certainly not a process in continual flux, as it is a body of rules binding all, rules that can be changed only by the same formal method by which they were enacted.[36]

The alternative, preferred by Bickel, is pragmatic philosophy applied to law and government. As Bickel put it:

> Limits are set by culture, by time-and-place-bound conditions, and with these limits the task of government informed by the present state of values is to make a peaceable, good, and improving society. That, and not anything that existed prior to society itself and that now exists independently of society, is what men have a right to. The Whig model obviously is flexible, pragmatic, slow-moving, highly political. It partakes, in substantial measure, of the relativism that pervades Justice Oliver Holmes' theory of the First Amendment, although not to its ultimate logical exaggeration. Lacking a catechism of shared values, such as religious societies may cherish, it has no choice but relativism.[37]

The Black view is related here in the language of a sharp critic, because if we eliminate the somewhat disparaging tone, the state-

---

32. A. BICKEL, THE MORALITY OF CONSENT 3 (1975).
33. *Id.*
34. *Id.*
35. I am in doubt as to Bickel's meaning of this word.
36. *Id.*
37. *Id.*

ment is about right. Black, of course, is not drawing his standards of free speech from a concept of "a natural, if imagined, contract." As far as he is concerned, he is dealing with a contract which was made, signed, and delivered, that contract being the Declaration of Independence, the Constitution, and the Bill of Rights. Nonetheless, this perfectly substantial and tangible contract did come into existence in an intellectual milieu described by Bickel.

In taking his positions, Black speaks to the law with a voice which has not been seriously heard for a long time. As Mortimer Adler put it in a 1976 lengthy and almost passionate letter to the Aspen Institute:

> The two most critical phrases in the Declaration of Independence—"inalienable rights" and "the pursuit of happiness"—are generally misunderstood or are just not understood by intelligent, well-educated Americans. [They] rest on doctrines and moral philosophy that are no longer taught in our universities, or, if ever referred to, are cavalierly dismissed.[38]

He concludes:

> The rejected premise can be compactly expressed in the following proposition: there is a human nature, common to all members of the human species; inherent in it are certain specific properties which we can know and understand well enough to be able to determine the needs and rights which are inherently human. If that proposition is true, everything else I have said follows. If it is not true, then this letter is not worth the paper it is written on.[39]

The pragmatists would discard the letter.

Carl Becker made the classic analysis of the Declaration of Independence from which I quote and paraphrase a little.[40] The Declaration of Independence perfectly achieves a fusion of historic and natural rights.[41] Take James Wilson's paper written in 1770 in which Wilson, on the North American continent on the eve of the Revolution, merges his own views with Locke:

> All men are, by nature, equal and free: No one has a right to any authority over another without his consent: All lawful government is

---

38. Letter X from M. Adler to J. Slater, Aspen Institute for Humanistic Studies (Apr. 1976).

39. *Id.*

40. C. BECKER, THE DECLARATION OF INDEPENDENCE (1942) [hereinafter cited as BECKER]. Becker accounts for the use of the word "unalienable" rather than "inalienable" as possible inadvertence or, alternatively, a possible difference of form in the eighteenth century. *Id.* at 142, 175. In any case, John Adams appears responsible for it.

41. BECKER, *supra* note 40, at 105.

founded in the consent of those who are subject to it: Such consent was given with a view to insure and to increase the happiness of the governed, above what they would enjoy in an independent and unconnected state of nature.[42]

The First Continental Congress, two years before the Declaration of Independence, declared the rights of "the inhabitants of the English colonies in North America, by the immutable laws of nature, the principles of the English Constitution, and the several charters or compacts" as "entitled to life, liberty and property."[43] Two years later, the concept had been materially refined to "life, liberty, and the pursuit of happiness"[44] and these "rights" had become "inalienable."

The fundamental concept of the Declaration was that governments derive their just powers from the consent of the governed. This was the wisdom of the Enlightenment as developed by Locke from the law of nature and accepted by Jefferson.[45] It was, as Becker develops, a political theory spin-off of Newtonian physics, a concept that truth could be found from sufficiently close observation of nature. At the heart of it is an eighteenth century optimism that improving humanity will have an ever-growing capacity to govern itself if given a fair chance to do so.[46]

Clearly the little handful of rebels who challenged the power of

---

42. *Id.* at 108 (quoting from Wilson's pamphlet *Considerations on the Nature and Extent of the Legislative Authority of the British Parliament*). As Jefferson put the same thought, "Every man and every body of men on earth possesses, the righ[t] of self government: They receive it with their being from the hand of nature." 17 PAPERS OF T. JEFFERSON 195 (J. Boyd ed. 1965); implicit here "are the rights of thinking, and publishing our thoughts by speaking or writing." 14 PAPERS OF T. JEFFERSON 678 (J. Boyd ed. 1958).

43. BECKER, *supra* note 40, at 122.

44. *See* Newman, *supra* note 7, at 54 (presents Jefferson's development of this concept from Locke's *Essay on Human Understanding*).

45. BECKER, *supra* note 40, at 62-63. This is not to underestimate the contribution of Montesquieu on the structure of government or Rousseau on the theory of liberty through self-government. *See generally* 10 W. & A. DURANT, THE STORY OF CIVILIZATION: ROUSSEAU AND REVOLUTION (1967) [hereinafter cited as 10 DURANT]. For the essence of the Social Contract: "Obedience to a law which we prescribe to ourselves in liberty." *Id.* at 173 (quoting Rousseau, *Social Contract*, Book 1 ch. viii).

46. *See* BECKER, *supra* note 40, at 40-51 (develops the Newtonian influence). Illustrative of the perfectionist concept is the influential Marquis de Condorcet (1743-1794), described by the Durants as *"The Last Philosophe."* 10 DURANT, *supra* note 45, at 894-97. Condorcet's *Progrès de l'esprit humain* (1795) shows the continuous progression of the human race to an ultimate perfection. To this end, he sponsored a new educational system for Revolutionary France, later adopted by Napoleon, "to establish among citizens an actual equality." Condorcet, *Report on Education in* A DOCUMENTARY SURVEY OF THE FRENCH REVOLUTION 347 (J. Stewart ed. 1951). As Becker says, "[t]o Condorcet, as to Jefferson, the political philosophy of the Declaration of Independence was just the common sense of the whole matter." BECKER, *supra* note 40, at 233.

a great nation were optimists; they had to be to carry their concept of truth to the wager of the battle. They were young, astonishingly young, energetic, and very optimistic indeed; but they were neither naive nor of short memory. They were revolting against what they sincerely regarded as English oppression, but the leadership was studious and thoroughly well acquainted with Stuart tyranny.[47]

The heavy majority did not believe that those "inalienable rights" could survive a strong central government unless that government were limited by express restrictions on abuses they had known or which were part of recent heritage. This was not the contemporaneous popular fancy that somehow there is a folk "out there" and an octupus at the capital; the eighteenth century recognized that in short term the people themselves might in gusts of passion persecute each other. It was with just such recognition that Black wrote his prayerful invocation of a calmer day at the conclusion of *Dennis v. United States:*[48] "Public opinion being what it now is, few will protest. . . . There is hope, however, that in calmer times, when present pressures, passions and fears subside," freedom will be restored.[49]

The Founding Fathers had no intention of leaving free speech to the turn of time's wheel. Hence, the Bill of Rights as an attempt at a written restriction to guarantee that constitutional government created in 1787 would not trench on the natural rights recognized in 1776. To use the word which the eighteenth century favored, they created a compact.

As Professor Emerson has observed, the natural law theory of the consent of the governed faded in the nineteenth century. Becker enlarges on this theme: The Founding Fathers and the philosophers

> no doubt took it for granted that this philosophy, being but the common sense of the matter, would rapidly win universal approval and become the sure foundation of governments throughout the world. But in fact the United States had scarcely assumed that equal station to which the laws of nature entitled it, before the laws of

---

47. To Black and to Chafee elimination of contemporary eighteenth century practices of suppression of free speech were the object of the amendment; it did not transfer English liberties, such as they were, but enlarged them. Z. Chafee, Free Speech in the United States 9-17 (1941). For illustration of Black's feeling see his correspondence with Edmond Cahn sharply critical of L. Levy, Legacy of Suppression (1960) in Newman, *supra* note 7.

48. 341 U.S. 494 (1951).

49. *Id.* at 58 (Black, J., dissenting). As Jefferson expressed the same thought, "It is still certain tho' written constitutions may be violated in moments of passion or delusion, yet they furnish a text to which those who are watchful may again rally and recall the people." Letter from Jefferson to Dr. Priestly (June 19, 1802) reprinted in Bureau of Rolls and Library, 5 A Documentary History of the Constitution 259-60 (1905).

nature, in the sense in which the Declaration of Independence had announced them, began to lose their high prestige. . . . What seems but common sense in one age often seems but nonsense in another. Such for the most part is the fate which has overtaken the sublime truths enshrined in the Declaration of Independence.[50]

The truth of this observation is the foundation of the ultimate drama of Black's intellectual life as a champion of free speech. Black was the first member of the Supreme Court to attempt to apply the Bill of Rights in terms of its intellectual purposes.

III. PRAGMATISM VS. IDEALISM: CLEAR AND PRESENT DANGER

When free speech questions first reached the Supreme Court, eighteenth century philosophy was virtually extinct. Locke and his compacts had become curios, and new gods were ascendant in the intellectual heavens. The host of free speech controversies in America between George Washington and World War I were not Court controversies. The Alien and Sedition Act conflict was settled by the election of 1800; the rights of abolitionists not allowed to urge an end to slavery and the rights of slaves not even allowed to read were resolved on political battlegrounds or, finally, by war. The Civil War, the Haymarket riots, the IWW—none forced the Supreme Court to confront the meaning of the first amendment.[51]

Congress adopted the first direct speech control statutes in World War I, and these statutes brought the first free speech cases to the Supreme Court. For pratical purposes the slate was clean. It is a safe hazard that no member of the Court thought for one minute about inalienable rights, or that there was a contract of the people to condition acceptance of central government upon a guarantee that speech and press be untrammeled. By 1919 a national government was proved by succcess, and no one seriously considered any more that its initial establishment was a close thing. In the first case to reach the Court it was enough for Holmes, speaking for the rest, that "when a nation is at war" there are utterances which "will not be endured so long as men fight."[52] The old soldier, his own body marked with repeated bullets it had borne more than fifty years before, laid down the test: "The question in every case is whether the words used are used in such circumstances and are of such a nature as to create a clear and present danger that they will bring

50. BECKER, *supra* note 40, at 233.

51. Frank, *Review and Basic Liberties,* SUPREME COURT AND SUPREME LAW 109, 113-14 (E. Cahn ed. 1954).

52. Schenck v. United States, 249 U.S. 47, 52 (1919).

about the substantive evils that Congress has a right to prevent."[53]

The clear and present danger test remained the liberal rallying point in the history of free speech for more than thirty years until Meiklejohn from the speaker's platform and Black on the bench began to attack it. I do not here pause to trail its ups and downs, because I am concerned about two other things: the history of ideas and Justice Black's relation to that history. Suffice it to say that this approach swiftly proved to lack tangible meaning so that Holmes, and Brandeis with him, were very soon in conflict with the Court majority in applying Holmes' standard.[54]

Without pausing over the cases decided between 1917 and 1950, I note as before that Professor Bickel in the passage earlier quoted was exactly right. He classifies the eighteenth century approach as "contractarian," and I would prefer and will use the less clumsy and more traditionally philosophic term, idealist. I usurp this splendidly broad philosophic term in part because it is what Dr. Meiklejohn called it when I was his student forty years ago. The term reflects a willingness to accept *a priori* values (inalienable rights, for example) coupled with the capacity for human improvement as in Condorcet's *Progres de l'esprit humain* which interrelates with both Locke and Rousseau on the social compact.[55] Black probably accepted the ideal and certainly accepted the particular compact.

Holmes' philosophy of free speech moves from fundamentals wholly different from the idealists'. When Holmes expresses himself with great care and precision on freedom of speech, he has nothing to say about "inalienable rights," or "the dignity of man," or the underlying moral values of freedom. He instead bespeaks a philosophy of utility, and was in that philosophical movement we call pragmatism. Indeed, as a member of the Metaphysical Club at Cambridge he was part of the group which with Charles Peirce and William James gave birth to pragmatism.[56] It is no accident that

---

53. *Id.* Far and away the most illuminating essay and materials on this World War I phase of free speech development is Gunther, *Learned Hand and the Origins of Modern First Amendment Doctrine*, 27 STAN. L. REV. 719 (1975). A brilliant, short introductory essay, followed by Hand-Holmes and Hand-Chafee correspondence fully demonstrates Holmes' insensitivity to free speech values in the early cases. It also demonstrates, as noted in my own text above, that not one of this trio, while building the twentieth century law of free speech, ever thought for one instant of Jefferson, or the Declaration, or the compact theory of government. The pure pragmatism of *Abrams* is reflected in the equally pure pragmatism of the Hand-Holmes correspondence. The worthlessness from a free speech standpoint of pre-*Abrams* Holmes is noted in Prude, *Portrait of a Civil Libertarian: The Faith and Fear of Zechariah Chafee, Jr.*, 60 J. AM. HIST. 633, 640-41 (1974) [hereinafter cited as Prude].

54. *See, e.g.*, Gitlow v. New York, 268 U.S. 652 (1925).

55. *See* note 46 *supra*.

56. 2 M. HOWE, JUSTICE OLIVER WENDELL HOLMES, THE PROVING YEARS 1870-1882, at 151 (1963).

John Dewey, our foremost formal philosopher of pragmatism, is able to underwrite Holmes' philosophy of free speech with complete agreement.[57]

The classic Holmes expression of his view is in his dissent in *Abrams v. United States*:[58]

> Persecution of the expression of opinions seems to me perfectly logical. If you have no doubt of your premises or your power and want a certain result with all your heart you naturally express your wishes in law and sweep away all opposition. To allow opposition by speech seems to indicate that you think the speech impotent, as when a man says that he has squared the circle, or that you do not care whole-heartedly for the result, or that you doubt either your power or your premises. But when men have realized that time has upset many fighting faiths, they may come to believe the very foundations of their own conduct that the ultimate good desired is better reached by free trade in ideas—that the best test of truth is the power of the thought to get itself accepted in the competition of the market, and that truth is the only ground upon which their wishes safely can be carried out.[59]

Holmes says here that we should not persecute those with whom we disagree because we may be wrong about it; because the persecuted may be right; and because the only way to find out is to leave ideas to the sifting process of the intellectual marketplace. In short, Holmes would let speech be free without regard to moral considerations or historic commitments by a process of balancing, because it is socially useful to do so.[60] This is the straight utilitarian-

---

57. J. Dewey, Problems of Men 118-21 (1946). Dewey's statement of the Holmes philosophy which he embraces on freedom of speech is the sharpest possible denial of Meiklejohn's own thesis. Dewey says: "Holmes and Brandeis are notable not only for their sturdy defense of civil liberties but even more for the fact that they based their defense on the indispensable value of free inquiry and free discussion to the normal development of public welfare, not upon anything inherent in the individual as such." *Id.* at 120.

58. 250 U.S. 616 (1919).

59. *Id.* at 630 (Holmes, J., dissenting).

60. This is too much for even a stout supporter like Professor Bickel who says, "The theory of truth of the market place, determined ultimately by a count of noses—this total relativism—cannot be the theory of our Constitution; there would be no Bill of Rights in it, and certainly no Supreme Court to enforce it." A. Bickel, The Morality of Consent 77 (1975). Meiklejohn says:

> I have never been able to share the Miltonian faith that in a fair fight between truth and error, truth is sure to win. And if one had that faith, it would be hard to reconcile it with the sheer stupidity of the policies of this nation—and of other nations—now driving humanity to the very edge of final destruction. In my view, "the people need free speech" because they have decided, in adopting, maintaining and interpreting their Constitution, to govern themselves rather than to be governed by others.

Meiklejohn, *The First Amendment is an Absolute*, 1961 Sup. Ct. Rev. 245, 263.

ism of John Stuart Mill, who in his *Essay on Liberty* spoke with
close parallel to Holmes in *Abrams*.[61]

But in this balance of utility Holmes admitted that sometimes,
in particular crises, the balance might be cast the other way.
Schenck, the Holmes opinion first quoted, did hold that words could
be suppressed when there was "a clear and present danger." In the
case of *Debs,*[62] Holmes permitted imprisonment for simple expression of an opinion about government policies because the opinion
was radically against the current of popular belief.

The *Debs* case points up the difference in both philosophy and
result between pragmatic and idealist thinking. In the idealist view,
Debs had an inalienable right to say his say; and in the Holmes
view, he could be sent to prison. The clear and present danger
theory grew and was molded into its ultimate form as the years
passed sometimes by Holmes and sometimes by Brandeis. In the
Whitney v. California[63] concurrence, Brandeis, with Holmes concurring, put the proper rule thus:

> To courageous, self-reliant men, with confidence in the power of free
> and fearless reasoning applied through the processes of popular gov-
> ernment, no danger flowing from speech can be deemed clear and
> present, unless the incidence of the evil apprehended is so imminent
> that it may befall before there is opportunity for full discussion. If
> there be time to expose through discussion the falsehood and falla-
> cies, to avert the evil by the processes of education, the remedy to be
> applied is more speech, not enforced silence.[64]

The clear and present danger test was born in utilitarianism,
and, by its proved inutility, it has died. It made a valuable contribution to the development of free speech doctrine.[65] Between 1918 and

---

61. *Compare* Holmes in *Abrams*:
   If you have no doubt of your premises or your power and want a certain result with all
   your heart you naturally express your wishes in law and sweep away all opposition
   . . . . But when men have realized that time has upset many fighting faiths, they may
   come to believe even more than they believe the very foundations of their own conduct
   that the ultimate good desired is better reached by free trade in ideas. . . .
Abrams v. United States, 250 U.S. 616, 630 (1919) (dissenting opinion) *with* Mill:
   All silencing of discussion is an assumption of infallability. The opinion which it is
   attempted to suppress may be true . . . every age having held many opinions which
   subsequent ages have deemed not only false but absurd. . . . Complete liberty of
   contradiction and disproving our opinion [is indispensible]; on no other terms can a
   being with human faculties have any rational assurance of being right.
J.S. Mill, *On Liberty*, 43 Britannica Great Books 267, 275-76 (1952); Prude, *supra* note 53,
at 642-43 makes much the same point of the Mill base for Holmes-Chafee.
   62. Debs v. United States, 249 U.S. 211 (1919).
   63. 274 U.S. 357, 372 (1927) (concurring opinion).
   64. *Id.* at 377.
   65. The friendliest and ablest exponent is Z. Chafee, Freedom of Speech (1941),

1950, those who were pragmatists, who doubted the existence of any truths apart from their consequences, and who believed in the theory of experimentalism in the social sciences as that theory was raised to legal philosophy by, for example, Justice Holmes and Chief Justice Stone, could follow Holmes. But certainly not all Americans were in this cool-headed group and, indeed, without Holmes' personal verve and sparkle, this emotionless concept could never have achieved legal currency.[66]

The real troubles with the theory, even for its devotees, are twofold. First, courts are wholly unequipped to assess realistically the probability of dangers. As the concept was reworked by Judge Learned Hand and adopted by the Supreme Court in a leading Communist prosecution, "In each case [courts] must ask whether the gravity of the 'evil,' discounted by its improbability, justifies such invasion of free speech as is necessary to avoid the danger."[67] Are the leaders of a national political party to be imprisoned because a particular jury of twelve is persuaded of the existence of a danger? Who makes the discount for improbability? How do the "discounters," whether judge or jury, know? It is easy enough for Holmes to make light of some earnest zealots tossing leaflets out of a window, as he did in *Abrams*, but how are judges equipped to assess a possible national fascist, racist drive?

Second, if the Holmes-Hand approach is coupled with the rule that all deference is to be paid to legislative enactments, supported by a presumption of constitutionality, there is no protection to free speech at all. If the Court is basically unable to determine the facts, and if in any case the facts must be presumed in aid of the legislation, repression will always win.

---

passim, himself an advocate of the pragmatic approach. Prude, *supra* note 53, at 651. The sharpest terse criticism is Meiklejohn's:

> That ruling annuls the most significant purpose of the First Amendment. It destroys the intellectual basis of our plan of self-government. The court has interpreted the dictum that Congress shall not abridge the freedom of speech by defining the conditions under which such abridging is allowable. Congress, we are now told, is forbidden to destroy our freedom except when it finds it advisable to do so.

A. MEIKLEJOHN, POLITICAL FREEDOM 30 (1961).

66. Z. Chafee, in reviewing Meiklejohn's *Free Speech*, says "[the Meiklejohn criticism] is like the mother in F.D.R.'s story, whose boy was rescued far out from shore by a lifeguard. She went after the lifeguard and scolded him for losing her son's cap." Chafee, Book Review, 62 HARV. L. REV. 891, 901 (1949). A few years later, he might have been less flip; in a private letter written in 1953, he said, "Meiklejohn is right in a way—things ought never to have got to this pass where freedom of thought and expression depend on distinctions as thin as a hair." Angell, *Zechariah Chafee, Jr.,* 70 HARV. L. REV. 1341 (1957).

67. The Supreme Court adoption is Dennis v. United States, 341 U.S. 494, 510 (1951) (quoting United States v. Dennis, 183 F.2d 201, 212 (2d Cir. 1950)).

A leading illustrator of this dooming inevitability was Justice
Frankfurter. It was satirically popular, particularly after its speedy
overthrow, to refer to the First Flag Salute Case,[68] in which Justice
Frankfurter for the Court upheld a requirement that Jehovah's Witnesses children salute the flag, as Felix's Fall of France opinion.
This was unfair; for this Justice, the presumption of constitutionality did require this result.[69] Put it all together and the consequence
is a washout for free speech.

And so in fact it was. Holmes, who did have a pragmatic dedication to free speech, flinched from the application of that ideal only
in the crunch of war. Followers, such as Justices Frankfurter and
Jackson, flinched with regularity. In terms of the history of ideas,
by the 1950's the Supreme Court, believing itself to be applying the
clear and present danger test, had moved 180 degrees from the
philosophy of inalienable rights. The Communist leaders sent to
prison were exercising the activities of speech and press only.[70] They
were both too canny and, I suspect, too puny to attempt anything
else. Their convictions were upheld squarely, said Judge Hand, as
a necessary invasion of free speech.[71] These decisions of the 1950's
epitomize the prevailing peak of Professor Bickel's point of view; a
free speech approach devoid of historical commitment, in which
"limits are set by culture, by time-and-place-bound conditions."[72]

Justice Black dissented from these decisions. His thought process, though worded differently, is similar to that of Pastor Dietrich
Bonhoeffer. In his *Letters From Prison*, Bonhoeffer, as he awaited
execution by the Nazis for his part in resisting Hitlerism, regretted
that in contemporary theology

> the area of freedom has receded into the background: Your reference
> to Socrates' remarks about culture and death may be very valuable;
> I must give it further thought. The only thing I am really clear about
> at the moment is that education that breaks down in the face of

---

68. Minersville School Dist. v. Gobitis, 310 U.S. 586 (1940).

69. It is a curio of history that Justice Stone, in the famous footnote 4 in United States
v. Carolene Products Co., 304 U.S. 144, 152 n.4 (1938) suggested that a counterpresumption
should apply in cases involving civil liberties and especially free speech. The then Professor
Frankfurter wrote Justice Stone strongly extolling the suggestion. Without detouring to the
details here the Stone proposal was a sound implementation of the pragmatic philosophy
which Stone personally espoused. This early conversion of Justice Frankfurter did not last,
and by First Flag Salute and for the rest of his life he was firmly committed to an opposite
point of view. *See* R. Newman, Hugo Black and Edmond Cahn, A Philosophical Friendship
(1976) (unpublished MA thesis, Univ. of Va.).

70. Dennis v. United States, 341 U.S. 494 (1951).

71. *Id.* at 510 (citing Judge Hand in United States v. Dennis, 183 F.2d 201, 212 (2d Cir.
1950)).

72. A. BICKEL, THE MORALITY OF CONSENT 4 (1975).

danger is no education. . . . Education must be able to face death and danger—*impravidum feriunt ruinae*: "the ruins will strike the fearless man" (Horace)—even if it cannot "conquer" them. . . .[73]

Whether or not it is too severe to say that the culture espoused by Professor Bickel is no culture at all, it is at least inescapable that Judge Hand's tolerated "invasion of free speech" conflicts with James Madison. It was Madison who declared the first amendment liberties to be "beyond the reach of this government;" who said that the federal government had "no power whatever"[74] in the premises. Hand cannot be squared with Jefferson's first inaugural:

If there be any among us who would wish to dissolve this Union or to change its republican form, let them stand undisturbed as monuments of the safety with which error of opinion may be tolerated where reason is left free to combat it.[75]

When the chips were down, the doctrine of utility proved to be not very useful. Hugo Black set himself decisively in the opposite direction. He would accept the challenge of Horace to let the ruin come; he would recall the country to Madison and Jefferson.

IV.   BLACK ON THE FIRST AMENDMENT: THE BIG PICTURE

Black's professional career falls into four pre-Court phases. In the beginning he was a youngster with a little civil and criminal practice and, shortly, a city judge in Birmingham for minor criminal matters. Then he became prosecuting attorney. Upon his return from World War I, Captain Black had a substantial personal injury and criminal practice, enough to permit him to take off almost all of 1925-26 to run for the Senate. As a Senator, he began to be a constitutional theorist; his views on due process and the commerce clause were molded in those years.[76] His greatest legal exercise, however, was in the extension of his superb trial skills. By 1937, when he went to the Court, Black was one of the Senate's ablest and most seasoned investigators.[77]

---

73.   D. BONHOEFFER, LETTERS AND PAPERS FROM PRISON 25-26 (E. Bethge ed. 1953).

74.   1 ANNALS OF CONG. 458-60 (Gales & Seaton eds. 1789).

75.   1 J. RICHARDSON, MESSAGES AND PAPERS OF THE PRESIDENTS 322 (1897).

76.   On Black's pre-Court life, see J. FRANK, MR. JUSTICE BLACK (1949); on Black's development as a constitutionalist in the Senate, see Frank, *The New Court and the New Deal*, in HUGO BLACK 39 (S. Strickland ed. 1967).

77.   As a Senator, Black enforced the right of the Senate to punish for contempt. Jurney v. MacCracken, 294 U.S. 125 (1935). On July 24, 1966, the Justice made an extensive file note that an article he had written for Harper's Magazine, Feb. 1936, as to the need of such a legislative power was quite wrong.

None of these experiences made Black, the Senator become Justice, a surefooted master of first amendment theory. What is remarkable is that he made so few mistakes in terms of later-expressed beliefs. Fortunately, in the first years first amendment cases were few. There were mistakes; the First Flag Salute Case was the greatest, and within three years, Black had reversed himself.[78] In conversation with me between First Flag Salute and the reversal, he expressed regret that he had not known until he was committed to Justice Frankfurter that Stone would dissent or he would have joined him. The apologia was unworthy of the Black I knew in 1942, who did not need companionship from anyone to take a stand. He joined in an opinion of Justice Murphy which contained an incidental passage that the first amendment does not apply to libel or obscenity,[79] a view the reverse of one he later preached for twenty years. He also joined the landmark Murphy opinion in *Thornhill v. Alabama*[80] that picketing is free speech. He later came to regard "the marching element of picketing" as primarily conduct rather than speech.[81]

This exhausts the list of instances in which Black had to alter early first amendment stands. He necessarily operated within the orbit of the clear and present danger test as it emerged in battered but still sturdy shape from the 1930's; but as early as 1941 he had induced a majority of the Court to reach for something much more. The seeds of his final position grow from his 1941 opinion in *Bridges v. California*:[82]

> What finally emerges from the "clear and present danger" cases is a working principle that the substantive evil must be extremely serious and the degree of imminence extremely high before utterances can be punished. Those cases do not purport to mark the furthermost constitutional boundaries of protected expression, nor do we here. They do no more than recognize a minimum compulsion of the Bill of Rights. For the First Amendment does not speak equivocally. It prohibits any law "abridging the freedom of speech, or of the press." It must be taken as a command of the broadest scope that explicit language, read in the context of a liberty-loving society, will allow.[83]

---

78. Minersville School Dist. v. Gobitis, 310 U.S. 586 (1940) (First Flag Salute Case). Justices Black and Douglas repented in Jones v. Opelika, 316 U.S. 584 (1942), and Board of Educ. v. Barnette, 319 U.S. 624 (1943), overruled *Gobitis*.

79. Chaplinsky v. New Hampshire, 315 U.S. 568, 571-72 (1942).

80. 310 U.S. 88 (1940).

81. H. BLACK, A CONSTITUTIONAL FAITH 54, 57 (1968).

82. 314 U.S. 252 (1941).

83. *Id.* at 263 (footnote omitted).

The period between 1949 and 1954 was a bleak span in Black's life. The premature deaths of Justices Murphy and Rutledge in 1949 destroyed Black's effective power on the Court in Bill of Rights matters. Where previously the quadrumvirate of Black, Douglas, Murphy and Rutledge could prevail on a free speech issue,[84] after 1949 Black and Douglas were at a discount. The replacement justices, Black's old Senate ally Sherman Minton and then Attorney General Tom Clark, gave Black happy personal ties; Clark remained a warm friend for the rest of Black's life. However, the new justices' civil liberties views were not at all similar to his. Moreover, in 1951, Black's wife died, and he, a man who had sacrificed social life for work, was terribly lonely. At this moment of loneliness and ineffectiveness came the great wave of illiberalism usually synopsized under the label McCarthyism. In case after case the Court upheld what Black regarded as ultimate inequities. In the relative calm of twenty years later, a calm in the free speech which exists in part because Black lived and fought his fight, it is hard to grasp the overwhelming emotion of those days. Black was powerless; he could do little more than scream.

In 1950, the Court upheld a statute for practical purposes barring from labor unions any officer who not merely might be a Communist but who might "support any organization that believes in or teaches the overthrow of the United States government."[85] Black passionately protested the power of Congress to proscribe beliefs and political affiliations.[86] The statute required labor union officials to take certain oaths. Black saw this as a "test oath" and with his sense of history he recalled the use of such oaths

> against the Huguenots in France, and against "heretics" during the Spanish Inquisition. It helped English rulers identify and outlaw Catholics, Quakers, Baptists, and Congregationalists—groups considered dangerous for political as well as religious reasons. And wherever the test oath was in vogue, spies and informers found rewards far more tempting than truth.[87]

The Justice laid down the principle which guided him time after time for the rest of his life; it was his answer, his alternative to the clear and present danger test:

> These experiences [the historical experiences referred to] underline the wisdom of the basic constitutional precept that penalties

---

84. *See, e.g.,* Schneiderman v. United States, 320 U.S. 118 (1943).
85. American Communications Ass'n v. Douds, 339 U.S. 382, 446 (1950).
86. *Id.* at 452.
87. *Id.* at 447 (footnote omitted).

should be imposed only for a person's own conduct, not for his beliefs
or for the conduct of others with whom he may associate. Guilt should
not be imputed solely from association or affiliation with political
parties or any other organization, however much we abhor the ideas
which they advocate. . . . Like anyone else, individual Communists
who commit overt acts in violation of valid laws can and should be
punished. But the postulate of the First Amendment is that our free
institutions can be maintained without proscribing or penalizing political belief, speech, press, assembly, or party affiliation.[88]

The next year the Court upheld the Smith Act under which
numerous persons were convicted of knowingly and willfully teaching and advocating the duty and necessity of overthrowing the government.[89] No overt acts were charged other than teaching and advocating this "duty and necessity." The other members of the
Court, in majority and in dissent, spoke much of the clear and
present danger test.[90]

Justice Douglas directed himself squarely to that concept and
turned some devastating sentences. He recognized Communism on
the world scene as a real menace to democracy:

> Communism in the world scene is no bogeyman; but Commun-
> ism as a political faction or party in this country plainly is. Commun-
> ism has been so thoroughly exposed in this country that it has been
> crippled as a political force. Free speech has destroyed it as an effec-
> tive political party. . . .
> How it can be said that there is a clear and present danger that
> this advocacy will succeed is, therefore, a mystery. . . . [I]n America
> they are miserable merchants of unwanted ideas; their wares remain
> unsold. The fact that their ideas are abhorrent does not make them
> powerful.
> . . . [T]he invisible army of petitioners is the best known, the
> most beset, and the least thriving of any fifth column in history. Only
> those held by fear and panic could think otherwise.[91]

Black spoke more briefly; his departure from the majority was
"a fundamental difference in constitutional approach." These petitioners have not been charged with any overt acts of any kind:

> They were not even charged with saying anything or writing anything
> designed to overthrow the Government. The charge was that they
> agreed to assemble and to talk and publish certain ideas at a later

---

88. *Id.* at 452-53 (citation and footnote omitted).
89. Dennis v. United States, 341 U.S. 494 (1951).
90. *Id.* at 581-91 *passim.*
91. *Id.* at 588-89.

date: The indictment is that they conspired to organize the Communist Party and to use speech or newspapers and other publications in the future to teach and advocate the forcible overthrow of the Government.[92]

He noted that the majority in various ways was cutting back on the concept of clear and present danger. For himself he reiterated his position in the *Bridges* case of a decade earlier. With a momentary and exceptional reservation reflecting a desire to think more about Professor Meiklejohn's recently published concepts, Black said, "at least as to speech in the realm of public matters,"[93] he believed that the clear and present danger test did not protect enough. Justice Jackson, referring to the "clear and present danger" language as making "our Government captive in a judge-made verbal trap," would substitute a "rule of reason."[94] Black, in response, took a position which in countless other matters culminated his thinking for the rest of his life:

> I cannot agree that the First Amendment permits us to sustain laws suppressing freedom of speech and press on the basis of Congress' or our own notions of mere "reasonableness." Such a doctrine waters down the First Amendment so that it amounts to little more than an admonition to Congress.[95]

The decisions of the 1950's continued, from Black's standpoint, to be almost all bad, although the appointments of Chief Justice Warren and Justice Brennan restored an intellectual compatibility for Black which made him less a Jeremiah, his tone less plaintive. In 1959, with the four Justices dissenting, the Court decided *Barenblatt v. United States.*[96] The issue was whether a person could be held in contempt of Congress for refusal to state whether he had ever been a member of the Communist Party or had certain knowledge about possible Communist activities on the University of Michigan campus when he had been a student. Justice Black's dissent held that the Committee was abridging freedom of speech "through exposure, obloquy and public scorn."[97]

Black here gave his most mature expression of the distinction between the control of conduct and the control of speech. He recognized that there are instances in which a law "primarily regulates

---

92. *Id.* at 494.
93. *Id.* at 580 (quoting Black, J. in Bridges v. California, 314 U.S. 252, 263 (1941)).
94. *Id.* at 568-69.
95. *Id.* at 580.
96. 360 U.S. 109, 134, 166 (1959).
97. *Id.* at 141.

conduct" and yet "might also indirectly affect speech"[98] and acknowledged that in such cases the law could be upheld "if the effect on speech is minor in relation to the need for control of the conduct."[99] Control of the streets to facilitate traffic or avoid litter are illustrations. But here no conduct was involved—the petitioner's views and associations, his membership in this campus club or another were simply matters of his beliefs.

The *Barenblatt* majority had upheld the requirement on the basis that the public interest in gaining the knowledge was greater than the individual's interest in free speech. To Black there was no capacity in the Congress to make any such judgment. Madison had said that the Bill of Rights made it the duty of the courts "to resist *every* encroachment"[100] upon the Bill of Rights, not just some of them. The government in its brief had spoken of the "communication of unlawful ideas;"[101] Black denied that ideas could ever be proscribed under the Constitution. So far as the Communist Party is concerned, "we cannot outlaw it, as a group, without endangering the liberty of all of us."[102] Hence, said Justice Black (and now it was one-third of the Court speaking through him):

> the First Amendment sought to leave Congress devoid of any kind or quality of power to direct any type of national laws against the freedom of individuals to think what they please, advocate whatever policy they choose, and join with others to bring about the social, religious, political and governmental changes which seem best to them.[103]

Two years later Justice Black observed that the clear and present danger test, though advanced in its day, "does not go as far as my own views as to the protection that should be accorded" the rights of freedom of speech and press and reiterated that these freedoms were "completely out of the area of any congressional control."[104]

There were better days coming, partly from changing personnel and partly from changing circumstance. Repression in America his-

---

98. *Id.*

99. *Id.*

100. 1 ANNALS OF CONG. 459 (Gales & Seaton eds. 1789).

101. 360 U.S. at 145.

102. *Id.* at 149.

103. *Id.* at 151.

104. Konigsberg v. State Bar, 366 U.S. 36, 56, 61, 63 (Black, J., dissenting) (1961). My friendly informal critic of a draft of this paper, Mr. Roger Newman, feels that I inadequately treat *Konigsberg*'s companion case, *In re* Anastaplo, 366 U.S. 82, 97 (1961), in which on an even clearer record than *Konigsberg*, Black for a minority of four attacks the "balancing" theory of the first amendment. But either case will make the key points.

torically is cyclical.[105] As I have observed on other occassions courts love liberty most when it is under pressure least.[106] The repressionist fervor abated in the placid Eisenhower years, particularly after the Senate censure of Senator McCarthy, and the community tone changed. With new appointments a Warren Court finally truly emerged, and as Professor Bickel has very gracefully said, "the Warren Court in its heyday was Hugo Black writ large."[107]

No complete majority ever adopted the full Black position on free speech, but it moved strongly in that direction. In *Schneider v. Smith*,[108] Justice Douglas writing for the Court, the issue was the power of the Coast Guard to condition licenses of seamen on consideration of their beliefs, or reading habits, or social, educational, or political associations. In holding that there was no such power, the Court declared that the first amendment "creates a preserve where the views of the individual are made inviolate."[109] It quoted Jefferson for precisely the proposition Black advocated: "It is time enough for the rightful purposes of civil government for its officers to interfere when principles break out into overt acts against peace and good order. . . ."[110]

In *Brandenburg v. Ohio*,[111] the Court in a per curiam opinion invalidated the Ohio Criminal Syndicalism Act and in so doing overruled *Whitney v. California*.[112] It was in *Whitney* that Justice Brandeis, dissenting and joined by Holmes, gave the ultimate and best statement of the pragmatic clear and present danger test; a statement which as a practical matter Professor Meiklejohn, as a leading intellectual idealist, was able wholly to accept. The *Brandenburg* Court confined the *Dennis* decision to the proposition that the states may not "forbid or proscribe advocacy of the use of force or of law violation except where such advocacy is directed to inciting or producing imminent lawless action and is likely to incite or produce such action."[113] Had *Dennis* in truth applied that standard, the result would have been different. Black concurred briefly simply to note that the Court had, in citing *Dennis*, indicated no

---

105. For brief exposition of this thesis see Frank, *United States Supreme Court: 1949-50*, 18 U. Chi. L. Rev. 1, 20 (1950), and J. Frank, *Review and Basic Liberties*, in Supreme Court and Supreme Law 109, 113-39 (E. Cahn ed. 1954).

106. *See generally* references cited in note 105 *supra*.

107. A. Bickel, The Morality of Consent 9 (1975).

108. 390 U.S. 17 (1968).

109. *Id.* at 25.

110. *Id.*

111. 395 U.S. 444 (1969).

112. 274 U.S. 357 (1927).

113. 395 U.S. at 447.

approval of its intellectual underpinnings; he was perhaps entitled to this small chortle.

Again, in *Baird v. Arizona*,[114] Black fell just short of total victory. Mrs. Baird, a Stanford Law School graduate, was barred from Arizona bar admission solely because she declined to answer whether she had ever been a member of the Communist Party or any organization that "advocates" overthrow of the United States. Black for four Justices, a fifth concurring specially, wrote that the government could "not inquire about a man's views or associations solely for the purpose of withholding a right or benefit because of what he believes."[115] As he cheerfully added, "[s]ome of what has been written is reconcilable with what we have said here and some is not."[116]

And, finally, the end. The *Pentagon Papers* case[117] was the government's unsuccessful effort to enjoin the *New York Times* and the *Washington Post* from publishing a history of Viet Nam policymaking. With Black as the senior Justice opposing the injunction, he might have marshaled a Court and obtained a single majority opinion. His strength was gone and only spirit remained; he and the Court splintered into nine opinions, only Justices Black and Douglas wholly agreeing with each other.

> I believe that every moment's continuance of the injunctions against these newspapers amounts to a flagrant, indefensible, and continuing violation of the First Amendment. . . . A [contrary] holding would make a shambles of the First Amendment.
> . . . When the Constitution was adopted, many people strongly opposed it because the document contained no Bill of Rights to safeguard certain basic freedoms. . . . In response to an overwhelming public clamor, James Madison offered a series of amendments to satisfy citizens that these great liberties would remain safe and beyond the power of government to abridge. . . . The Bill of Rights changed the original Constitution into a new charter under which no branch of government could abridge the people's freedoms of press, speech, religion, and assembly. . . .
> . . . In other words, we are asked to hold that despite the First Amendment's emphatic command, the Executive Branch, the Congress, and the Judiciary can made laws enjoining publication of current news and abridging freedom of the press in the name of "national security." . . . The Framers of the First Amendment . . .

---

114.   401 U.S. 1 (1971). *Baird* is treated in the Memorial Service for Justice Black as overruling the earlier bar admission cases, 405 U.S. at 27 (1971).

115.   401 U.S. at 7.

116.   *Id.*

117.   New York Times Co. v. United States, 403 U.S. 713 (1971).

and in depth; Black knew Macaulay better than any other judge of our times.[142] He dug back to the classical era as well; his personal Tacitus and his Livy are physically marked throughout for episodes of abuses of civil liberties.[143] Of nothing was he more sure than that the Bill of Rights was not intended to preserve the very limited English common law of free speech as of 1790; he was exceedingly clear, both in lecture and in opinion, that this is precisely what the amendment sought to avoid.

For Black it would have been enough if he were interpreting an historical document, but his choice of illustrations might obscure the fact that for Black this was living history. Black did not think of the rack and the screw as curious antiquities. Seventeenth century torture had been occurring in Birmingham, Alabama, when he was prosecuting attorney, and he knew all about it. Suspects have been forced to incriminate themselves by torture in America repeatedly, and the Wickersham Report of 1931 fully demonstrated this.[144] Black embraced the prohibition on self-incrimination with a passion and strenuously repudiated forced confessions because he understood perfectly well the brutalities, ancient and modern, which made the defendants talk.

In the forties Black fought the possibility, to use the phrase of the times, that it could happen here. Hitlerism and Stalinism were real contemporary illustrations to him in our own world and in our own time of the tyranny he sought to resist; and in the repression of the late 1940's and 1950's he sincerely believed that those very abuses, particularly of free speech, were occurring in the United States.[145] During the last five years of Black's life the Soviet Union conducted the monstrous trials of Sinyavski and Daniel for "anti-Soviet publications" in which the findings of Glavlit, of the Soviet

---

142. In Joint Anti-Fascist Refugee Comm. v. McGrath, Justice Black said:
[S]ince prejudice manifests itself in much the same way in every age and country and since what has happened before can happen again, it surely should not be amiss to call attention to what has occurred when dominant governmental groups have been left free to give uncontrolled rein to their prejudice against unorthodox minorities.
341 U.S. 123, 145 (1951) (Black, J., concurring).

143. Meador gives a substantial illustration of Tacitus as a Black source and notes that Black's Livy was "heavily marked, personally indexed." D. MEADOR, MR. JUSTICE BLACK AND HIS BOOKS 11, 15, 84 (1974).

144. NATIONAL COMMISSION ON LAW OBSERVANCE AND ENFORCEMENT, REPORT ON THE ENFORCEMENT LAWS OF THE UNITED STATES 46 (1931) (commonly known as the Wickersham Report).

145. In remarks on receipt of an award for service to libertarian goals on April 3, 1945, as World War II was ending, Black said, "The principles of fascism, and all that fascism stands for with its barbaric denial of human values, must be obliterated and destroyed. To accomplish this there must be an emphatic reassertion of democratic values and a resurgence in democratic faith at home and throughout the world." Black Mss., Library of Congress.

Domestic Censorship Agency, were used as the basis of the indictment and were read as evidence in the courtroom.[146] Black was
keenly aware of these contemporary monstrosities. While his illustrations were ancient, his thought was contemporary, for to him
tyranny was recrudescent; the English rack for the extortion of confessions, and the Nazi secret police were all of a piece.

   In not merely his goals but in his predictions, I believe the
Justice to have been right. We live in a world of tyranny and of
torture. For three-quarters of the people on the earth, there is no
political freedom; in our own hemisphere in Chile and Brazil, as well
as in Russia, the tortures of the rack are intensified by the wonders
of contemporary science. Solzhenitsyn may not have been welcome
at the White House in recent years, but he would have been welcome at the Black home.

D.   New Techniques

   The methods and circumstances of communication have
changed in ways the eighteenth century could not possibly contem-
plate. The eighteenth century did not have labor unions, much less
picketing; there was no question as to that kind of communication.
The eighteenth century had no sound trucks. There was of course
no radio. The whole economic order was different. It was vividly
apparent by the middle of Black's lifetime that the real limit on a
free press was money. The first amendment was adopted when the
press was virtually a store-front industry, when almost anyone could
buy a simple press, a font of type, and with it talk to his fellow
townsmen. That was a long yesterday ago.

   Black took his swing at applying the antitrust laws to monopoly
press.[147] As *Pentagon Papers* reveals, he upheld freedom of content
with his dying breath. Yet as a practical matter freedom of content,
apart from economic controls, has been under only specialized pressure in recent years, as in quarrels over news coverage of criminal
trials. A printers' union frantically resisting automation suppresses
more publication in a week than the Supreme Court is called upon
to undo in a decade. In responding to these changes Black sought
to adapt first amendment principles to the new situations. On con-

---

   146.   Hayward, *The Trial of Sinyavsky and Daniel,* N.Y. Times, Apr. 17, 1966, § 6
(Magazine) at 20.
   147.   *See, e.g.,* Associated Press v. United States, 326 U.S. 1 (1945); Citizen Pub. Co.
v. United States, 394 U.S. 131 (1969); *see also* T. EMERSON, THE SYSTEM OF FREEDOM OF
EXPRESSION 627-96 (1970) (developing the problems of access of the public to communication
more fully than Black ever dealt with it.)

tent protection he made some headway; on the larger restraints inherent in the one-newspaper city or the monopoly network he was essentially ineffective.[148]

Just as there was methodology in the technique of communication so there was new technology in oppression; the twentieth century has been ingenious in ways which did not occur to our fathers in disabling those with whom we disagree. While individuals have doubtless long dismissed other individuals with whom they disagreed from their employment, the device of large-scale governmental systematic barring from public or private employment for opinion is quite new.[149] These were the massive devices of the loyalty programs of the House Committee on Un-American Activities and the McCarthy Committed.[150] Black found an extreme instance of this, the removal of three named persons from public employment, to be a bill of attainder, a lonely contemporary illustration of an ancient concept.[151] The creative leap here lay in the perception that the principles of the first amendment should bear as heavily on starving or disgracing the dissenter as on the more traditional device of imprisoning him.[152] In this respect Black recovered from the reverses of the 1950's, and the contemporary shape of the law confirms as one of Black's most effective contributions this adaptation of first amendment principles to a new situation.[153]

E. *"Reasonable" Standards*

A definition not only includes but it also excludes, and Black was as rigorous with his exclusions as with his inclusions. It was here, in particular, that on occasion he pulled away from Justice Douglas.

Specifically, Black believed that the prohibitions of the Consti-

---

148. *See, e.g.,* The Aspen Institute Program on Communications and Society, unpublished paper (August, 1976, conference) ("Particular concern exists with regard to the dominant position of three commercial networks in controlling what the nation sees and hears over television.") Black never affected that concern. Because his brother-in-law, Clifford Durr, was an FCC Commissioner, for many years Black disqualified himself in all FCC cases.

149. For a concise, excellent statement with numerous citations, see T. EMERSON, TOWARD A GENERAL THEORY OF THE FIRST AMENDMENT 95-100 (1963); T. EMERSON, THE SYSTEM OF FREEDOM OF EXPRESSION 161-204 (1970). I have relied on both these works very heavily in preparing this essay.

150. From the large literature, I choose one high quality, illustrative citation, R. BROWN, LOYALTY AND SECURITY (1958).

151. United States v. Lovett, 328 U.S. 303 (1946).

152. For another grim illustration, in which failure to disclose political affiliation became "good cause" for discharge under a union agreement, see Black v. Cutter Laboratories, 351 U.S. 292 (1956). Justice Douglas wrote the dissent in which Chief Justice Warren and Black joined. *Id.* at 300.

tution should be applied to the hilt; the only functions of judges
were to determine whether a particular bit of conduct was prohibited, and then act. The corollary of this for him was that for activity
not clearly prohibited by the Constitution, the government might
proceed, and this no matter how distasteful he personally thought
the government action might be. In Black's mind, the judges themselves could easily be the real enemy of freedom, and this by judicial
importation of standards of "reasonableness" in the application of
the amendments. So far as he was concerned (except as to searches
and seizures where the Constitution itself delegates determination
of reasonableness to the judges), "reasonableness" of legislation was
no concern of the Court. In response to "overwhelming public
clamor," James Madison offered his amendments to satisfy those
citizens who felt insecure under the Constitution. Black read the
government's argument in the *Pentagon Papers* case as a contention
that provisions in the body of the Constitution should, as necessary,
override the Bill of Rights; he could "imagine no greater perversion
of history."

Wholly outside any matter of the Bill of Rights, this question
arose in connection with substantive due process before Black came
to the Court. In its halcyon days, the old Court invalidated social
legislation as unreasonable under the due process clause over the
dissents of Holmes and Brandeis on the Court and Black in the
Senate.[154]

This identical phenomenon of judicial determination of reasonableness was doubly unappetizing to Black in relation to the Bill of
Rights because he saw it as a watering down of what should be
absolute security of the citizen. Hence his drive toward hard constitutional interpretation became almost frenzied when his brethren
were deciding what regulations were "reasonable" or what conduct
"shocked the conscience."

An extreme illustration is *Rochin v. California*,[155] in which the
opinion of the Court held invalid a conviction obtained by pumping
out the stomach of the defendant and presenting the evidence thus
found. The opinion of the Court found this was "conduct that
shocks the conscience" and that it was therefore unconstitutional.
Justice Black concurred on the ground that the fifth amendment
prohibition on self-incrimination was applicable to the states, that

---

153. For illustration of a sharp limit of ideological criteria for employment, see Schneider v. Smith, 390 U.S. 17 (1968) (Douglas, J.).

154. *See generally* J. FRANK, MR. JUSTICE BLACK (1949); *see also* Frank, *The New Court
and the New Deal* in HUGO BLACK 39 (S. Strickland ed. 1967).

155. 342 U.S. 165 (1952).

this was self-incrimination, and that the conviction therefore was *Rochin* unconstitutional. In a terse opinion, one which, in terms of the intellectual conviction which it reflected, was one of the most important he ever wrote, he objected to leaving it to the judges to decide constitutional questions in terms of conscience.

To Black, the vice of the "reasonableness" approach was most brilliantly illustrated by its bearing on first amendment cases. "I long ago," he said, "concluded that the accordian-like qualities of this philosophy must inevitably imperil all the individual liberty safeguards specifically enumerated in the Bill of Rights. Reflection and recent decisions of this Court sanctioning abridgment of the freedom of speech and press have strengthened this conclusion."[156] In this view, Justice Black had the strong support of Professor Meiklejohn, who felt that the *Rochin* concurrence

> goes straight to the heart of the matter and I'm daring to hope that, sooner or later, what you are saying will have decisive influence in the direction of better understanding. The philosophy of the majority opinion is, as you say, radically unsound, but it has a very strong appeal to the "American mind," as it now functions, and it is dominant and dangerous in every phase of our life.[157]

Oddly enough, Black on stomach pumps requires Black on birth control. Conviction by stomach pump is appalling. It is unconstitutional, not because it is obnoxious, distasteful, grotesquely abusive, but because it violates the perfectly clear mandate of the fifth amendment that no person shall be required to incriminate himself. Anti-birth control legislation Black felt was "offensive;" but unlike the majority, he could not accept the conclusion that "the evil qualities they see in the law make it unconstitutional,"[158] citing his own concurrence in *Rochin*. The other justices invalidated the law on the ground that the first amendment had a "penumbra" protecting privacy. Black could be as passionate in favor of privacy as the next one, but he could not make it a constitutional standard. He had no desire

> to keep the Constitution in tune with the times. The idea is that the Constitution must be changed from time to time and that this Court is charged with a duty to make those changes. For myself, I must with all deference reject that philosophy. The Constitution makers knew the need for change and provided for it.[159]

---

156. *Id.* at 177 (Black, J., concurring).
157. Letter from Meiklejohn to Black (Jan. 28, 1952) Meiklejohn file, Black Mss.
158. Griswold v. Connecticut, 381 U.S. 479, 507 (1965) (Black, J., dissenting).
159. *Id.* at 522.

If Justice Black had his way, every last bit of the Bill of Rights would have been applicable to the states, which as a concrete matter would have included the seventh amendment. This would have required the use of a jury in every civil case involving twenty dollars. Justice Black knew that this was absurdly intolerable; it would throw every small claims court in America into the ashcan. It would have done an immense disservice to small claimants and small defendants, and would have made the whole process of dispute settling excessively costly. When he and I discussed this consequence his response always was: "A constitutional amendment will be easy enough."

In other words, so far as he was concerned, the Bill of Rights requires a civil jury in small cases, the fourteenth amendment makes the entire Bill of Rights applicable to the states: there can be no picking or choosing in terms of reasonableness. If the law is distasteful, change it. The other side of that same coin is *Griswold*. Restrictions on birth control may be foolish but they are not unconstitutional; if the public dislikes them, let the Constitution be changed.

To Black, both these positions were absolutely essential to his stand on free speech, and hence the warm concurrence which he received from Professor Meiklejohn. If the first amendment is to be enforced as it should be, it was up to the judges, in Madison's language, "to resist every encroachment upon rights expressly stipulated for in the Constitution by the Declaration of Rights."[160] Let judges decide whether they like birth control legislation, or "twenty dollar" juries, or stomach pumps, and they can also decide whether they like free speech. This, to Black, was intolerable.

VI.   CRIMINAL CONDUCT TEST

Where, if anywhere, would Black stop free speech? No one supposes that a conspiracy to commit murder is free of control and, indeed, punishment simply because it is done with words. Nobody supposes, to take the classic example, that one can with impunity falsely shout "fire" in a crowded theatre. No one, including Justice Black, believes that speech is absolutely free.

What, then, is the limitation? The Holmes-Brandeis view of clear and present danger was that emerging from pragmatic philosophy earlier discussed: speech could be restrained only where a lawfully prohibitable danger was so imminent that counter speech

---

160.   1 ANNALS OF CONG. 450 (Gales & Seaton eds. 1789).

could not prevail. Black, because of the "accordion-like qualities" of this approach found this concept wholly useless.[161] On the other hand he also agreed that not every word would be blessed in the sanctuary of the law. What were his limitations?

We come back to the absolute approach. Taken at its simplest for purposes of example, key words in the first amendment are: "Congress shall make no law . . . abridging the freedom of speech. . . ."[162] One can decide, as does Black, that "no law" means "no law" and still have problems left as to what is abridgment and what is speech. As was suggested in the preceding section of this paper both Professor Anastaplo and Dean Griswold clearly raise the question,[163] even given the absolute concept, of exactly what it is that is absolutely prohibited. In formulating doctrine under the first amendment one can give a specific and hence somewhat narrow definition of "speech" and then give that "speech" full protection; or one can give a very loose and broad definition of "speech," and give it only partial protection.

Black never thought with the same comprehensive exhaustiveness and historical attention on the meaning of either "abridgment" or "speech" that he gave to the concept of "no law." He did think closely on the relationship of "speech" and "conduct," a distinction about to be developed; but he never thoroughly analyzed or historically investigated whether either obscenity or libel were "speech" at all as that phrase is used in the first amendment. On abridgment, while he did not use the term as a key to decision, his decisions can be rationalized on the basis that he did not consider certain restrictions as "abridgments" at all. This is illustrated in the concept articulated by Meiklejohn, and accepted by Black, that while speech is not subject to control for its content, it is controllable in terms of time, place, and manner. Not everyone can talk at once. There is a right of speech in parliamentary bodies, but only subject to the procedures of parliamentary law. A defendant can not so carry on in a courtroom as to make his trial impossible, a matter on which Black was categorically firm.

As was his position with attempts to intimidate court proceedings by mobs in the courtyard. Where a mob wished to demonstrate near a courthouse, Black found it completely proper

to protect courts and court officials from the intimidation and dangers that inhere in huge gatherings at courthouse doors and jail doors

---

161. Konigsberg v. State Bar, 366 U.S. 36, 56 (1961) (Black, J., dissenting).
162. U.S. CONST. amend. I.
163. *See* note 135 *supra*.

to protest arrests and to influence court officials in performing their duties. . . . Justice cannot be rightly administered, nor are the lives and safety of prisoners secure, where throngs of people clamor against the processes of justice right outside the courthouse or jailhouse doors. . . . Use of the streets for such purposes has always proved disastrous to individual liberty in the long run, whatever fleeting benefits may have appeared to have been achieved.[164]

Black's observation was stated in a dissent, but the same view moved into the majority when the Court, in a Black opinion, upheld the conviction of members of a mob demonstrating at a jail and blocking its flow of traffic. Black's opinion flatly rejected the proposition that demonstrators have a right to express their views "whenever and however and wherever they please."[165] He continued, "The United States Constitution does not forbid a state to control the use of its own property for its own lawful nondiscriminatory purpose."[166]

In the cases just discussed, the restrictions were not on the content of the expression, which may have been innocuous enough; rather the restrictions went to time, place, and manner. But the ultimate test is whether the first amendment permits restrictions on content, and there were circumstances in which Black upheld such restrictions. These were the cases in which speech becomes the conduct which itself is illegal.[167] The conspiracy to commit murder is the classic example. Thus Black upheld restrictions on speech aimed at violation of the antitrust laws with no compunction at all; the speech was simply incidental to the actual illegal conduct presently underway.[168] As Justice Douglas put it, speech may become illegal when it is "brigaded with action."[169]

Black joined in upholding the convictions of persons who burned their draft cards, accepting Chief Justice Warren's proposition that "when 'speech' and 'nonspeech' elements are combined in the same course of conduct, a sufficiently important governmental

---

164. Cox v. Louisiana, 379 U.S. 536, 583 (1965) (Black, J., dissenting).
165. Adderley v. Florida, 385 U.S. 39, 48 (1966).
166. *Id.*
167. A searching criticism of this approach is L. HAND, THE BILL OF RIGHTS 56-77 (1958). *See, e.g.,* Yates v. United States, 354 U.S. 298 (1957), in which Justice Harlan for the Court sought to distinguish between words that advocate "concrete action" and those that advocate "principles divorced from action." Bickel briskly tosses the whole approach into the waste basket as "absurd." He says, "There is no bright line between communication and conduct. What is a live sex show—communication or conduct?" A. BICKEL, THE MORALITY OF CONSENT 74 (1975). Chafee rejects the view that "all speech is free, and only action can be restrained and punished." Z. CHAFEE, FREEDOM OF SPEECH 7 (1920).
168. *See* Giboney v. Empire Storage & Ice Co., 336 U.S. 490 (1949).
169. Speiser v. Randall, 357 U.S. 513, 536 (1958) (Douglas, J., concurring).

interest in regulating the nonspeech element can justify incidental limitations on First Amendment freedoms."[170] On the other hand, he upheld the symbolic speech involved in the wearing of arm bands to protest the Viet Nam War because it was symbolic speech which involved no illegal conduct whatsoever.[171] He believed that a defendant could be punished for burning a flag despite the fact that the burning may have been accompanied by statements or had some symbolic value: "It is immaterial to me that words are spoken in connection with the burning. It is the *burning* of the flag that the State has set its face against."[172] The first amendment gives no protection to speech or writing used " 'as an integral part of conduct in violation of a valid criminal statute.' "[173]

In the conduct cases Black inescapably slipped into the very type of balancing to which he objected in connection with more general speech. For example, he would uphold only tightly restrictive anti-littering laws where they interfered with handbills which might convey ideas, thus to some extent balancing the litter control against the distribution of ideas. His own limitation on this score he set forth thus: "[T]his kind of balancing should be used only where a law is aimed at conduct and indirectly affects speech; a law directly aimed at curtailing speech and political persuasion can, in my opinion, never be saved through a balancing process."[174]

When Black required overt acts, he meant it; for him, mere "incitement" was not enough. He borrowed directly here from Meiklejohn:

I believe that the First Amendment forbids Congress to punish people for talking about public affairs, whether or not such discussion incites to action, legal or illegal. . . . As the Virginia Assembly said in 1785, in its "Statute for Religious Liberty," written by Thomas Jefferson, "it is time enough for the rightful purposes of civil government, for

---

170. United States v. O'Brien, 391 U.S. 367, 376 (1968).

171. Tinker v. Des Moines Community School Dist., 393 U.S. 503, 515 (1969). Although Justice Black dissented in *Tinker*, he did so because he believed the area and time restrictions on the symbolic speech at issue were reasonable. This makes for some tight distinctions. *See* Cohen v. California, 403 U.S. 15 (1971) (Black, J., joined in dissent holding immune from punishment someone who went through a courthouse wearing a jacket bearing the words, "Fuck the Draft."). The dissenters thought this "mainly conduct and little speech." *Id.* at 27.

172. Street v. New York, 394 U.S. 576, 610 (1969).

173. *Id.*

174. H. BLACK, A CONSTITUTIONAL FAITH 61 (1968). For discussion of the complexities of "conduct" vs. "speech" (to me not always persuasive), see T. EMERSON, THE SYSTEM OF FREEDOM OF EXPRESSION 405-12 (1970); and for illustrations of illegal speech/action, see *id.* at 332-35.

its officers to interfere when principles break out into overt acts against, peace and good order. . . ."[175]

VII. HOLMES OR BLACK?

What is the signigicant difference between the fully developed Holmes-Brandeis clear and present danger approach and the Black restriction on conduct only approach to the first amendment? As a purely personal matter, I feel some special obligation to wrestle with this problem because, with the passage of time, I have reversed myself altogether. When the Meiklejohn work first appeared in 1949, it seemed to me that the country would happily live with the Holmes-Brandeis approach as developed in *Whitney v. California.*[176] As I thought then the thirty years' experience with the clear and present danger test and the broadly permissive stance adopted by Chief Justice Hughes in *De Jonge v. Oregon*[177] presented a "well enough" which should have been left alone.

As it now seems to me, I was wrong. The clear and present danger test did not stand the test of time. In the decade subsequent to that expression of personal opinion the test eroded to nothing. As Justice Black said, this was because of the accordion-like quality of the concept.

Perhaps this would be true of any test. Jefferson never guaranteed us absolute security; he said only that the first amendment would become a rallying point around which patriots could gather. But the absolute test, limited fundamentally only by immediately illegal conduct, is easier to apply and harder to evade. Under that test, the result in *Dennis* could never have been reached; the defendants were charged with no illegal overt acts at all. Either test will be stretched a little to fit emergencies; no one needs to allow publication of troop movements. For the most part the conduct test gives maximum security to cherished ideals; and it is supported with the buttressing effect of a glorious, if ancient, American tradition.

VIII. TOMORROW

What of the future? Is Black's philosophy of free speech to become a quaint anachronism? Will it be exhumed from time to

---

175. Yates v. United States, 354 U.S. 298, 340 (1957) (citing A. MEIKLEJOHN, *Free Speech and Its Relation to Self-Government*, in POLITICAL FREEDOM (1960)). By illegal conduct, Black meant illegal conduct other than speech by the speaker. In Terminiello v. Chicago, 337 U.S. 1 (1949), the Court (Douglas, J.) held that a person could not be punished for stirring people to anger quite possibly against himself or others in the crowd.

176. 274 U.S. 357 (1927).

177. 299 U.S. 353 (1937).

time by decreasing numbers of graduate students until finally it will
be known by a handful of political scientists approximately equal
to the number of philosophers who understand the distinctions
among Plato's dialogues?

There are, of course, pressures in that direction. Black on libel
and Black on obscenity go marching on, but it would be a sour
triumph if only these remained. They were never more than pawn
positions to protect the king: free discussion of the meaningful issues of the day.[178]

Not only has the complexion of the Supreme Court radically
changed so that the salesman of Black's ideas faces a diminishing
market for his wares, but there has been a change in the nature of
oppression; new techniques are already post-Black. He died without
ever imagining that an American President might be orchestrating
burglaries and enemies lists to control the spread of differing opinions. He would, I think, have been able to adapt the concepts of free
speech to these new devices as he earlier did to the use of economic
measures of repression.

To some, Black's approach was losing its charm even before he
died. There was much talk that he was "changing." It was true that
in the later years of his life, times, values, and public opinion
changed, and he did not change with them. As liberal impulses
shifted, particularly in relation to race and Viet Nam, and as many
persons sought to affect government policy by direct action, there
was a change in Black's relation to his constitutional era. He was
out of joint with shifting cycles in much the same sense that a
Republican of Weimar was out of joint with the Third Reich. He was
personally wholly opposed to the Viet Nam War and wholly opposed
to those who sacked college buildings to demonstrate the new freedom. He was, in short, an old liberal standing firm to the values of
a lifetime. This wheel has turned so quickly that he is very nearly
in currency again.

Whatever the winds of change, Black's constitutional views
continued in accord with Lilburne's, or Udall's, or Wilkes', or Madison's, and his belief in inalienable rights on the one hand and duties
to the state on the other were at one with Plato. Those views were
absolutely out of accord with the overwhelming congressional ap-

---

178. Black's essential concept of first amendment primacy is well caught up in the title
of Cahn, *The Firstness of the First Amendment*, 65 YALE L.J. 464 (1956), and the text
discussion as to Black's view, *id.* at 471, 477. As Black wrote Allan Barth, "All the constitutional protections you mention are important but I am myself still of the idea that the First
Amendment freedoms are the ones without which no government can possibly retain its
liberty." Letter from Hugo Black to Allan Barth (Feb. 17, 1959) Box 17, Black Mss.

proval of Title II of the Safe Streets Act in 1968, or with a mob destroying property, or with the proposal of recent years for "preventive custody" in the District of Columbia, or with resegregation of universities from a black racial point of view.

America has no magic which keeps it from succombing to the torments of the rest of the world. We do have traditions and institutions of deep roots which we hope to keep building.[179] Black's voice will have force so long as any remnant of our population believes in the inalienable rights of free people and in the concept that government requires the consent of the governed. Holmes and Brandeis were long dead before McCarthyism, but their ideals and their eloquence gave a rallying point to the resistance. Hugo Black's dedication, his firm tie to our deepest roots, and his eloquence will be a sustaining strength in another storm.

When the Court met for its first session after Justice Black's death, Chief Justice Burger said:

> Throughout his entire life he never wavered in his unbounded faith in the people and in the political processes of a free people under the American Constitution. He loved this Court as an institution, and contributed mightily to its work, to its strength, and to its future. He revered the Constitution; he had enormous respect for the Presidency and for the Congress, but above all else, he believed in the people.[180]

The Chief Justice's bright insight far transcends moral platitude to reach the heart of the matter. Hugo Black truly believed in a people worthy of self-government, in the inalienable rights of life, liberty, in the pursuit of happiness, and in government with the consent of the governed. He believed in a compact. He devoted the most urgent efforts of his life to upholding it.

In this Bicentennial year, the democratic ideals of the Declaration of Independence are not dead yet!

---

179.   For illustration of the continuity of Black's ideals in the first year after his death, see Chicago v. Mosley, 408 U.S. 92 (1972), a case involving school picketing in Chicago, "[A]bove all else, the First Amendment means that government has no power to restrict expression because of its message, its ideas, its subject matter, or its content. . . . [O]ur people are guaranteed the right to express any thought, free from government censorship." Chief Justice Burger concurred alone to note that he did not accept the passage quoted. *Id.* at 95-96.

180.   404 U.S. at VII (1971).

PHILIP KURLAND

JUSTICE ROBERT H. JACKSON— IMPACT ON CIVIL RIGHTS AND CIVIL LIBERTIES†

*Philip B. Kurland**

I. INTRODUCTION

The Baum Memorial Lectures, although of comparatively recent origin, have already gained great significance for their celebration of the protection of civil rights and civil liberties as a primary endeavor of those dedicated to the rule of law. The lectureship has, therefore, come to honor the lecturer no less than the subject. And I am, of course, pleased to assume the mantle of those who have preceded me.

I must, nevertheless, confess to being somewhat uncomfortable in the role. For surely there is something gauche about preaching heterodoxy from a pulpit which, like all pulpits, is by definition dedicated to orthodoxy. Let me state my problem.

Civil liberties in the context of the law, and particularly Supreme Court law, reveals to me two distinct modes of thought which, for convenience rather than description, I would label the "libertarian tradition" and the "liberal tradition." (I speak not at all here of the "conservative tradition.") There is, I think, not much difference between the goals of the legal libertarian and the legal liberal. For both, the objective is a free people in a democratic society. But freedom and democracy are not words without multiple meanings. Indeed, there are societies that call themselves democratic and their people free which nevertheless epitomize the very opposite of what most of us would mean when we use those words. And there is, as well, a substantial difference between the libertarian and the liberal as to the appropriate means to their jointly defined goal.

As I see it, the legal libertarian tends to think in terms of the absolute and unconditioned protection of asserted civil liberties, almost without acknowledgement of the possibility of any legiti-

---

† *These remarks were originally delivered at the University of Illinois College of Law, October 14, 1976, as the second 1976-77 lecture of the David C. Baum Lectures on Civil Rights and Civil Liberties.*

* *William R. Kenan, Jr., Distinguished Service Professor, The University of Chicago. A.B. 1942, Univ. of Pennsylvania; LL.B. 1944, Harvard Law School.*

mate competing values. For many of them, the mere assertion of a
claim labeled civil liberties is sufficient to justify its encompass-
ment within the protection of our Constitution. I would say here
that the tradition is represented by such great jurists as Hugo Black
and William Douglas, as Wiley Rutledge and Frank Murphy, as
Earl Warren and William Brennan, as Henry Edgerton and Skelly
Wright. You may derive from this roster that the libertarian tradition, for the most part, includes also a commitment to judicial activism, particularly in support of civil liberties. But you will recognize,
too, that, while all libertarians may be judicial activists, not all
judicial activists are libertarians. In gross, then, the libertarian as I
perceive him is dedicated to a creed that societal salvation lies in
the maintained primacy of all claimed civil rights and that the
saviour is the judicial branch of government.

My discomfort lies in the fact that I believe the Baum Lectures
to have been founded to further this libertarian creed. Yet neither
my subject, Mr. Justice Jackson, nor I, properly can be called an
adherent of the faith. We belong rather to the liberal tradition, a
tradition that earned the first Lord Halifax the opprobrious sobri-
quet, "The Trimmer."[1] For the liberal tradition is, indeed, a tradition born in doubt rather than faith, and maintained by skepticism
rather than by belief.

Perhaps the American tradition does not derive, as Professor
Bickel would have it, from Edmund Burke. But surely Bickel, the
foremost academic apologist for the liberal tradition, accurately
described it in his posthumously published book, *The Morality of
Consent,* when he wrote:

> The Age of Reason continues, if not quite as pretentiously and self-
> confidently as it began. Precisely for that reason, however, the prob-
> lem of which Burke spoke is even more acute for us. A valueless
> politics and valueless institutions are shameful and shameless and,
> what is more, man's nature is such that he finds them, and life with
> and under them, insupportable. Doctrinaire theories of the rights of
> man, on the other hand, serve us no better than Burke thought they
> would. The computing principle is still all we can resort to, and we
> always return to it following some luxuriant outburst of theory in the
> Supreme Court, whether the theory is of an absolute right to contract,
> or to speak, or to stand mute, or to be private. We find our visions of

---

1. "A Constitution cannot make itself; some body made it; not at once but at several
times. It is alterable; and by that draweth nearer Perfection; and without suiting itself to
differing Times and Circumstances, it could not live. Its Life is prolonged by changing season-
ably the several Parts of it at several times." THE COMPLETE WORKS OF GEORGE SAVILE, FIRST
MARQUESS OF HALIFAX 211 (Raleigh Ed. 1912).

good and evil and the denominations we compute where Burke told us to look, in the experience of the past, in our tradition, in the secular religion of the American republic. The only abiding thing, as Brandeis used to repeat . . . is change, but the past should control it, or at least its pace. We hold to the values of the past provisionally only in the knowledge that they will change, but we hold to them as guides.

* * *

Our problem . . . is that we cannot govern, and should not, in submission to the dictates of abstract theories, and that we cannot live, much less govern, without some "uniform rule and scheme of life," without principles, however provisionally and skeptically held. . . .

Since few principles are inscribed sharply in the Constitution itself, the Supreme Court speaking in the name of the Constitution fills, in part, the need for middle-distance principles. . . . It proffers, with some important exceptions, a series of admonitions, an eighteenth-century checklist of subjects; it does this cautiously and with some skepticism. It recognizes that principles are necessary, have evolved, and should continue to evolve in the light of history and changing circumstance. That . . . is the Constitution as the Framers wrote it. And that is what it must be in a secular democratic society, where the chief reliance for policy-making is placed in the political process.

. . . Few definite, comprehensive answers on matters of social and economic policy can be deduced from it. The judges, themselves abstracted from, removed from political institutions by several orders of magnitude, ought never to impose an answer on the society merely because it seems prudent and wise to them personally, or because they believe that an answer—always provisional—arrived at by the political institutions is foolish. . . .

Yet in the end, and even if infrequently, we do expect the Court to give us principle, the limits of which can be sensed but not defined and are communicated more as cautions than as rules. Confined to a profession, the explication of principle is disciplined, imposing standards of analytical candor, rigor, and clarity. The Court is to reason, not feel, to explain and justify principles it pronounces to the last possible rational decimal point. It may not itself generate values, out of the stomach, but must seek to relate them—at least analogically—to judgments of history and moral philosophy. . . .[2]

For the liberal tradition, the representative jurists are not less than those of the libertarian camp. They include Holmes, Brandeis, and Cardozo, Frankfurter and Stone, Learned Hand and Henry

---

2. BICKEL, THE MORALITY OF CONSENT 24-26 (1975).

Friendly, and certainly Robert Jackson, the subject of this essay.

Those of you who know the extrajudicial writings of Judge Learned Hand[3]—and I commend them to everyone who cherishes the high style of a great essayist—will find their echoes in my quotation from Bickel. You will also find those echoes in Paul Freund's conclusion of an essay devoted to the same subject that I address here,[4] an essay that makes all I am about to say redundant. Probably because it would be difficult to speak of Jackson as a civil libertarian, Freund ended his paper with praise of Jackson's investment in the uniqueness of each case that came before him, and next with compliments for the style and wit with which his opinions were written. Freund's third conclusory point demonstrated the contemporary relevance of Jackson's work: "The Justice contrived to focus on the twin evils that are most corrupting in a legal order: secrecy where there should be disclosure; publicity where there should be privacy."[5]

Finally, Professor Freund concluded:

> More generally, he left a legacy of concern for the inner self, the free mind and spirit on which a free society ultimately depends. In an era of growing exploration and manipulation of the deepest recesses of the mind, as well as the far reaches of outer space, a time of increasing anonymity and submersion in the mass, a period of a morality of statistics, a poignant reminder from Justice Jackson of who each of us is—the vagrant, mysterious, unservile, yet responsible self—is a heritage to be husbanded and treasured.[6]

It is significant that Freund titled his piece "Mr. Justice Jackson and Individual Rights." For in the concern for the individual rather than the class or group, the concern for "the vagrant, mysterious, unservile, yet responsible self," is to be found one of the essential separations of the liberal from the libertarian tradition. It is the singularity of the individual, what I have elsewhere called "The Private I,"[7] that makes the tradition for which Hand and Jackson were the most elegant judicial spokesmen in an era in which the individual has become more and more subordinated to the collective, whether it be the state or some other form of Leviathan.

Obviously I cannot, in the space of a single lecture, hope to

---

3. HAND, THE SPIRIT OF LIBERTY (1952). A new paperback edition has just been published by The University of Chicago Press.

4. Freund, *Mr. Justice Jackson and Individual Rights,* in MR. JUSTICE JACKSON: FOUR LECTURES IN HIS HONOR 29 (1969).

5. *Id.* at 56.

6. *Id.*

7. KURLAND, THE PRIVATE I: SOME REFLECTIONS ON PRIVACY AND THE CONSTITUTION (1976).

replicate the contents of Jackson's judicial efforts on the Supreme Court, even limited to the single field of civil liberties and civil rights. Mr. Justice Jackson's opinions epitomized the individuality that he so clearly cherished. They defy both summary and easy classification. His was probably the best writing that a Justice of the Supreme Court has ever produced. It is not readily captured in the prosaic and deadening words of a mere critic. I shall endeavor, therefore, to deal with but a few examples of his opinions and to allow his voice to come through directly by means of extensive quotation. If I succeed in my purpose, you may then seek out the corpus of his work for yourself to gain understanding, where I can offer only direction.

II. Of Flag Salutes and Similar Matters

A clear distinction between libertarian and liberal is to be found in the latter's notion that the Constitution afforded protection to individuals and, therefore, to all, rather than to classes and, therefore, only to some. For Jackson, it would seem, constitutional liberties could not derive from or be confined to membership in a group or a class. Such liberties as the Constitution afforded to members of a group or class must be liberties claimable by everyone. Moreover, it would seem possible for a class or group jointly not to have the constitutional rights that each individual in that class or group may have by himself.

The judicial origins of such propositions as these, so far as Mr. Justice Jackson's tenure on the Court is concerned, came during his second term, when the Jehovah's Witnesses were being given so much attention by the Court. Indeed, Mr. Justice Jackson's most famous civil liberties decision was rendered in 1943 in his opinion in the second flag salute case, *West Virginia State Board of Education v. Barnette.*[8] Three years earlier the Court, through Mr. Justice Frankfurter, who was joined by Justices Black, Douglas, and Murphy, among others, and over the lone dissent of then Mr. Justice Stone, held that the Jehovah's Witnesses were not entitled to exemption from compulsory flag salute laws because the compulsory flag salute was not an invasion of their freedom of religious exercise.[9]

The case came back to the Court after, in the interim, Justices Black, Douglas, and Murphy had changed their minds.[10] They had changed their minds about the answer to the question that had been

---

8. 319 U.S. 624 (1943).
9. Minersville School District v. Gobitis, 310 U.S. 586 (1940).
10. Jones v. Opelika, 316 U.S. 584, 623 (1942).

raised in *Gobitis,* the first flag salute case: "We believe that the statute before us fails to accord full scope to the freedom of religion secured to the appellees by the First and Fourteenth Amendments."[11] But, according to Jackson, the spokesman for the Court, the question in *Gobitis* was not the proper question to be addressed in *Barnette:*

> Nor does the issue as we see it turn on one's possession of particular religious views or the sincerity with which they are held. While religion supplies appellees' motive for enduring the discomforts of making the issue in this case, many citizens who do not share these religious views hold such a compulsory rite to infringe constitutional liberty of the individual. It is not necessary to inquire whether nonconformist beliefs will exempt from the duty to salute unless we first find power to make the salute a legal duty.[12]

Although the majority opinion frequently is misread even today as a religious freedom ruling, perhaps because of the concurring opinions of Black, Douglas, and Murphy, Jackson's different position could not have come as a surprise to his brethren. It was clear to them that Jackson would espouse no such cause as special privilege for Jehovah's Witnesses. Earlier in the term, the Court had dealt with a series of Jehovah's Witnesses cases involving municipal restrictions on their right to proselytize by ringing doorbells, soliciting funds, and seeking allegiance to church doctrine that those of more conventional religious faiths found totally abhorrent. It was in these cases that Mr. Justice Jackson dissented from finding special constitutional protections in the religious freedom clause.

In a composite minority opinion, filed in *Douglas v. City of Jeannette,*[13] Jackson wrote: "I had not supposed that the rights of secular and non-religious communciations were more narrow or in any way inferior to those of avowed religious groups."[14] He went farther, thus putting himself beyond the pale of some modern academic and judicial dogmas that minorities are entitled to preferences that may be denied to majorities—however one defines those terms—as he wrote in *Jeanette:*

> The First Amendment grew out of an experience which taught that society cannot trust the conscience of a majority to keep its religious zeal within the limits that a free society can tolerate. I do not think it any more intended to leave the conscience of a minority

---

11.   319 U.S. at 643.
12.   *Id.* at 634-35.
13.   319 U.S. 157 (1943).
14.   *Id.* at 179.

to fix its limits. Civil government cannot let any group ride rough-
shod over others simply because their "consciences" tell them to do
so.[15]

For Jackson, if not his libertarian brethren, there was a weighing
of interests to be conducted. The claims of the Jehovah's Witnesses
in the solicitation cases impinged on the claims of those on whom
they imposed their message. Jackson would find the balance in
favor of the latter, the imposed on rather than the imposers. If the
Court's valid precedents precluded such activities as those of the
Jehovah's Witnesses when indulged by others, as they did, even
those who could aspire to Mr. Justice Douglas's colorful appellation
of "colporteur," were not specially privileged.

> These Witnesses, in common with all others, have extensive rights to
> proselyte and propagandize. These of course include the right to op-
> pose and criticize the Roman Catholic Church or any other denomi-
> nation. These rights are, and should be held to be, as extensive as any
> orderly society can tolerate in religious disputation. The real question
> is where their rights end and the rights of others begin.[16]

For Jackson, therefore, the flag-salute case was easier. At least
it was easier in one respect:

> The freedom asserted by these appellees does not bring them into
> collision with rights asserted by any other individual. It is such con-
> flicts which most frequently require intervention of the State to deter-
> mine where the rights of one end and those of another begin. But the
> refusal of these persons to participate in the ceremony does not inter-
> fere with or deny rights of others to do so. Nor is there any question
> in this case that their behavior is peaceable and orderly. The sole
> conflict is between authority and the rights of the individual.[17]

Stating the question that way, Jackson answered it. In a conflict
between rights of the individual and the claims of Leviathan, the
Constitution insists that the individual prevail.

In *Gobitis,* Frankfurter had stated the same issue but had come
down with a different conclusion.[18] For Frankfurter, the conflict
between the interests of the nation and the interests of the individual were for resolution by the legislature not the judiciary. But
neither Frankfurter, nor Stone, nor Black, nor Douglas, nor Murphy
had asked the right question. And there is no way to get the right

---

15. *Id.*
16. *Id.* at 178.
17. 319 U.S. at 630.
18. *Id.* at 636-37.

answer except by asking the right question. "The question which underlies the flag salute controversy is whether such a ceremony so touching matters of opinion and political attitude may be imposed upon the individual by official authority under powers committed to any political organization under our Constitution."[19]

The question was not whether an individual was entitled to exemption from a valid legislative order, the question was whether the legislative order was valid. And surely, the Jacksonian question was a properly Jeffersonian question to be addressed to a national government under a Constitution of delegated powers. It did not quite fit with the notion of state authority whose powers were not delegated to it by the national Constitution. So Jackson had to resort quickly, as he did, to the limitations on state authority to be found in the First Amendment. But it was not a religious freedom proposition, nor even an orthodox free speech construction. He had both to deny the liberal notion of judicial self-abnegation and to create a First Amendment principle to support a right of disobedience to an invalid law.

First, the Bill of Rights was promulgated to remove certain subjects from the legislative realm. Or, in Jackson's words:

> The very purpose of a Bill of Rights was to withdraw certain subjects from the vicissitudes of political controversy, to place them beyond the reach of majorities and officials and to establish them as legal principles to be applied by the courts.[20]

Second, it is clear that mere rationality of legislative purpose cannot justify legislative action that was beyond the legislative ken. It did not matter, therefore, that judges were not specially competent to judge the wisdom of the legislation:

> True, the task of translating the majestic generalities of the Bill of Rights, conceived as part of the pattern of liberal government in the eighteenth century, into concrete restraints on officials dealing with the problems of the twentieth century, is one to disturb self-confidence. These principles grew in soil which also produced a philosophy that the individual was the center of society, that his liberty was attainable through mere absence of governmental restraints, and that government should be entrusted with few controls and only the mildest supervision over men's affairs. We must transplant these rights to a soil in which the *laissez-faire* concept or principle of non-interference has withered at least as to economic affairs, and social

---

19. *Id.* at 635-36.
20. *Id.* at 638.

advancements are increasingly sought through closer integration of society and through expanded and strengthened governmental controls. These changed conditions often deprive precedents of reliability and cast us more than we would choose upon our own judgment. But we act in these matters not by authority of our competence but by force of our commissions.[21]

It was not a proper objective of the state to achieve uniformity. "Compulsory unification of opinion achieves only the unanimity of the graveyard."[22] "If there is any fixed star in our constitutional constellation, it is that no official, high or petty, can prescribe what shall be orthodox in politics, nationalism, religion, or other matters of opinion or force citizens to confess by word or act their faith therein."[23] One must wonder what Mr. Justice Jackson would think about the uniformities imposed today in the name of egalitarianism.

Here is the liberal judicial creed with all its internal conflicts showing. They are the conflicts of our democratic society. The individual is free and supreme, subject to majority rule in those areas where the majority is authorized to rule, and the realm of majority rule has been greatly extended, but not with regard to matters of faith, or speech or ideas unless that speech or ideas or faith does specific harm to others. Above all, for the liberal jurisprude, responsibility was an attribute of liberty. There was a duty to the society, but that did not include an obligation to submit to compulsion of thought. No little red book, not even a red-white-and-blue one, can be tolerated.

We can have intellectual individualism and the rich cultural diversities that we owe to exceptional minds only at the price of occasional eccentricity and abnormal attitudes. . . . [F]reedom to differ is not limited to things that do not matter much. That would be a mere shadow of freedom. The test of its substance is the right to differ as to things that touch the heart of the existing order.[24]

III. The Aliens in Our Midst

The Jacksonian concern for the individual is shown in still another context. Since I am limited here to a sampling of the Justice's opinions, I have selected some from his individual expressions about the treatment of aliens. The alien is probably the least privileged of persons to seek succor from the courts of the United States, at

21. *Id.* at 639-40.
22. *Id.* at 641.
23. *Id.* at 642.
24. *Id.* at 641-42.

least if he is an alien not yet legally admitted to our borders. I have
selected these not only because they are idiosyncratic factual situations, but because Jackson used these opinions to state some of his
more basic notions about the fundamentals of our jurisprudence.

It would appear—both from the document itself and the relevant decisions—that the Constitution affords the unadmitted alien
no comfort whatsoever. And so, for the most part, Jackson speaking
frequently on behalf of these woebegone creatures was speaking in
dissent. When he did speak, he did not attempt to force the Constitution to cover what it clearly did not cover. He did, however, put
congressional legislation into the press of common sense in order to
squeeze from it humane conclusions.

Two opinions are of primary interest here. Both are concerned
with the admission to the country of aliens. The first is the "German
war bride case," *United States ex rel. Knauff v. Shaughnessy,*[25] in
which Jackson's appeal to his brethren failed, but ultimately succeeded in securing relief by executive and legislative clemency.[26]
The second was *Shaughnessy v. Mezei,*[27] the man-without-a-country
story, whose ultimate outcome I do not know.

The Ellen Knauff case involved a congressional act of compassion which provided that war brides of American servicemen could
be admitted to this country without meeting the qualifications imposed on other aliens. As a safeguard, however, Congress provided
that the Attorney General could deny admission in any particular
case to protect the security of the United States. Ellen Knauff was
a German war bride who was denied admission by the Attorney
General, without hearing and without stated reason for the exclusion. Jackson spoke in dissent on behalf of himself and Justices
Black and Frankfurter.

No constitutional argument was raised by the dissenters, perhaps because 1960 preceded in time the notion of constitutional
penumbras and haloes. And Jackson's opinion opened with a dis-
claimer:[28]

> I do not question the constitutional power of Congress to author-
> ize immigration authorities to turn back from our gates any alien or
> class of aliens. But I do not find that Congress has authorized an
> abrupt and brutal ρxclusion of the wife of an American citizen with-
> out a hearing.

---

25.   338 U.S. 537 (1950).
26.   *See* KNAUFF, THE ELLEN KNAUFF STORY (1974).
27.   345 U.S. 206 (1953).
28.   338 U.S. 537, 550 (1950) (Jackson, J., dissenting).

Due process of law is a rule of construction as well as a constitutional doctrine. Given the opportunity to read the statute as affording elementary procedural due process or denying it, Jackson set out reasons for rejecting procedures that suggested origins in Franz Kafka's novels:

> [T]he government tells the Court that not even a court can find out why the girl is excluded. But it says we must find that Congress authorized this treatment of war brides and, even if we cannot get any reason for it, we must say it is legal; security requires it.
>
> Security is like liberty in that many are the crimes committed in its name. The menace to the security of this country, be it great as it may, from this girl's admission is as nothing compared to the menace to free institutions inherent in procedures of this pattern. In the name of security the police state justifies its arbitrary oppressions on evidence that is secret, because security might be prejudiced if it were brought to light in hearings. The plea that evidence of guilt must be secret is abhorrent to free men, because it provides a cloak for the malevolent, the misinformed, the meddlesome, and the corrupt to play the role of informer undetected and uncorrected.[29]

This was a lesson which, had it been learned, would have stood us in good stead from then to now, from the pre-McCarthy period to the post-Watergate period. But Jackson did not prevail. Another alien case, argued the same day as *Knauff,* but decided a month later, saw Mr. Justice Jackson writing for the majority. The case was *Wong Yang Sung v. McGrath*[30] and the question was whether the procedural hearing requirements of the Administrative Procedure Act were applicable to deportation proceedings against an alien who was alleged to have entered the country illegally. Once again the issue was made one of statutory construction, but that construction was forced in part because its opposite would raise constitutional difficulties:

> But the difficulty with any argument premised on the proposition that the deportation statute does not require a hearing is that, without such hearing, there would be no constitutional authority for deportation. The constitutional requirement of procedural due process of law derives from the same source as Congress' power to legislate and, where applicable, permeates every valid enactment of that body. . . .
>
> * * *
>
> . . . When the Constitution requires a hearing, it requires a fair one,

---

29. *Id.* at 551.
30. 339 U.S. 33 (1950).

one before a tribunal which meets at least currently prevailing standards of impartiality. A deportation hearing involves issues basic to
human liberty and happiness and, in the present upheavals in lands
to which aliens may be returned, perhaps to life itself. It might be
difficult to justify as measuring up to constitutional standards of
impartiality a hearing tribunal for deportation proceedings the like
of which has been condemned by Congress as unfair even where less
vital matters of property rights are at stake.[31]

It was, however, the *Knauff* attitude and not the *Wong Sung*
position that prevailed when the *Mezei* case came before the Court
a few years later. Again Justices Black and Frankfurter were in
dissent with Jackson, but only Frankfurter joined the Jackson opinion. The facts are even now hard to believe. In Jackson's words:

> What is our case? In contemplation of law, I agree, it is that of
> an alien who asks admission to the country. Concretely, however, it
> is that of a lawful and law-abiding inhabitant of our country for a
> quarter of a century, long ago admitted for permanent residence, who
> seeks to return home. After a foreign visit to his aged and ailing
> mother that was prolonged by disturbed conditions in Eastern Eu-
> rope, he obtained a visa for admission issued by our consul and re-
> turned to New York. There the Attorney General refused to honor his
> documents and turned him back as a menace to this Nation's secu-
> rity. This man, who seems to have led a life of unrelieved insignific-
> ance, must have been astonished to find himself suddenly putting the
> Government of the United States in such fear that it was afraid to
> tell him why it was afraid of him. He was shipped and reshipped to
> France, which twice refused him landing. Great Britain declined, and
> no other European country has been found willing to open its doors
> to him. Twelve countries of the American Hemisphere refused his
> applications. Since we proclaimed him a Samson who might pull
> down the pillars of our temple, we should not be surprised if peoples
> less prosperous, less strongly established and less stable feared to
> take him off our timorous hands. . . . For nearly two years he was
> held in custody of the immigration authorities of the United States
> at Ellis Island, and if the Government has its way he seems likely to
> be detained indefinitely, perhaps for life, for a cause known only to
> the Attorney General.[32]

The question was whether the unwanted man could secure release from custody by habeas corpus. The Government argued that
he was not detained by them. He was free to leave Ellis Island at
any time, except to enter the United States. Jackson had little

---

31. *Id.* at 49-51.
32. 345 U.S. at 219-20 (footnotes omitted).

doubt that he was effectively in custody and that the Great Writ was appropriate to the circumstances:

> Fortunately it is still startling, in this country, to find a person held indefinitely in executive custody without accusation of crime or judicial trial. Executive imprisonment has been considered oppressive and lawless since John, at Runnymeade, pledged that no free man should be imprisoned, dispossessed, outlawed, or exiled save by the judgment of his peers or by the law of the land. The judges of England developed the writ of habeas corpus largely to preserve these immunities from executive restraint. Under the best tradition of Anglo-American law, courts will not deny hearing to an unconvicted prisoner just because he is an alien whose keep, in legal theory, is just outside our gates. Lord Mansfield, in the celebrated case holding that slavery was unknown to the common law of England, ran his writ of habeas corpus in favor of an alien, an African Negro slave, and against the master of a ship at anchor in the Thames.[33]

What then was the constitutional question posed by the detention of this alien? The standard is that of the Due Process Clause of the Fifth Amendment, which Jackson saw as having two attributes, substantive and procedural. There was no substantive due process right to be relieved of custody. If the Government had cause for his detention, it could not be denied that power.

> Substantively, due process of law renders what is due to a strong state as well as to a free individual. It tolerates all reasonable measures to insure the national safety, and it leaves a large, at times a potentially dangerous, latitude for executive judgment as to policies and means.
>
> After all, the pillars which support our liberties are the three branches of government, and the burden could not be carried by our own power alone. . . .
>
> * * *
>
> I conclude that detention of an alien would not be inconsistent with substantive due process, provided—and this is where my dissent begins—he is accorded procedural due process of law.[34]

Procedural due process is a different matter. And procedural due process, unlike substantive due process, is essentially in the keeping of the judicial branch. It invoked the special expertise that was not available to either the executive or the legislative branches to determine:

---

33. *Id.* at 218-19.
34. *Id.* at 222, 224.

Procedural fairness, if not all that originally was meant by due process of law, is at least what it most uncompromisingly requires. Procedural due process is more elemental and less flexible than substantive due process. It yields less to the times, varies less with conditions, and defers much less to legislative judgment. Insofar as it is technical law, it must be a specialized responsibility within the competence of the judiciary on which they do not bend before political branches of the Government, as they should on matters of policy which comprise substantive law.[35]

Jackson saw the evils of executive detention in the recent history of the totalitarian states, both Nazi Germany, the recent menace to civilization, and Communist Russia, then regarded as the current menace to civilization. Jackson conceded his anti-Russian bias, but suggested that bias extended to detesting imitation of their procedures, as well as their substantive principles. He concluded *Mezei* as he had begun *Knauff*:

Congress has ample power to determine whom we will admit to our shores and by what means it will effectuate its exclusion policy. The only limitation is that it may not do so by authorizing United States officers to take without due process of law the life, the liberty or the property of an alien who has come within our jurisdiction; and that means he must meet a fair hearing with a fair notice of the charges.

It is inconceivable to me that this measure of simple justice and fair dealing would menace the security of this country. No one can make me believe that we are that far gone.[36]

Allow me to shift from the somber mood by invoking two other opinions of Mr. Justice Jackson in this area of alien rights.

In *McGrath v. Kristensen*,[37] the question was whether an alien, whose temporary visitor status was altered because the outbreak of war prevented his return to his homeland, had thus become a permanent alien subject to military service. If he had thus become a resident and chosen not to enter military service, he was subject to deportation. The Court charitably held that the temporary visitor was not subject to such conscription and therefore not subject to deportation.

Jackson's concurring opinion is noteworthy not for its substantive law—it contains none—but as a felicitous form of confession of

---

35. *Id.* at 224.
36. *Id.* at 228.
37. 340 U.S. 162 (1950).

error. I quote it in part, for its lightening as well as enlightening effects:

> I concur in the judgment and opinion of the Court. But since it is contrary to an opinion which, as Attorney General, I rendered in 1940, I owe some words of explanation. . . . I am entitled to say of that opinion what any discriminating reader must think of it—that it was as foggy as the statute the Attorney General was asked to interpret. . . .
>
> * * *
>
> It would be charitable to assume that neither the nominal addressee nor the nominal author of the opinion read it. That, I do not doubt, explains Mr. Stimson's acceptance of an answer so inadequate to his questions. But no such confession and avoidance can excuse the then Attorney General.
>
> Precedent, however, is not lacking for ways by which a judge may recede from a prior opinion that has proven untenable and perhaps misled others. . . . Baron Bramwell extricated himself from a somewhat similar embarrassment by saying, "The matter does not appear to me now as it appears to have appeared to me then." . . . Perhaps Dr. Johnson went to the heart of the matter when he explained a blunder in his dictionary—"Ignorance, sir, ignorance." But an escape less self-depreciating was taken by Lord Westbury, who, it is said, rebuffed a barrister's reliance upon an earlier opinion of his Lordship: "I can only say that I am amazed that a man of my intelligence should have been guilty of giving such an opinion." If there are other ways of gracefully and good naturedly surrendering former views to a better considered position, I invoke them all.[38]

In *Jordan v. De George*,[39] the Court held that conspiracy to defraud the United States of taxes on distilled spirits is a "crime involving moral turpitude" and the alien twice convicted must be banished from our shores. Justices Jackson, Black and Frankfurter dissented in an opinion written by Jackson. As usual, Jackson quickly and concisely stated the question:

> Respondent, because he is an alien, and because he has been twice convicted of crimes the Court holds involve "moral turpitude," is punished with a life sentence of banishment in addition to the punishment which a citizen would suffer for the identical acts. Mr. Justice Black, Mr. Justice Frankfurter and I cannot agree, because we believe the phrase "crime involving moral turpitude," as found in the Immigration Act, has no sufficiently definite meaning to be a constitutional standard for deportation.[40]

---

38. *Id.* at 176-78 (citations omitted).
39. 341 U.S. 223 (1951).
40. *Id.* at 232 (footnote omitted).

Jackson's opinion is written in lighthearted tones that deride the sanctimonious and self-righteous grounds for Chief Justice Vinson's majority opinion. But the lightness of touch does not conceal the seriousness of his propositions:

. . . The Court concludes that fraud is "a contaminating component in any crime" and imports "moral turpitude." The fraud involved here is nonpayment of a tax. The alien possessed and apparently trafficked in liquor without paying the Government its tax. That, of course, is a fraud on the revenues. But those who deplore the traffic regard it as much an exhibition of moral turpitude for the Government to share its revenues as for respondents to withhold them. Those others who enjoy the traffic are not notable for scruples as to whether liquor has a law-abiding pedigree. So far as this offense is concerned with whiskey, it is not particularly un-American, and we see no reason to strain to make the penalty for the same act so much more severe in the case of an alien "bootlegger" than it is in the case of the native "moonshiner." I have never discovered that disregard of the Nation's liquor taxes excluded a citizen from our best society and I see no reason why it should banish an alien from our worst.

But it is said he has cheated the revenues and the total is computed in high figures. If "moral turpitude" depends on the amount involved respondent is probably entitled to a place in its higher brackets. Whether by popular test the magnitude of the fraud would be an extenuating or an aggravating circumstance, we do not know. We would suppose the basic morality of a fraud on the revenues would be the same for petty as for great cheats. But we are not aware of any keen sentiment of revulsion against one who is a little niggardly on a customs declaration, or who evades a sales tax, a local cigarette tax, or fails to keep his account square with a parking meter. But perhaps what shocks is not the offense so much as the conviction.

We should not forget that criminality is one thing—a matter of law—and that morality, ethics and religious teachings are another. Their relations have puzzled the best of men. Assassination, for example, whose criminality no one doubts, has been the subject of serious debate as to its morality. This does not make crime less criminal, but it shows on what treacherous grounds we tread when we undertake to translate ethical concepts into legal ones, case by case. We usually end up by condemning all that we personally disapprove and for no better reason than that we disapprove it. In fact, what better reason is there? Uniformity and equal protection of the law can come only from a statutory definition of fairly stable and confined bounds.[41]

---

41. *Id.* at 240-42 (footnote omitted).

I do not mean to tell you that Jackson was always on the side of angels, even in this area of the law. He had no difficulty writing a persuasive opinion for the Court that Congress could "constitutionally . . . deport a legally resident alien because of membership in the Communist Party which terminated before enactment of the Alien Registration Act, 1940."[42] But he continued to insist, if still in dissent, that, before an alien may be deported, or convicted for not making himself available for deportation, the premises of the governmental act must be proved to a court in accordance with the requirements of due process of law.[43]

The opinions of Jackson in this field reveal again that the essential feature of the liberal judge is his commitment to procedural due process, not as a technical device for having his way on the merits, but as the real safeguard for the individual against the impositions of government. Here the liberal doctrine requires little if any bowing to legislative authority, for it is here that the charge of the Constitution to the judiciary is the clearest. The opinions also reveal that, if a true judicial liberal will not rewrite a statute contrary to the clear language, intent, and purpose of the legislature, he may nevertheless, where the statute affords equal authority for two or more readings, choose that meaning which most closely corresponds with the benevolent concepts of substantive as well as procedural due process.

IV. THE ROYAL PREROGATIVE

You may find it difficult to think of the next case that I will discuss as a civil liberties case. After all, it involved a seizure of property, not life or liberty, and it was a contest between government and a huge corporate enterprise. Nevertheless, I think that the opinion is probably the most important that Jackson ever composed and is directed at a more fundamental issue of liberty than construction of any of the Bill of Rights. I speak, of course, of the *Steel Seizure Case,*[44] in which Jackson wrote only a concurring opinion, while Mr. Justice Black spoke for the Court's majority.

The case arose during the course of a "police action" conducted by United Nations forces in Korea. Immediately before a strike call by the Steelworkers was to go into effect, President Truman issued an executive order directing the Secretary of Commerce to seize the steel mills and to keep them operating. The justification for the

---

42. Harisiades v. Shaughnessy, 342 U.S. 580, 581 (1952) (footnote omitted).
43. United States v. Spector, 343 U.S. 169, 174 (1952).
44. Youngstown Sheet & Tube Co. v. Sawyer, 343 U.S. 579 (1952).

order was that steel was an indispensable element for war produc-
tion and that a work stoppage would endanger the national security.
He relied on a conglomerate of powers set forth in Article II of the
Constitution, but particularly on the Commander-in-Chief power.

One difficulty with the Truman exercise in implied powers of
the Presidency that caused some concern to at least some of the
Justices was that in the then recent controversy over the Taft-
Hartley Law, the executive branch had sought a seizure power and
been turned down by Congress.

Justice Black's opinion for the Court, on the question of prerogative raised by the steel companies effort to enjoin the seizure, was
simple. There is some anomaly in the fact that his position was that
of William Howard Taft, while the dissenters, led by Chief Justice
Vinson, espoused the point of view of Theodore Roosevelt, about the
powers of the Presidency.

For Justice Black, "The President's power, if any, to issue the
order must stem either from an act of Congress or from the Constitution itself."[45] There was, indeed, no statutory authority for the President's action. Nor was there any Constitutional authority. The Government's claim was one that has become all too familiar. "[I]t is
not claimed that express constitutional language grants this power
to the President. The contention is that presidential power should
be implied from the aggregate of his powers under the Constitution."[46] His authority could not be inferred from the Commander-
in-Chief Clause, that is concerned with military operations in the
"theater of war." "In the framework of our Constitution, the President's power to see that the laws are faithfully executed refutes the
idea that he is to be a lawmaker."[47]

Thus, Mr. Justice Black in fact framed an opinion that stated
there were no implied powers of the Presidency. The President was
the agent of the legislature and had no lawmaking powers of his
own. As Mr. Justice Frankfurter noted in his concurrence: ". . . the
considerations relevant to the legal enforcement of the principle of
separation of powers seem to me more complicated and flexible
than may appear from what Mr. Justice Black has written, ..."[48]

The dissent of Mr. Chief Justice Vinson was equally uncomplicated. The President had found an emergency that required emergency action, at least until Congress acted. This power may be

---

45. *Id.* at 585.
46. *Id.* at 587.
47. *Id.*
48. *Id.* at 589.

inferred not only from the Commander-in-Chief provision but also from the President's duty to "take Care that the Laws be faithfully executed, ..."[49]

Mr. Justice Jackson, with his experience as Attorney General at the outbreak of World War II, was cognizant of the realities as well as the theories of presidential action. He was unable to reduce the issues to the simple question that had been the subject of the majority and the dissenters' opinions. He suggested an outline that has since become regarded as the rule of the case, despite the fact that he wrote only for himself:

> 1. When the President acts pursuant to an express or implied authorization of Congress, his authority is at its maximum, for it includes all that he possesses in his own right plus all that Congress can delegate. In these circumstances, and in these only, may he be said (for what it may be worth) to personify the federal sovereignty. . . .
>
> 2. When the President acts in absence of either a congressional grant or denial of authority, he can only rely upon his own independent powers, but there is a zone of twilight in which he and Congress may have concurrent authority, or in which its distribution is uncertain. Therefore, congressional inertia, indifference or quiescence may sometimes, at least as a practical matter, enable, if not invite, measures on independent presidential responsibility. In this area, any actual test of power is likely to depend on the imperatives of events and contemporary imponderables rather than on abstract theories of law.
>
> 3. When the President takes measures incompatible with the expressed or implied will of Congress, his power is at its lowest ebb, for then he can rely only upon his own constitutional powers minus any constitutional powers of Congress over the matter. Courts can sustain exclusive presidential control in such a case only by disabling the Congress from acting upon the subject. Presidential claim to a power at once so conclusive and preclusive must be scrutinized with caution, for what is at stake is the equilibrium established by our constitutional system.[50]

Mr. Justice Jackson then went into an extensive analysis and concluded that in light of the refusal of Congress to give the President the power of seizure when he asked for it, the present situation fell into the third category and the seizure was invalid. Again, a reading of the full opinion will demonstrate to the reader the strength of the mind of an advocate with keen analytic skills and

---

49. U.S. CONST. art. II, § 3.
50. 343 U.S. 579, 635-38 (1952) (footnotes omitted).

extraordinary powers of rhetoric. But he was an advocate for the Constitution and not for either of the contending parties or other interests. It was not the steel mills nor the steel workers nor the legislature nor the executive that weighted his arguments. It was rather a realization that no more fundamental question about our democratic system in a modern age could be raised. He demonstrated that, however casebook editors might classify the case, it was a case of civil liberties because freedom was at stake.

Since then we have gained further experience with the problem of the imperial presidency. None should think that the Korean War was not an immediate precedent for the Viet Nam War. None should think that Watergate was an idiosyncratic event caused by the eccentricities of an egocentric President with royal pretensions. Recent history reveals that the Watergate syndrome, with its secret acts and enemy lists, with its Louis XIV complex—*l'etat, c'est moi*—may be found to a greater or lesser degree in each of Nixon's predecessors, even back to the President that Jackson served as Attorney General.

What Jackson understood and stated here was a concept that is fundamental to the cause of the liberal jurists: Democracy and a constitutional system of checks and balances are also relevant to the liberty of Americans. The failure of democracy and the consequent failure of limited authority in any of the three branches of the national government could be catastrophic. And yet, even now we approach the catastrophe without recognizing the need for fundamental changes in the existent distribution of powers. Choosing men of good will for leadership is not sufficient, as Madame Gandhi has taught us so well.

Jackson's conclusion was

> that emergency powers are consistent with free government only when their control is lodged elsewhere than in the Executive who exercises them. That is the safeguard that would be nullified by our adoption of the "inherent powers" formula. Nothing in my experience convinces me that such risks are warranted by any real necessity, although such powers would, of course, be an executive convenience.[51]

It is important that everyone at least see the portrait of government as painted by Jackson in his opinion in the *Steel Seizure* case. For it will be ignored only at the price of all civil rights and civil liberties:

---

51. *Id.* at 652.

In view of the ease, expedition and safety with which Congress can grant and has granted large emergency powers, certainly ample to embrace this crisis, I am quite unimpressed with the argument that we should affirm possession of them without statute. Such power either has no beginning or it has no end. If it exists, it need submit to no legal restraint. I am not alarmed that it would plunge us straightway into dictatorship, but it is at least a step in that wrong direction.

As to whether there is imperative necessity for such powers, it is relevant to note the gap that exists between the President's paper powers and his real powers. The Constitution does not disclose the measure of the actual controls wielded by the modern presidential office. That instrument must be understood as an Eighteenth-Century sketch of a government hoped for, not as a blueprint of the government that is. Vast accretions of federal power, eroded from that reserved by the States, have magnified the scope of presidential activity. Subtle shifts take place in the centers of real power that do not show on the face of the Constitution.

Executive power has the advantage of concentration in a single head in whose choice the whole nation has a part, making him the focus of public hopes and expectations. In drama, magnitude and finality his decisions so far overshadow any others that almost alone he fills the public eye and ear. No other personality in public life can begin to compete with him in access to the public mind through modern methods of communcation. By his prestige as head of state and his influence upon public opinion he exerts a leverage upon those who are supposed to check and balance his power which often cancels their effectiveness.

. . . I cannot be brought to believe that this country will suffer if the Court refuses further to aggrandize the presidential office, already so potent and so relatively immune from judicial review, at the expense of Congress.

But I have no illusion that any decision by this Court can keep power in the hands of Congress if it is not wise and timely in meeting its problems. A crisis that challenges the President equally, or perhaps primarily, challenges Congress. If not good law, there was worldly wisdom in the maxim attributed to Napoleon that "The tools belong to the man who can use them." We may say that power to legislate for emergencies belongs in the hands of Congress, but only Congress itself can prevent power from slipping through its fingers.

The essence of our free Government is "leave to live by no man's leave, underneath the law"—to be governed by those impersonal forces which we call law. Our Government is fashioned to fulfill this concept so far as humanly possible. The Executive, except for recommendation and veto, has no legislative power. The executive action we have here originates in the individual will of the President and represents an exercise of authority without law. No one, perhaps not even the President, knows the limits of the power he may seek to exert in this instance and the parties affected cannot learn the limit of their rights. W.e do not know today what powers over labor or property would be claimed to flow from Government possession if we should legalize it, what rights to compensation would be claimed or recognized, or on what contingency it would end. With all its defects, delays and inconveniences, men have discovered no technique for long preserving free government except that the Executive be under the law, and that the law be made by parliamentary deliberations.

Such institutions may be destined to pass away. But it is the duty of the Court to be last, not first, to give them up.[52]

And so endeth the text of the liberal judges' creed on separation of powers, or more correctly checks and balances, as the *sine qua non* for a democratic society with freedom for individuals in that society, which is, as I have suggested the goal of both liberals and libertarians.

V.   Equality as Civil Liberty

It is since Jackson's time that the Supreme Court has turned its attention to imposing an egalitarianism on American life. Equal protection of the laws, prior to the decision of the Court in *Brown v. Board of Education*,[53] was a narrow conception of comparatively little moment in the life of the Constitution. As known to that time, it was a concept that Jackson liked as a lesser restraint on the states than the due process clause with its substantive content. Thus, he said in *Railway Express Agency, Inc. v. New York:*

My philosophy as to the relative readiness with which we should resort to these two clauses is almost diametrically opposed to the philosophy which prevails on this Court. While claims of a denial of equal protection are frequently asserted, they are rarely sustained. . . .

. . .Invalidation of a statute or an ordinance on due process grounds leaves ungoverned and ungovernable conduct which many people find objectionable.

Invocation of the equal protection clause, on the other hand, does not disable any governmental body from dealing with the subject at hand. It merely means that the prohibition or regulation must have a broader impact. I regard it as a salutary doctrine that cities, states and the Federal Government must exercise their powers so as not to discriminate between their inhabitants except upon some reasonable

---

52. *Id.* at 653-55 (footnotes omitted).
53. 347 U.S. 483 (1954).

differentiation fairly related to the object of regulation. This equality is not merely abstract justice. The framers of the Constitution knew, and we should not forget today, that there is no more effective practical guaranty against arbitrary and unreasonable government than to require that the principles of law which officials would impose upon a minority must be imposed generally. Conversely, nothing opens the door to arbitrary action so effectively as to allow those officials to pick and choose only a few to whom they will apply legislation and thus to escape the political retribution that might be visited upon them if larger numbers were affected. Courts can take no better measure to assure that laws will be just than to require that laws be equal in operaton.[54]

Those with any familiarity with the development of the equal protection clause since Jackson's departure will readily see that his concept of the standard and reason for the equal protection clause is no longer deemed appropriate. His was a notion of equal treatment by the law. The later notions are more concerned with the use of the law—the unequal use of the law—to bring about equality of condition. Substantive equal protection has been substituted for substantive due process as a means by which the courts undertake to make policy determinations about the wisdom and desirability of statutes. The equal protection clause no longer serves merely to void laws that are not equal in their application. The choice is no longer left to the legislature to decide to enlarge or diminish the class to bring about equality of treatment. The laws are themselves rewritten by the courts to conform to judicial notions of social justice.

I find it difficult to believe that Mr. Justice Jackson would have taken kindly to the changed concept of equal protection of the laws. In a recent lecture at the University of Chicago, Professor Paul A. Freund noted Oliver Wendell Holmes's remark that the Constitution did not incorporate Herbert Spencer's *Social Statics* and went on to suggest that neither does the Constitution incorporate Professor John Rawl's "Social Ecstatics."[55] But Holmes was wrong and so, too, is Freund. The Constitution of Holmes's day, with its concepts of liberty of contract and substantive due process, did indeed incorporate Spencer's *Social Statics,* and the current Constitution, at least through the Warren Court, may as easily be said to invoke Rawl's *A Theory of Justice.* Rawl's proposition is that any inequality of condition has to be justified and if it cannot be justified it has to be rectified. We have come a very long way from the Jacksonian

---

54. 336 U.S. 106, 111-13 (1949) (Jackson, J., concurring).
55. *See* RAWLS, A THEORY OF JUSTICE (1971).

notion of the purpose and effect of the equal protecton clause.

Let this not be taken to suggest dissent by Jackson from the decision in the *Brown* case. Clearly the exclusion of children from a public school because of the color of their skins would fall afoul of the standard stated by Jackson in the *Railway Express* case. Mr. Justice Jackson must have thought so. He was in a hospital bed suffering from a heart attack when the time came to hand down the *Brown* decision. He left that bed—it is said against doctors' orders—to demonstrate that the decision of the Court in *Brown* was one supported by all nine Justices by sitting with his brethren on the fateful day of that decision. He died before the Court was faced with the problems of executing its judgment.

I am sure, too, that Mr. Justice Jackson had qualms about the *Brown* decision. They did not, however, go to the merits of the judgment, but rather to the lack of justification for it in the Court's opinion, a lack of candor as well as a lack of authority. And even more was he troubled by the question whether the substantial revision of the social structure of the nation could be achieved through judicial rather than legislative and executive action.[56] With the power of hindsight, can we say, even today, that his troubles were not real ones?

VI. CONCLUSION

Let me conclude by attempting to respond to the question implicit in my assignment for tonight. It was the sponsors of this lecture who stated the title: "Justice Robert Jackson—Impact on Civil Rights and Civil Liberties." They might have ended the title with a question mark, although in fact they did not. Assuming that they had invoked the inquisitive mood and asked what effect did Justice Jackson have on the consitutional law of civil rights and civil liberties, I should have to respond by saying that Jackson's impact has been very small indeed.

Jackson's tenure on the Court ended on 9 October 1954 with his sudden death shortly after the Court reconvened for its 1954 term. Clearly his work was far from finished. But had he remained, it would probably have merely been an extension of the frustrations that he suffered throughout most of his judicial tenure.

The Warren Court, as it has come to be called, was clearly a libertarian court, with the ideas of Justices Black and Douglas in the ascendant. There was no room here for the liberal mode.

---

56. *See* KLUGER, SIMPLE JUSTICE (1975).

Absolutes of constitutional meaning precluded the balances and conditions that Jackson asserted. Rules were no longer tailored to the resolution of particular cases. They were now "prophylactic" as the modern jargon would have it, promulgated not to cure existent ills but to foreclose future ailments, real and imaginary. True, Mr. Justice Black, toward the end of his career, often looked more like a liberal than a libertarian.[57] But by then, the Court had passed its leader.

Now, the Warren Court, too, is dead. But Jackson and judicial liberalism are not revived. On its way from Warren Court doctrine to Burger Court doctrine, if it can be called that, the Court has again bypassed the liberal tradition. It tends to write absolutes of its own. The Jacksonian dedication to reason, to the need to explain constitutional opinions, especially those that make changes in the law, weighs very lightly, if at all, on the current Court's membership. Suffice it for them that judgments are reached together with a lengthy exegesis that more often hides than reveals reasons for the decision.

I would say that neither Jackson's attitudes nor his craftsmanship, whether in the realm of civil liberties or elsewhere, has left a deep mark on the jurisprudence of the Supreme Court. But he has left an intellectual inheritance that may, like a phoenix, rise again.

This lecture was not, therefore, intended as a testimonial to the present importance of the judicial efforts of Robert H. Jackson. But, as Mr. Justice Holmes once wrote:

> When his work is finished it is too late for praise to give the encouragement which all need, and of which the successful get too little. Still, there is a pleasure in bearing one's testimony even at that late time, and thus in justifying the imagination of posthumous power on which all idealists and men not seeking the immediate rewards of success must live.[58]

Mr. Justice Jackson was such an idealist, although a practical one. He saw that individual responsibility was the necessary concomitant of individual freedom. He saw that, in the end, the errors of representative government were more tolerable for free men, than the perfections of the corporate Leviathan.

Let me close with Jackson's own last words of testament. He died after preparing but before delivering the Godkin lectures at Harvard. His peroration for those lectures should be meaningful, in light of current events, for both liberal and libertarian:

---

57. *See* Snowiss, *The Legacy of Justice Black*, 1973 SUP. CT. REV. 187.
58. HOLMES, COLLECTED LEGAL PAPERS 283 (1920).

. . . In Great Britain, to observe civil liberties is good politics and to transgress the rights of the individual or the minority is bad politics. In the United States, I cannot say that this is so. Whether the political conscience is relieved because the responsibility here is made largely a legal one, I cannot say, but of this I am sure: any court which undertakes by its legal processes to enforce civil liberties needs the support of an enlightened and vigorous public opinion which will be intelligent and discriminating as to what cases really are civil liberties cases and what questions really are involved in those cases. I do not think the American public is enlightened on this subject.

Sometimes one is tempted to quote his former self, not only to pay his respects to the author but to demonstrate the consistency of his views, if not their correctness. On the 150th anniversary of the Supreme Court, speaking for the executive branch of the Government as Attorney General, I said to the Justices:

"However well the Court and its bar may discharge their tasks, the destiny of this Court is inseparably linked to the fate of our democratic system of representative government. Judicial functions, as we have evolved them, can be discharged only in that kind of society which is willing to submit its conflicts to adjudication and to subordinate power to reason. The future of the Court may depend more upon the competence of the executive and legislative branches of government to solve their problems adequately and in time than upon the merits which is its own."[59]

Mr. Justice Jackson was not a man for all seasons. At least his was not the dominant voice on the Court that he graced. Nor was it the voice of the Warren Court that succeeded his. And it appears not to be that of the present Court that falls outside the teachings both of our liberal and our libertarian Justices. But perhaps his can be the mode of the Court of the future. That can be so, however, only if his efforts and ideas are kept alive by continued study of them by new generations of lawyers and law teachers. It is to encourage that possibility that I have offered these remarks. It is to you that I give the charge. And so I wish you Godspeed.

---

59.   JACKSON, THE SUPREME COURT IN THE AMERICAN SYSTEM OF GOVERNMENT 82-83 (1955).

WILLIAM T. COLEMAN, JR.

MR. JUSTICE FELIX FRANKFURTER: CIVIL LIBERTARIAN AS LAWYER AND AS JUSTICE: EXTENT TO WHICH JUDICIAL RESPONSIBILITIES AFFECTED HIS PRE-COURT CONVICTIONS†

William T. Coleman, Jr. *

WHEN FRAGMENTS OF Mr. Justice Felix Frankfurter's diaries were published not long ago, a distinguished reviewer, Leonard Boudin, ventured an all too facile opinion, unfortunately representative of those held by many of Justice Frankfurter's critics—that his judicial commitment to civil liberties and civil rights did not live up to the expectations engendered by his pre-Court career.[1] Boudin summarized the conventional wisdom:

> In light of Frankfurter's brilliant pre-Court career, what did the country—and Frankfurter himself—expect from him on the bench? What were his role and accomplishments on the Court? Given Frankfurter's early liberalism, could one have foreseen, and can we now explain, his later shift to conservatism? Is there a consistent philosophical thread between the younger Frankfurter and the Justice? . . .
>
> Frankfurter's unusual combination of scholarship and activism should have made him a dominating figure on the Supreme Court, and one who in a period of stress, would protect the rights of political and religious minorities. But neither occurred. Instead, Frankfurter emerged as the paradigm rationalist, the academics' Justice. His primary concerns were with regularity,

---

† These remarks were originally delivered at the University of Illinois College of Law on October 12, 1977, as the first 1977-78 lecture of the David C. Baum Lectures on Civil Rights and Civil Liberties.

* A.B. 1941, University of Pennsylvania; LL.B. 1946 (as of 1943), Harvard Law School; Law Clerk to Mr. Justice Frankfurter, October Term 1948; Secretary of the U.S. Department of Transportation 1975-77; Member of the American College of Trial Lawyers and the Pennsylvania and District of Columbia Bars.

1. Boudin, Book Review, 89 HARV. L. REV. 282 (1975) (reviewing J. LASH, FROM THE DIARIES OF FELIX FRANKFURTER (1975)).

neutrality, and judicial humility. He deferred to administrative expertise, the political processes, and stare decisis.[2]

Tonight I would like to discuss with you whether the judicial decisions of Mr. Justice Frankfurter did in fact fail to show the same sensitivity to civil liberties and civil rights that had characterized his earlier career.[3]

To set the stage, let me remind you briefly of Justice Frankfurter's renowned pre-Court career. In between brief stints as a private practitioner, he held several government positions, including that of an Assistant United States Attorney under Mr. Henry L. Stimson, then became a Harvard law professor for a quarter of a century, taking out time during World War I to return to government. At Harvard he became the nation's leading authority on the federal courts, the federal system, and labor injunctions, while remaining a stimulating and popular professor who sent many of his brightest students into the government. Eventually he acted as an unofficial advisor to President Franklin D. Roosevelt, a role he would continue to some extent as a Justice. His closest professional conversational companions were Justices Holmes and Brandeis, Harold Laski, Dean Acheson, Henry Stimson, and his law clerks.[4]

Throughout his early career Frankfurter manifested a strong concern for civil rights and civil liberties. He was counsel to the NAACP. Soon after arriving at Harvard he became involved with the National Consumers League and eventually argued several important minimum wages and maximum hours cases to the Supreme Court. During World War I he recommended that President Wilson intercede on behalf of Tom Mooney, the labor leader given a death sentence in California for allegedly planting a bomb, and he condemned the action of vigilante groups against I.W.W. miners. In reaction to the anticommunist hysteria that followed World War I, reflected in the *Abrams v. United States*[5] convictions for publication of allegedly seditious leaflets, he joined a group of distinguished lawyers in a report condemning

---

2. *Id.* at 284-85.

3. In addition to Justice Frankfurter's opinions and other writings, I am indebted to many other authorities in the preparation of this lecture. In addition to sources cited elsewhere in the footnotes, I have consulted M. Freedman, Roosevelt and Frankfurter, Their Correspondence 1928-1945 (1967); W. Mendelson, Felix Frankfurter: A Tribute (1964); W. Mendelson, Justices Black and Frankfurter: Conflict in the Court (2d ed. 1966); H. Phillips, Felix Frankfurter Reminisces (1960).

4. The Justice took an interest in his law clerks which continued long after their service to the Court. He would provide social occasions for conversation and was a thought-provoking correspondent, providing a continuing flow of advice. Once, for example, he wrote me about an offer I had received to codify the laws of Liberia:

Chance is a most influential—I think almost a decisive—factor in the career of men. What is important is that one should have a direction of purpose as you have and not aim for a particular realization of it, through a particular job. That is almost fatal, for the contingencies of life are too many.

Letter from Felix Frankfurter to the author (Feb. 9, 1950).

5. 250 U.S. 616 (1919).

illegal activities by the Department of Justice.[6] He participated in the founding of the American Civil Liberties Union, and his 1927 book, *The Case of Sacco and Vanzetti*,[7] incurred the wrath of conservatives at Harvard and elsewhere.

On January 30, 1939, after his nomination to the Supreme Court of the United States by President Roosevelt had subjected him to stormy confirmation hearings during which he was accused of being a socialist and a communist, Professor Felix Frankfurter took Mr. Justice Cardozo's place on the Court. Justice Frankfurter would often speak of January 30, as the most important date in the English-speaking world. I hasten to add that the reason for the date's importance to the Justice was that it was the date on which Charles I was beheaded, an event which, for Frankfurter, established the proposition that in a free society no man is above the law.

Frankfurter's nomination to the Supreme Court prompted Archibald MacLeish to predict that Frankfurter would protect the Bill of Rights against legislative erosion because, among other things, his work in the Sacco and Vanzetti case had demonstrated "his peculiar sensitivity to attacks on civil rights and his deep and passionate devotion to their defense."[8] As the earlier quotation of Leonard Boudin indicates, however, many libertarians feel that Frankfurter's performance on the Court did not live up to this prediction. It is my conviction that Felix Frankfurter's commitment to civil liberties and civil rights during his pre-Court years was constantly reaffirmed during his twenty-three years as a Justice. I believe that his contribution on the Court was essential to the nation's continuing progress toward equality and fuller protection of human rights. I believe that his contribution will endure and I predict that his opinions will outlive some of those by other Justices who received higher marks from liberal scholars during the fifties and sixties.

Why, then, has Frankfurter's reputation as a judicial defender of civil liberties been characterized as a retreat from his pre-Court commitment? Many have said that as a Justice he was paralyzed by the lesson that he had learned from the spectacle of the Nine Old Men of the pre-Roosevelt era commandeering the Court in an effort to incorporate Herbert Spencer's *Social Statics* into the fourteenth amendment.[9] Frankfurter's own pre-Court advocacy of protection for working people and of responsible federal and state social and economic legislation frequently had met with defeat at their hands. Many have said that attorney Frankfurter's commitment to judicial deference to legislative judgments became so strong that Justice Frankfurter

---

6. *See* J. Lash, From the Diaries of Felix Frankfurter 31 (1975).
7. F. Frankfurter, The Case of Sacco and Vanzetti (1927).
8. MacLeish, *Foreword* to Law and Politics: Occasional Papers of Felix Frankfurter, 1913-1938 at xxiii (A. MacLeish & E. Prichard eds. 1939).
9. *See* Lochner v. New York, 198 U.S. 45, 75 (1905) (Holmes, J., dissenting).

could not shake it when the need for judicial checks on legislative action arose.

Indeed, the danger of judicial arrogance taught by these judicial political-economic philosophers was not easily forgotten. For Frankfurter as a Justice, the process of reconciling his unwavering faith in the people's legislature as the essence of democratic government with his empathy with those who "have few friends"[10] was often a process of personal agony. Nevertheless, by 1939 Frankfurter had put behind him his most extreme views on judicial deference, such as his comment to Mr. Henry L. Stimson in 1924 that "the Fourteenth Amendment is too powerful an instrument of uncertain centralization. I think the due process clauses ought to go."[11] He was fully prepared to assert judicial authority against the legislative will when appropriate.

I believe his reputation has suffered not because he was paralyzed, but because the lesson of judicial humility constantly tempered his judgments. Some of his colleagues—Chief Justice Warren and Justices Black, Douglas, Murphy, and Rutledge—were often bolder, more on the cutting edge of dramatic advances, more sweeping in their outraged condemnation of the violation of human rights. Frankfurter, on the other hand, brought a unique historical perspective to each problem, seeking always to ensure that the changing currents of contemporary judicial conviction did not overwhelm the steady trend toward responsibile democracy. Frankfurter believed that our government is a constitutional democracy—with the emphasis on "democracy." Although we fortunately do not have to make the choice, it is intriguing to debate whether the protection of minorities from the tyranny of the majority is best ensured by the democratic ideal in which the people are ultimately responsible through their legislature, or by the Constitution, the prescripts of which are interpreted by a judicial elite.

The Justice was not prone to platitudes or simplistic ringing phrases that would echo among the halls of academia, reinforcing the spirited convictions of our nation's moralist elite. Frankfurter's judicial opinions on civil liberties were not designed to gratify libertarian colleagues or scholars. Nevertheless, his articulation of principles and methods in the interpretation of our Constitution remains the ratchet that will prevent a less bold Court from receding from the gains for human dignity and human rights which we achieved during Frankfurter's tenure. Although we may disagree with some of the applications of his constitutional theories—I, for one, think he was wrong on a few first amendment decisions[12]—we must agree that his quest for the realization of those "canons of decency and fairness which express the

---

10. Letter from Felix Frankfurter to Frank Murphy (Feb. 15, 1947) (Frankfurter Papers, Library of Congress).

11. Letter from Felix Frankfurter to Henry Stimson (Oct. 6, 1924) (Stimson Papers, Sterling Memorial Library, Yale University).

12. *See, e.g.,* West Virginia State Bd. of Educ. v. Barnette, 319 U.S. 624, 646 (1943) (Frank-

notions of justice of English-speaking peoples"[13] was reasoned, objective, and impersonal. For this reason, I believe that his legacy to the American people will persevere. But before commenting upon some of his major decisions on civil liberties, I would like to elaborate on the principles of constitutionalism that the Justice advanced during his tenure on the Court. In my judgment, it is these principles that have shaped a jurisprudence deeply committed to human dignity and that will be an enduring heritage for the nation.

Contrary to what some have said, the literal language and the pre-ratification history of the Constitution and the Bill of Rights seldom provide a clear basis for the resolution of disputes over civil rights or civil liberties. Because "it is a Constitution we are expounding," its language is necessarily general and often vague. The contemporary significance of the Constitution's vague commands, Frankfurter frequently demonstrated, must be derived from "the totality of a man's nature and experience,"[14] from a knowledge of history, and from an understanding of the fundamentals of a dynamic, open, democratic society. Moreover, Frankfurter believed that this judgment should not be exercised by "those who express their private views or revelations, deeming them, if not *vox dei*, at least *vox populi*,"[15] but rather by

> those who feel strongly that they have no authority to promulgate law by their merely personal view and whose whole training and proved performance substantially insure that their conclusions reflect understanding of, and due regard for, law as the expression of the views and feelings that may fairly be deemed representative of the community as a continuing society.[16]

However courageous or righteous a judgment may seem at the time it is rendered, its lasting value and the credibility of the court which delivers it depend upon its foundation in history and its acceptance by the public. As personalities and philosophies on the Court change like an ever-turning kaleidoscope, only the tradition and the authority of the institution endure. An opinion cut loose from those traditions—however well intended—leaves the institution subject to the whims and predilections of those unknown personalities who will one day take the bench, each with an appointment for life and without any direct responsibility to the people. Subject to such stewardship, the Constitution becomes a drifting vessel, its meaning constantly changing direction like a burgee with the "shifting political winds."[17]

---

furter, J., dissenting); Minersville School Dist. v. Gobitis, 310 U.S. 586 (1940). For a discussion of the Flag Salute Cases, see text accompanying notes 76-81 *infra*.

13. Adamson v. California, 332 U.S. 46, 67 (1947) (Frankfurter, J., concurring).

14. F. FRANKFURTER, *The Judicial Process and the Supreme Court*, in OF LAW AND MEN 39-40 (1956).

15. *Id.* at 40.

16. *Id.*

17. Berger, *The Imperial Court*, N.Y. Times, Oct. 9, 1977, § 6 (Magazine), at 38.

To Justice Frankfurter, constitutional litigation presented few absolutes, only relative values to be articulated, weighed, and compared. Constitutional law was formulated not so much by the choice between right and wrong as by the reconciliation of competing rights that often did not lend themselves to easy or graceful comparison. Thus, Frankfurter rejected attempts to make constitutional doctrine turn on easy formulas, such as Justice Black's belief that the first eight amendments are incorporated into the fourteenth[18] or Black's assertion "I read 'no law . . . abridging' to mean *no law abridging* [speech]."[19] Frankfurter maintained that decisions must be carefully reasoned for law is "the institutionalized medium of reason" and "fragile as reason is . . . that's all we have standing between us and the tyranny of mere will and the cruelty of unbridled, undisciplined feeling."[20] Consequently, Justice Frankfurter's approach to decision writing is not noted for its brevity. Upon learning that Mrs. Frankfurter often edited her husband's nonjudicial writings, Justice Jackson once remarked: "why don't you extend the censorship?"[21]

Frankfurter believed that judicial restraint was necessary because constitutionality was not synonymous with wisdom or personal legislative desires.[22] He believed that as the least democratic branch of government, the judiciary should not act "as a super-legislature."[23] Thus, although his commitment to civil rights and liberties had not changed after his elevation to the bench, Frankfurter argued that the liberal spirit cannot

> be enforced by judicial invalidation of illiberal legislation . . . . Reliance for the most precious interests of civilization . . . must be found outside of their vindication in courts of law. Only a persistent positive translation of the faith of a free society into the convictions and habits and actions of a community is the ultimate reliance against unabated temptations to fetter the human spirit.[24]

Put more bluntly, a nation that must resort to the Supreme Court for the final definition of its civil liberties is a benign autocracy, in which the people have relinquished their responsibilities as citizens. In the words of Rauol Berger, "Better the risk of misgovernment by the people than the prospect of Utopia under the reign of nine—often only five—Platonic Guardians."[25]

---

18. Adamson v. California, 332 U.S. 46, 68 (1947) (Black, J., dissenting).
19. Smith v. California, 361 U.S. 147, 157 (1959) (Black, J., concurring).
20. TIME, Sept. 7, 1962, at 15.
21. N.Y. Times, Mar. 19, 1947, at 27 *quoted in* L. BAKER, FELIX FRANKFURTER 90 (1964).
22. The Justice put his philosophy pungently when he wrote me from Charlemont, Massachusetts: "Without strict adherence to reason and a refraining from permitting personal biases to enter adjudication, judges become covert little Hitlers." Letter from Felix Frankfurter to the author (Aug. 27, 1949).
23. N.Y. Times, Nov. 13, 1942.
24. West Virginia State Bd. of Educ. v. Barnette, 319 U.S. 624, 670-71 (1943) (Frankfurter, J., dissenting).
25. Berger, *The Imperial Court*, N.Y. Times, Oct. 9, 1977, § 6 (Magazine), at 118.

What is most striking about Justice Frankfurter's contribution is that despite his emphasis on tradition and detached reason, despite his recognition that there are few absolutes, only relative values to be compared, and despite his cautious restraint in approaching constitutional doctrine out of deference due to the Congress and the states, he nevertheless remained exceedingly capable of expressing the outrage of the Court at encroachments upon individual liberty that offended principles of justice "so rooted in the traditions and conscience of our people as to be ranked as fundamental."[26] The Justice would not tolerate an intrusion upon those rights "implicit in the concept of ordered liberty."[27]

His opinion in *Rochin v. California*[28] illustrates his capacity for outrage. In *Rochin* the Court reversed a decision of the Supreme Court of California affirming a conviction for possession of morphine. After describing vividly how the evidence was pumped from the stomach of the defendant against his will, Frankfurter wrote:

> the proceedings by which this conviction was obtained do more than offend some fastidious squeamishness or private sentimentalism about combating crime too energetically. This is conduct that shocks the conscience. Illegally breaking into the privacy of the petitioner, the struggle to open his mouth and remove what was there, the forcible extraction of his stomach's contents—this course of proceeding by agents of government to obtain evidence is bound to offend even hardened sensibilities. They are methods too close to the rack and the screw to permit of constitutional differentiation . . . . It would be a stultification of the responsibility which the course of constitutional history has cast upon this Court to hold that in order to convict a man the police cannot extract by force what is in his mind but can extract what is in his stomach.[29]

Rochin is a typical example of Frankfurter jurisprudence. For him the threshold of constitutional offense was most easily crossed by a disregard of fair procedure, because the historic requirements and proper role of the courts are best defined in the area of procedure and there is less danger in that area that judicial policymaking will supplant the role of the legislature. Yet by concentrating on procedure, the courts ensure that legislative policies are implemented fairly and that people are not denied the right to participate in the democratic processes by which policy is formulated. This is no small contribution. If we agree on the process, then we may disagree about the policies without fear. Ultimately, if we believe that reason will prevail over prejudice, then fair process will ensure that the rights of the individual are protected.

---

26. Snyder v. Massachusetts, 291 U.S. 97, 105 (1934) (opinion by Cardozo, J.).
27. Palko v. Connecticut, 302 U.S. 319, 325 (1937) (opinion by Cardozo, J.) *quoted in* Rochin v. California, 342 U.S. 165, 169 (1952) (opinion by Frankfurter, J.).
28. Rochin v. California, 342 U.S. 165 (1952).
29. *Id.* at 172-73.

It was with this perspective in view that Justice Frankfurter addressed some of the more difficult civil liberties and civil rights issues of his time. Although many cases illustrate how, within principles of judicial responsibility, Frankfurter continued his lifetime commitment to the enhancement of human rights, I will address three areas of particular significance: his concept of the fourteenth amendment in contrast to that of Justice Black, his reconciliation of first amendment freedoms with the legitimate needs of the state, and his dedication to a society free of racial bias.

With the ratification of the fourteenth amendment in 1868, the Constitution commanded that no state deprive any person of life, liberty, or property without due process of law nor deny any person the equal protection of the laws. When Justices Frankfurter and Black reached the Supreme Court, they shared a common perception that the pre-Roosevelt Court's property and contract decisions had distorted the meaning of the fourteenth amendment. Yet the Justices reacted to this problem very differently.

Justice Black's solution was to devise a mechanistic formula that could be applied automatically and thus eliminate discretionary policymaking based on the fourteenth amendment. The formula was first announced in his dissenting opinion in *Adamson v. California*.[30] In 1947 the Supreme Court held that California had not denied Mr. Adamson due process of law when the prosecutor at his trial for murder was permitted to comment on his failure to take the stand. Although it assumed that such a comment in a federal court would have violated the fifth amendment's prohibition of compulsory self-incrimination, the majority of the Supreme Court concluded that the prohibitions of the fifth amendment did not necessarily extend to state action through the fourteenth amendment.

Justice Black's dissent traced the history of the Court's interpretation of the fourteenth amendment to invalidate regulation of property rights and business practices beginning with the Minnesota Rate Case of 1889, when a railroad rate regulation was declared unconstitutional,[31] through the *Lochner* case in 1905, when the Supreme Court overturned a state maximum hours law.[32] What was intended as an amendment to restrain and check "the powers of wealth and privilege," Justice Black maintained, had "become the Magna Charta of accumulated wealth and organized capital."[33] Justice Black argued that the fourteenth amendment had not been intended to impose such a judicial restraint on legislative power, but rather had been intended to incorporate the first eight amendments and apply them to state action.

---

30. Adamson v. California, 332 U.S. 46, 68 (1947) (Black, J., dissenting).
31. Chicago, M. & St. P. Ry. v. Minnesota, 134 U.S. 418 (1890).
32. Lochner v. New York, 198 U.S. 45 (1905).
33. 332 U.S. at 84 *quoting* C. COLLINS, THE FOURTEENTH AMENDMENT AND THE STATES 137-38 (1912).

In a lengthy concurring opinion responding to Justice Black's seductively simple and convenient formula, Frankfurter rejected the incorporation theory. He stated that "the fourteenth amendment inescapably imposes upon this Court an *exercise of judgment* upon *the whole course of the proceedings* in order to ascertain whether they offend [the] canons of decency and fairness."[34] Although many libertarians supported Black's position and criticized Frankfurter for failing to seize this opportunity to extend to all state proceedings in one fell swoop the precious guarantees of the Bill of Rights, I believe that the Frankfurter view represents a firmer foundation upon which to build an enduring commitment to procedural safeguards in our judicial system.

Because Frankfurter's rejection of the Black approach goes to the heart of his institutional commitment to civil liberties, I would like to consider in some detail why he rejected the incorporation theory and what he considered to be the wiser course. First, the attempt to curtail judicial discretion by the invocation of a simplistic formula was, to Frankfurter, a dangerous resignation of judicial responsibility. He believed that the excesses of the pre-Roosevelt Court in economic cases should be avoided not by eliminating reasoned judgment but by exercising judicial restraint when the Constitution did not command intervention by the Court.[35]

Second, the Bill of Rights guarantees some rights and remedies that are inapposite to state experience.[36] Mandatory grand juries in criminal cases and jury trials in all civil cases in which the amount in dispute exceeds twenty dollars would be unnecessary burdens on state court systems, resulting in delays and complications that would clog the courts and deny efficient and timely justice. These rights were established for the federal courts on the assumption, subsequently proved correct, that federal crimes would be few and that federal courts would exercise jurisdiction only over substantial civil cases.

Third, Frankfurter recognized that curbing judicial discretion curbs the potential for safeguarding civil liberties as well as the potential for abuse. Incorporation taken literally would restrict the four-

---

34. 332 U.S. at 67 (Frankfurter, J., concurring) (emphasis added).
35. *Rochin v. California*, 342 U.S. 165, 170-71 (1952). Unlike many other Justices, Frankfurter could not restrict the principle of restraint to property cases.

Judicial self-restraint is equally necessary whenever an exercise of political or legislative power is challenged. . . . Our power does not vary according to the particular provision of the Bill of Rights which is invoked. The right not to have property taken without just compensation has, so far as the scope of judicial power is concerned, the same constitutional dignity as the right to be protected against unreasonable searches and seizures, and the latter has no less claim than freedom of the press or freedom of speech or religious freedom.

. . . [R]esponsibility for legislation lies with legislatures, answerable as they are directly to the people, and this Court's only and very narrow function is to determine whether within the broad grant of authority vested in legislatures they have exercised a judgment for which reasonable justification can be offered.

West Virginia State Bd. of Educ. v. Barnette, 319 U.S. 624, 648-49 (Frankfurter, J., dissenting).
36. 332 U.S. at 64-65 (Frankfurter, J., concurring).

teenth amendment to concepts prevalent when the Bill of Rights was adopted in 1791. In approaching current issues, judges must either make strained interpretations of the Bill of Rights or leave violations of rights unredressed.[37] The Bill of Rights, for example, does not specifically prohibit vague and ambiguous criminal statutes[38] or a prosecutor's knowing use of false evidence to obtain convictions.[39] Literal application of the incorporation doctrine could therefore result in a retreat from some of the procedural safeguards on state action that are now required under the fourteenth amendment.

As a practical matter literal incorporation could not always be followed. Even its author, Justice Black, occasionally broadened considerably his interpretation of due process.[40] Because the Black formula cannot be applied literally, it fails in its original purpose of curtailing discretion and serves only to constrain reasoned judgment upon which enduring progress through the judicial system depends. Moreover, the straitjacket effect of Black's doctrine predicted by Frankfurter eventually revealed itself in several of Justice Black's later dissents. Among these were Justice Black's dissents to decisions holding that the fourth amendment governs electronic surveillance by government agents,[41] that a state may not punish the use of contraceptives by married couples,[42] that the government must establish guilt beyond a reasonable doubt when prosecuting a juvenile for an act which, if committed by an adult, would be criminal,[43] and that the government cannot terminate a welfare recipient's benefits without a prior evidentiary hearing.[44]

Frankfurter, on the other hand, recognized that the Bill of Rights simply does not provide specific guidance to either federal or state courts today on many of the procedural safeguards and civil rights that have now become deeply ingrained in our traditions and experience and that reflect the contemporary standards of the community. Frankfurter's emphasis on history and restraint did not deny the importance of incremental and evolutionary progress to fill gaps. The Bill of Rights "grew out of transient experience or formulated remedies which time might well improve. The Fourteenth Amendment did not mean to imprison the States into the limited experience of the eighteenth cen-

---

37. *See id.* at 46.
38. *See, e.g.,* Papachristou v. City of Jacksonville, 405 U.S. 156 (1972).
39. *See, e.g.,* Brady v. Maryland, 373 U.S. 83 (1963).
40. *See* Alcorta v. Texas, 355 U.S. 28 (1957) (per curiam); Williams v. New York, 337 U.S. 241 (1949).
41. Katz v. United States, 389 U.S. 347, 369 (1967) (Black, J., dissenting).
42. Griswold v. Connecticut, 381 U.S. 479, 507 (1965) (Black, J., dissenting).
43. *In re* Winship, 397 U.S. 358, 377 (1970) (Black, J., dissenting).
44. Goldberg v. Kelly, 397 U.S. 254, 271 (1970) (Black, J., dissenting). *See also* Sniadach v. Family Fin. Corp., 395 U.S. 337 (1969) (holding that an individual's wages may not be garnished without prior notice and an adversary hearing). Once again Justice Black was forced to dissent because of his rigid notion of incorporation. *See id.* at 344.

tury."[45]   What was important was that the Court progressed as if it were walking across a newly frozen pond, testing the firmness of the ice with each succeeding step.

We have learned that the incorporation doctrine poses another threat to the safeguarding of rights. To the extent that it creates a parallelism between the federal and state courts by applying the Bill of Rights to the procedures of each, it tends to dampen considerably the special federal prerogative to ensure the highest standards of procedural fairness in the federal courts. Thus, the Supreme Court has occasionally diluted constitutional requirements as it extended them from the federal government to the states because of its reluctance to impose requirements on all the states inconsistent with their diversity of experiences, traditions, and needs.[46]   To give content to the special constitutional purpose of the federal courts, the Supreme Court could confidently assert higher standards for the federal system if it were not constrained by the notion that the Bill of Rights requires that the same standards be applied in both the federal and state systems.[47]

Justice Frankfurter's own diligence in requiring the highest standards of procedure in the federal courts cannot be faulted. In *McNabb v. United States*,[48] the Supreme Court reversed the conviction for second degree murder of an alleged moonshiner because of the introduction into evidence of a confession obtained by revenue agents who failed to arraign the accused promptly. "The history of liberty," Frankfurter wrote for the Court, "has largely been the history of observance of procedural safeguards. And the effective administration of criminal justice hardly requires disregard of fair procedure imposed by law."[49]

Consistent with his view of constitutional federalism and his interpretation of the fourteenth amendment's due process requirements, Frankfurter accorded the state courts greater flexibility in establishing fair process. But greater flexibility did not extend to the denial of fundamental rights. In *Malinski v. New York*,[50] the Supreme Court reversed the conviction of a man who had been arrested by the police in New York and taken to a hotel room in Brooklyn where he was detained for more than seven hours, stripped, and eventually given only a

---

45.   Francis v. Resweber, 329 U.S. 459, 468 (1947) (Frankfurter, J., concurring).

46.   *See, e.g.*, Williams v. Florida, 399 U.S. 78 (1970) (abandoning long-standing sixth amendment requirement of 12-person juries after the extension of the sixth amendment right to trial to the states in Duncan v. Louisiana, 391 U.S. 145 (1968)). *See* Amsterdam, *The Supreme Court and the Rights of Suspects in Criminal Cases*, 45 N.Y.U.L. REV. 785, 797 (1970).

47.   *See* Williams v. Florida, 399 U.S. 78, 117 (1970) (Harlan, J., dissenting in part, concurring in part); Ker v. California, 374 U.S. 23, 44 (1963) (Harlan, J., concurring).

48.   318 U.S. 332 (1943).

49.   *Id.* at 347. Among his other contributions to federal procedure was his fierce insistence on the value of the fourth amendment and its exclusionary rule. *See, e.g.*, Harris v. United States, 331 U.S. 145, 155 (1947) (Frankfurter, J., dissenting). His dissent in *Harris* eventually was vindicated in Chimel v. California, 395 U.S. 752 (1969).

50.   324 U.S. 401 (1945).

blanket, shoes, socks, and underwear. Four days after his arrest he confessed at the police station. The confession was used as evidence at the trial. Frankfurter wrote in a concurring opinion:

> [T]he long and continuous questioning, the wilful and wrongful delay in his arraignment and the opportunity that gives for securing, by extortion, confessions such as were here introduced in evidence, the flagrant justification by the prosecutor of the illegality as a necessary police procedure, inevitably calculated to excite the jury—all these in combination are so below the standards by which the criminal law, especially in a capital case, should be enforced as to fall short of due process of law.[51]

Malinski and *Rochin* were easy for Justice Frankfurter because his commitment to civil liberties and to judicial restraint were not in conflict and neither had to be compromised. More difficult were those cases in which he personally believed that a human right had been violated, but could not find—using the external analytical standard that a disinterested judge was bound to apply—that the violation was of constitutional significance. In 1944, a fifteen-year-old black from Louisiana named Willy Francis killed a druggist in a holdup from which he received four dollars and a watch. He was tried, convicted, and sentenced to die in the electric chair. On May 3, 1946, the switch was thrown, but the chair malfunctioned and he was not killed. A second death warrant was issued for an execution scheduled for May 9. His counsel attacked the second warrant on the ground that it violated Francis's rights against "double jeopardy" and "cruel and unusual punishment," as applied to the state through the fourteenth amendment. Denials of relief were appealed through the state system to the Supreme Court, which declined by a vote of five-to-four to overrule the Supreme Court of Louisiana.[52]

Felix Frankfurter agonized over this decision, but ultimately concluded in his concurrence:

> I cannot bring myself to believe that for Louisiana to leave to executive clemency, rather than to require, mitigation of a sentence of death . . . because the first attempt to carry it out was an innocent misadventure, offends a principle of justice "rooted in the traditions and conscience of our people . . . ." Short of the compulsion of such a principle, this Court must abstain from interference with State action no matter how strong one's personal feeling of revulsion against the State's insistence on its pound of flesh . . . .[53]

He could not shake himself of the conclusion that "were I to hold that Louisiana would transgress the Due Process Clause . . . [in carrying] out the death sentence, I would be enforcing my private view rather

---

51. *Id.* at 417-18 (Frankfurter, J., concurring).
52. Francis v. Resweber, 329 U.S. 459 (1947).
53. *Id.* at 470-71 (Frankfurter, J., concurring).

than that consensus of society's opinion which, for purposes of due process, is the standard enjoined by the Constitution."[54]   Unable to make a disinterested finding that the fourteenth amendment had been violated, Frankfurter placed the responsibility where he thought it belonged—with the Governor of Louisiana who had the power to grant executive clemency. Having adhered to his judicial responsibilities with some remorse, however, Frankfurter wrote several times to an old classmate in New Orleans seeking his assistance in persuading the Governor to commute the sentence to life imprisonment. Clemency, he argued, would "strengthen the forces of goodwill, compassion, and wisdom in society."[55] Frankfurter's efforts were unsuccessful. Willy Francis was electrocuted on May 9. The price of constitutional integrity had been great. Nevertheless, Frankfurter's opinions on fair law enforcement procedures will have enduring value precisely because they are not products of personal passion but rather rest on a historical foundation and contemporary standards.

Justice Frankfurter's commitment to civil liberties also permeates his first amendment opinions and fourteenth amendment opinions applying related values to the states, though relatively few of them ring with the bold phrases of a Black or a Douglas. Frankfurter preferred not to preach constitutional ultimatums to the Congress or the states or to cast the issues in terms of first amendment values versus the will of the legislature, thus threatening the fragile consent upon which the Court's authority rests. Yet, as Joe Rauh points out, Justice Frankfurter found ways to hold illegal the challenged federal or state activity in almost every case involving official investigation of an individual's beliefs.[56] In a separate opinion in *American Communications Association v. Douds*,[57] Frankfurter upheld only part of a requirement in the Labor-Management Relations Act that required each union officer to sign an affidavit that

he is not a member of the Communist Party or affiliated with such party, and that he does not believe in, and is not a member of or supports [*sic*] any organization that believes in or teaches, the overthrow of the United States Government by force or by any illegal or unconstitutional methods.[58]

Frankfurter deferred to the power of Congress to require the "actual membership" portion of the affidavit.[59] The Justice concluded, however, that "Congress has cast its net too indiscriminately in some of the provisions" of the affidavit,[60] and he held unconstitutional the attempt by Congress to invade the thoughts and beliefs of the individual.

---

54. *Id.* at 471.
55. Letter from Felix Frankfurter to Monte Lemann (Feb. 3, 1947) (Library of Congress).
56. Rauh, Felix Frankfurter: Civil Libertarian (Francis Biddle Memorial Lecture).
57. 339 U.S. 382 (1950).
58. Labor-Management Relations Act of 1947, ch. 120, § 9(h), 61 Stat. 136, 146.
59. 339 U.S. at 421 (Frankfurter, J., concurring in part).
60. *Id.* at 419.

Frequently, he relied upon errors of process—holding, for example, that Congressional investigators inquiring into Communist affiliations had asked questions that were too broad or were not clearly authorized by Congressional action.[61] Rather than challenging the legislative authority directly, he sought to interpret it in the least offensive way and then to ensure that it was enforced that way. By correcting the procedural errors in investigations, he not only relied on precedents for which the judiciary's authority was strongest, but also exposed the banality and viciousness of legislative activities such as the House Un-American Activities Committee. Through such exposure, the Committee ultimately lost respect, and the Congress let it expire.

Even when Frankfurter reached substantive first amendment questions, he tended to avoid bold phrases because his principled jurisprudence demanded too careful a reconciliation of competing values. When in his judgment the constitutional command was explicit, he could be uncompromising. He was vigilant, for example, in pursuing his conviction that the Constitution decreed that "complete separation between state and religion is best for the state and best for religion."[62] When contending values were not explicitly weighed by the Constitution, however, he was careful to articulate those values, to give them definition and lasting substance, and then to weigh and compare them, often deferring to the legislature when its choice of a dominant value appeared reasonable.

His concurring opinion in *Sweezy v. New Hampshire*[63] is a good example of this careful weighing process. In *Sweezy* the Supreme Court reversed a New Hampshire contempt citation based on Mr. Sweezy's refusal to respond to questions asked by the state attorney general, under a legislative mandate, about his pro-Communist lectures at the University of New Hampshire and his work with the Progressive Party. Justice Frankfurter found that Sweezy could be compelled to answer questions on neither subject. Frankfurter found the questions about Sweezy's lecture improper, because interests in self-protection asserted by the state were outweighed by academic freedom. Frankfurter noted "the grave harm resulting from governmental intrusion into the intellectual life of the university,"[64] and concluded that

> [f]or society's good—if understanding be an essential need of society—inquiries into [economics, law, sociology, and other areas of academic thought and] speculations about them . . . must be left as unfettered as possible. Political power must abstain from intrusion into this activity of freedom pursued in the interest of wise

---

61. Watkins v. United States, 354 U.S. 178, 216 (1957) (Frankfurter, J., concurring).
62. Illinois *ex rel.* McCollum v. Board of Educ., 333 U.S. 203, 232 (1948) (separate opinion of Frankfurter, J.) *quoting* Everson v. Board of Educ., 330 U.S. 1, 59 (1947) (Rutledge, J., dissenting).
63. 354 U.S. 234 (1957).
64. *Id.* at 261 (Frankfurter, J., concurring).

government and the people's well-being . . . .[65]
Similarly, Frankfurter weighed Sweezy's interest in political autonomy
against the state's interest of self-protection to reach the conclusion that
the questioning about the Progressive Party was improper.

[T]his is a conclusion based on a judicial judgment in balancing
two contending principles—the right of a citizen to political privacy, as protected by the Fourteenth Amendment, and the right of
the State to self-protection. And striking the balance implies the
exercise of judgment. This is the inescapable judicial task in giving substantive content . . . to the Due Process Clause . . . .[66]

"For a citizen to be made to forego even a part of so basic a liberty
as his political autonomy, the subordinating interest of the State must
be compelling."[67] "In the political realm . . . thought and action are
presumptively immune from inquisition by political authority."[68]

By the very nature of his balancing process, Frankfurter would
sometimes conclude that governmental interests outweighed first
amendment values. In balancing the interests of the state to enforce
"the primary requirements of decency . . . against obscene publications"[69] with first amendment protections against prior censorship, the
Justice displayed the analytical craftsmanship that probed beneath the
surface of ringing absolutes. In *Kingsley Books, Inc. v. Brown,*[70] a New
York statute authorizing a "limited injunctive remedy" against the sale
of specific obscene materials was challenged as an impermissible prior
restraint. Frankfurter distinguished the statute from the broad prior
censorship of publications addressed in *Near v. Minnesota* and upheld
it. He carefully showed that despite the prior restraint label, the statute affected first amendment interests less directly than the state's admitted power to punish criminally for the sale of obscene matter. The
threat was less because a bookseller would know after civil judicial
process whether or not he could sell a book; under traditional criminal
enforcement, he could never have similar assurance.[71]

In the opinion for the Court, Frankfurter lectured his dissenting
colleagues:

The judicial angle of vision in testing the validity of a statute
like § 22-a is "the operation and effect of the statute in substance."
The phrase "prior restraint" is not a self-wielding sword. Nor can
it serve as a talismanic test. The duty of closer analysis and critical
judgment in applying the thought behind the phrase has thus been
authoritatively put by one who brings weighty learning to his sup-

65. *Id.* at 262.
66. *Id.* at 266-67.
67. *Id.* at 265.
68. *Id.* at 266.
69. Near v. Minnesota, 283 U.S. 697, 716 (1931).
70. 354 U.S. 436 (1957).
71. The force of Frankfurter's observations was recently acknowledged by Mr. Justice Brennan. McKinney v. Alabama, 424 U.S. 669, 679 (1976) (Brennan, J., concurring).

port of constitutionally protected liberties: "What is needed," writes Professor Paul A. Freund, "is a pragmatic assessment of its operation in the particular circumstances. The generalization that prior restraint is particularly obnoxious in civil liberties cases must yield to more particularistic analysis."[72]

Sometimes the values to be reconciled were each constitutionally protected rights. The *Times-Mirror* case,[73] for example, required the balancing of the defendant's right to impartial adjudication against freedom of the press to write about judicial proceedings. Relying heavily on history and on the need to preserve confidence in judicial proceedings, Justice Frankfurter's dissent found that California was entitled to favor the right to impartial adjudication if the facts showed a genuine threat to the defendant's right, and he would have sustained the validity of one of the charges of contempt against the Los Angeles Times,[74] while the majority hinted that contempt of court convictions for interference with judicial proceedings might never be valid.[75]

An assessment of Frankfurter's concept of the first amendment is not complete without an examination of his opinions in the Flag Salute and Communist Party Cases. On these cases, as with some of his opinions in the obscenity field, Frankfurter's detractors base their strongest criticisms. Nevertheless, these decisions, while subject to criticism, are not as far from the mainstream as some would have us think.

In 1940, he wrote an opinion for the Court upholding the right of a Pennsylvania school district to expel two children who refused to salute the flag in a daily school exercise because they were Jehovah's Witnesses and believed the salute denied the supremacy of God.[76] Two years later, the Supreme Court overruled this decision,[77] with Frankfurter dissenting.[78] Many explanations—even apologies—have been made for Frankfurter's stance in these cases. Some thought the decisions were an expression of super-patriotism by an immigrant Jew in the wake of Nazi victories at the Battle of Flanders.[79] Others thought the decisions expressed a "conception of the role of the public schools as secular, nationalizing agencies."[80]

Frankfurter's opinions cast the issue in terms of judicial restraint, legislative prerogative, and the balancing of contending values, including the legitimate interest of the state in national unity. Where the

---

72.   354 U.S. at 441-42.
73.   Times-Mirror Co. v. Superior Court was the companion case to Bridges v. California, 314 U.S. 252 (1941).
74.   314 U.S. at 279 (Frankfurter, J., dissenting).
75.   *See id.* at 268-71.
76.   Minersville School Dist. v. Gobitis, 310 U.S. 586 (1940).
77.   West Virginia State Bd. of Educ. v. Barnette, 319 U.S. 624 (1943).
78.   *Id.* at 646 (Frankfurter, J., dissenting).
79.   J. LASH, FROM THE DIARIES OF FELIX FRANKFURTER 68 (1975); H. THOMAS, FELIX FRANKFURTER 45-49 (1960).
80.   A. BICKEL, THE SUPREME COURT AND THE IDEA OF PROGRESS 33 (1970).

exercise of religious principles conflicts with the legitimate secular interests of society, there must inevitably be some giving of ground. Acknowledged judicial champions of civil liberties recognized this with the Blue Law Cases.[81] Ultimately, Frankfurter believed that the legislature is the proper forum for reconciliation of such competing values and that if the values the legislature deems worthy of preservation are reasonable, the Court should not substitute its judgment. His trust in the legislative process, not a lack of commitment to civil liberties, led him to weigh the competing values as he did.

In 1951, the Supreme Court, with no majority opinion, upheld the convictions of Eugene Dennis and ten other leaders of the Communist Party of the United States for conspiring to organize the party as a group to "teach and advocate the overthrow" of the government by force and violence.[82] Justice Frankfurter concurred.[83] For Frankfurter the *Dennis* case did not present first amendment values of a magnitude equal to those of academic freedom and the political autonomy presented in *Sweezy*. He believed, and the case law supported him,[84] that the advocacy of illegal behavior with which the defendants were charged ranked low "[o]n any scale of values which we have hitherto recognized"[85] and therefore was outweighed by governmental interests. Consequently, he again deferred to the determination of the legislature, reiterating a familiar theme:

> The wisdom of the assumptions underlying the legislation and prosecution is another matter [from their constitutionality]. In finding that Congress has acted within its power, a judge does not imply [approval].
>
> . . . .
>
> Civil liberties draw at best only limited strength from legal guaranties. Preoccupation by our people with the constitutionality, instead of with the wisdom, of legislation or of executive action is preoccupation with a false value . . . . Focusing attention on constitutionality tends to make constitutionality synonymous with wisdom. When legislation touches freedom of thought and freedom of speech, such a tendency is a formidable enemy of the free spirit.[86]

Although we may disagree with some of the results Frankfurter reached, his opinions gave lasting value to the simple phrases of the first amendment by articulating the pragmatic lessons of the history of a free and open society. He did not have to preach first amendment

---

81. *See, e.g.*, Braunfield v. Brown, 366 U.S. 599 (1961) (plurality opinion by Warren, C.J.) (Sunday closing laws may be enforced against Orthodox Jews).
82. Dennis v. United States, 341 U.S. 494 (1951).
83. *Id.* at 517 (Frankfurter, J., concurring).
84. *See, e.g.*, Abrams v. United States, 250 U.S. 616 (1919).
85. 341 U.S. at 545.
86. *Id.* at 553, 556. He first expounded this theme in 1925 in an article in the *New Republic*, which he paraphrased in the opinion in *Dennis*. *See* XLIII NEW REPUBLIC 8557 (1925).

values or absolute truths revealed only to the priests of the high Court, because the intrinsic worth of these freedoms became apparent as they were described and defined in terms of historical experience and practical effect. The judicial articulation that gave them substance speaks with enduring authority, because it did not confront unnecessarily the will of the people as expressed by their elected representatives or reach too far beyond that which the community could accept as common sense.

By contrast, Justice Black played a much easier role in his numerous dissents that eloquently defined the first amendment. In many ways, he could engage in the privileged hand-wringing of a dissenter who, because he was not speaking for the Court, could be less concerned with acceptance by the people and the Congress of the Court's pronouncements on issues of great public volatility. Of the 105 first amendment cases between 1937 and 1967, Justice Black wrote an opinion in fifty-four. In only ten cases, however, did he write the majority opinion. He dissented twenty-seven times and wrote a concurring opinion seventeen times.

Although more applauded at the time by civil libertarians, Justice Black's view of the first amendment has not had the lasting imprint of the Frankfurter approach. Justice Black's simple absolutism—"I read 'no law abridging' to mean *no law abridging*"[87] has never been accepted as constitutional doctrine. To cite but three examples, states may still, in appropriate circumstances, punish speech that is libelous,[88] obscene,[89] or subversive.[90] Thus, constitutional limitations ultimately depend on a balancing and reconciliation of competing interests. The Holmes-Frankfurter school has taught us how to approach these problems, and Frankfurter's careful efforts to articulate first amendment values assures that future Courts will have adequate guidance in resolving competing social claims. Moreover, the Frankfurter approach has preserved the investigative power of the legislature subject to the requirement of fair procedure. Although this power may have been misused in the past, it is also a vital source of protection—as the Watergate hearings demonstrate—against the abuse of power.

In contrast to the restraint he exercised in first amendment cases, Frankfurter's commitment to racial equality was absolute. According to Richard Kluger, the author of the definitive history of *Brown v. Board of Educaiton*,[91] Frankfurter "had voted on the black man's side in virtually every case involving Negro rights since he had come to the Court."[92] He paved the way toward racial equality on numerous

---

87. Smith v. California, 361 U.S. 147, 157 (1959) (Black, J., concurring).
88. Gertz v. Welch, 418 U.S. 323 (1974).
89. Miller v. California, 413 U.S. 15 (1973).
90. Brandenburg v. Ohio, 395 U.S. 444 (1969).
91. 347 U.S. 483 (1954).
92. R. KLUGER, SIMPLE JUSTICE 599 (1976).

paths.

Among his most significant contributions were the decisions that helped ensure effective participation by blacks in the political process, particularly in the South, where the techniques of exclusion were subtle and sophisticated. *Terry v. Adams*[93] and *Gomillion v. Lightfoot*[94] illustrate the Justice's strong conviction that the elimination of discrimination in the political process is essential to preserving the integrity of legislation upon which responsible democracy depends.

In *Terry v. Adams*, a private Democratic association that excluded blacks conducted a pre-primary election to determine which candidates it would support for local office. With few exceptions, those whom the Jaybird Party endorsed were victorious in the primary. In finding that the Jaybird-Democratic primary machinery had discriminated unconstitutionally on the basis of race, Frankfurter pierced through the subterfuge of a private association and found the necessary state action:

> [T]he Jaybird primary is as a practical matter the instrument of those few in this small county who are politically active—the officials of the local Democratic Party and, we may assume, the elected officials of the county. As a matter of practical politics, those charged by State law with the duty of assuring all eligible voters an opportunity to participate in the selection of candidates at the primary—the county election officials who are normally leaders in their communities—participate by voting in the Jaybird primary. They join the white voting community in proceeding with elaborate formality . . . to withdraw significance from the State-prescribed primary, to subvert the operation of what is formally the law of the State for primaries in this county.[95]

In the *Gomillion* case, Alabama had gerrymandered the boundaries of the City of Tuskegee to exclude some four hundred black voters from the local jurisdiction without excluding a single white voter, transforming the city's boundaries from a square into a twenty-eight-sided figure in the process. The district court and court of appeals dismissed a complaint alleging violations of the fourteenth and fifteenth amendments, citing *Colegrove v. Green*[96] in which Justice Frankfurter wrote the Court's opinion holding that congressional redistricting was a "political question" inappropriate for judicial review. Writing the opinion for the Court in *Gomillion*, Justice Frankfurter reversed the lower courts and declared the legislative redistricting an unconstitutional violation of the fifteenth amendment. He made short shrift of the argument that the issue before the Court was "political" in nature, asserting that "differentiation on racial lines . . . lift[s] this controversy out of the so-called 'political arena' and into the conventional sphere of con-

---

93. 345 U.S. 461 (1953).
94. 364 U.S. 339 (1960).
95. 345 U.S. at 473-74 (separate opinion of Frankfurter, J.).
96. 328 U.S. 549 (1946).

stitutional litigation."[97]

Frankfurter's restraint in supplanting the legislative process was clearly not manifested when that process disenfranchised persons on the basis of race. But this is not an inconsistency. Frankfurter regarded the command of the fifteenth amendment as clear, and his deep and abiding faith in the democratic process was clearly offended when, in some cases, that process did not represent black Americans. The contrast between his lofty opinion in *Gomillion* and his outraged dissent in *Baker v. Carr*[98] is dramatic evidence of the high value he placed on freedom from racial discrimination in the voting process.

Justice Frankfurter's role in the unanimous *Brown v. Board of Education*[99] decision may never be fully known, because of the tradition of confidentiality in the Court's internal deliberations. Joe Rauh "accords him the lion's share of [the] credit."[100] Enough has by now become public knowledge, however, to make clear that Frankfurter contributed four important dimensions to the deliberations. First, at his insistence the Court relied on empirical evidence so that the decision would be rooted firmly in facts. Second, Frankfurter recognized the difficulty of establishing an enforceable remedy, and, consequently, he urged the inclusion in the Court's opinion of the phrase "with all deliberate speed."[101] Third, Frankfurter helped to encourage the Court to join in an unanimous opinion. Finally, Frankfurter's influence helped create an opinion that used persuasion and education rather than inflamed rhetoric, because "[c]ompliance with the decisions of this Court, as the constitutional organ of the supreme Law of the Land, has often, throughout our history, depended on active support by state and local authorities."[102] "[T]he responsibility of those who exercise power in a democratic government is not to reflect inflamed public feeling," he later wrote, "but to help form its understanding, [and this] is especially true when they are confronted with a problem like a racially discriminating public school system."[103]

Having spent much of his life as a persistent but not always successful advocate for civil rights and liberties and as a teacher who instilled such values in his students, Justice Frankfurter approached his judicial responsibilities with patience and perspective. He recognized that the Supreme Court could not, in a democratic society, be ultimately responsible for advancing the most precious interests of civilization.

---

97. 364 U.S. at 346-47.
98. 369 U.S. 189, 266 (1962) (Frankfurter, J., dissenting).
99. 347 U.S. 483 (1954).
100. Rauh, Felix Frankfurter: Civil Libertarian (Francis Biddle Memorial Lecture).
101. Brown v. Board of Educ., 349 U.S. 301 (1955).
102. Cooper v. Aaron, 358 U.S. 1, 26 (1958) (Frankfurter, J., concurring).
103. *Id.*

For the Justice, government was essentially an educational process. He believed that by rooting interpretations of the Constitution in historical experience and reasoned analysis, the Supreme Court would contribute significantly to the public understanding that must precede public acceptance, which, in turn, would give sanction to the Court's commands. With public understanding, the steady gains toward a society that better reflects the canons of decency and fairness implicit in a concept of ordered liberty would be made permanent. With public understanding, the people would ensure that those advances are respected and nurtured by the legislative and executive branches. With public understanding, the protection and advancement of civil rights and liberties would not be the special, transitory prerogative of impassioned Justices, but would be knitted permanently into the fragile fabric of our society.

VERN COUNTRYMAN

JUSTICE DOUGLAS AND FREEDOM OF EXPRESSION†

Vern Countryman*

I. INTRODUCTION

Before William O. Douglas came to the Supreme Court in April 1939, the Court had not been extensively concerned with the first amendment. It had held that the fourteenth amendment incorporated the first, making its protections applicable to the states.[1] Additionally, in a series of World War I cases involving sedition laws, which forbade advocacy of ideas thought to be dangerous, Justices Brandeis and Holmes had formulated, and persuaded the Court to adopt, the "clear and present danger" test.[2] Although it was not to be the ultimate result, the original goal of the clear and present danger test may have been to give more constitutional protection to speech and press than the Court had previously indicated was warranted.[3] The other significant decision, prior to Douglas's joining the Court, was *Near v. Minnesota.*[4] In *Near*, Chief Justice Hughes, writing for the Court, held that a state could not abate a newspaper as a public nuisance, on an allegation that the paper published "malicious, scandalous and defamatory" matter about public officials, private citizens, and Jews. The abatement was held to violate the guaranty of a free press because it imposed a "previous restraint" on publication. The Court concluded that the first amendment guaranty required, among other things, "immunity from

---

† *These remarks were originally delivered at the University of Illinois College of Law, October 13, 1977, as the second 1977-78 lecture of the David C. Baum Lectures on Civil Rights and Civil Liberties.*

* *Royall Professor of Law, Harvard University. B.A. 1939, LL.B. 1942, University of Washington.*

1. In the first case it was assumed, without deciding, that the fourteenth amendment incorporated first amendment rights, but no violation of those rights was found. Gitlow v. New York, 268 U.S. 652, 666 (1925). But later state sedition prosecutions in Whitney v. California, 274 U.S. 357, 371 (1927), Fiske v. Kansas, 274 U.S. 380, 386-87 (1927), and Stromberg v. California, 283 U.S. 359, 368 (1931), were invalidated as violating the first amendment, which *Gitlow* was read to incorporate into the fourteenth amendment.

2. Schenck v. United States, 249 U.S. 47, 52 (1919); Frohwerk v. United States, 249 U.S. 204 (1919); Debs v. United States, 249 U.S. 211 (1919); Abrams v. United States, 250 U.S. 616, 624 (1919) (Holmes, J., dissenting); Schaefer v. United States, 251 U.S. 466, 482 (1920) (Brandeis, J., dissenting); Gitlow v. New York, 268 U.S. 652, 672 (1925) (Holmes, J., dissenting); Whitney v. California, 274 U.S. 357, 372 (1927) (Brandeis, J., concurring).

3. *See* Fox v. Washington, 236 U.S. 273, 277 (1915); Patterson v. Colorado, 205 U.S. 454, 462 (1907); Robertson v. Baldwin, 165 U.S. 275, 281 (1897).

4. 283 U.S. 697 (1931).

previous restraints" and that the state law on which the action was based was invalid even though the law recognized a defense for a publisher who could convince the court that what he had published was true and had been published with good motives.[5]

In contrast to earlier times, during the more than thirty-six years of Justice Douglas's service on the Court, which ended with his retirement because of ill health in November 1975, the Court was much concerned with the first amendment. And during that time Justice Douglas—whose prior professional experience consisted of two year's of private practice on Wall Street and one in Yakima, Washington, stints as a professor of corporate and bankruptcy law at Columbia and at Yale, and service as a member and later as chairman of the Securities and Exchange Commission—was the chief defender of the guaranties with which I am here concerned. Douglas found in the first amendment prohibitions against abridgement of freedom of speech, press, and religion more strength and more breadth than even his longtime ally, the redoubtable Justice Hugo L. Black, about whose views John Frank spoke in an earlier Baum lecture.[6]

In the first four freedom of expression cases that came before the Court after he had joined it,[7] Justice Douglas acquitted himself well. In each instance, he voted with the Court but did not write the opinion. The first, *Schneider v. State*,[8] invalidated, as applied, city ordinances that forbade the distribution of handbills on city streets. The ordinances had been applied to prohibit distributors from advertising a meeting to discuss the pending war in Spain and a meeting to protest the administration of state unemployment insurance, as well as to prevent a labor union picketer from distributing an appeal to pedestrians not to patronize the picketed employer. To the city's argument that the ordinances were designed to prevent littering of the streets, the Court replied that the solution was not to abridge the distributors' freedom of speech or press, but to punish those who received the circulars and then dropped them in the streets.[9] In the same case the Court also held unconstitutional another ordinance which forbade door-to-door canvassing without a written permit from the city police chief. The Court found the ordinance faulty because it gave the police chief unfettered discretion to grant or deny the permit. The ordinance had been applied to prohibit Jehovah's Witnesses from distributing that sect's literature. Protection of the public against trespassers, molesters, and

---

5. *Id.* at 701-23.
6. Frank, *Hugo L. Black: Free Speech and the Declaration of Independence*, 1977 U. ILL. L.F. 577.
7. Douglas did not participate in the decision in Hague v. Committee for Indus. Organization, 307 U.S. 496 (1939), which invalidated a city ordinance that infringed the rights of labor union representatives to distribute handbills and to hold public meetings in the city's streets and parks. The case was decided after, but argued before, he took his seat on the Court.
8. 308 U.S. 147 (1939).
9. *Id.* at 162.

fraudulent solicitors was held not to justify this police censorship of speech and press and interference with the free exercise of religion.[10] Such protection could be obtained without censorship by laws requiring door-to-door canvassers to register in advance and by prescribing penalties for fraud, molestation, and trespass.[11]

In the second of these four cases, *Cantwell v. Connecticut*,[12] the Court held that a state statute forbidding solicitation of contributions for religious causes without a license, with the licensing official to determine whether the cause was a religious one, also ran afoul of the first amendment. In *Cantwell*, Jehovah's Witnesses were convicted for going from house-to-house without licenses in a predominantly Roman Catholic neighborhood seeking contributions for their literature. In addition, the Witnesses played, for anyone who would listen, a phonograph record embodying a general attack on all organized religion with special strictures for the Roman Catholic. The licensing procedure, when applied to religious solicitation, was held to constitute an invalid prior restraint on the free exercise of religion even though the licensing official's decision was subject to later judicial review. The Court concluded that a judge's determination of what was a religious cause was as objectionable as a licensing official's.[13] In the same case the Court held that one of the defendants could not be convicted of the common law offense of inciting a breach of the peace merely because two persons who had listened to his playing of the phonograph record testified that they were incensed by it and were tempted to strike him. The Court held that such a conviction must be based on a narrowly drawn statute prohibiting specific conduct limited to that which constituted a clear and present danger to public peace and order.[14]

Thornhill v. Alabama[15] and a companion case[16] held that the first amendment forbade state interference with peaceful picketing during a labor dispute whether the pickets expressed their grievances to passersby and nonstriking fellow workers by word of mouth or by means of carried signs.[17]

---

10. *Id*. at 164-65.
11. *Schneider* went little beyond Lovell v. City of Griffin, 303 U.S. 444 (1938), which earlier had invalidated, as applied to another Jehovah's Witness, a city ordinance forbidding all distribution of literature anywhere in the city without first obtaining a permit from the city manager, who again had complete discretion to grant or deny the permit.
12. 310 U.S. 296 (1940).
13. *Id*. at 305-06.
14. *Id*. at 311.
15. 310 U.S. 88 (1940).
16. Carlson v. California, 310 U.S. 106 (1940).
17. In later cases Douglas voted with the Court when it upheld a state injunction against violence on a picket line, Hotel Employees' Local 122 v. Wisconsin Employment Relations Bd., 315 U.S. 437 (1942), and against peaceful picketing which was "more than . . . speech" and "an integral part" of union conduct designed to compel the employer to violate valid state laws. Giboney v. Empire Storage Co., 336 U.S. 490, 498, 502-03 (1949). But he has also dissented when he thought the Court was expanding or misapplying these two limited exceptions to constitutional protection. Milk Wagon Drivers Local 753 v. Meadowmoor Dairies, Inc., 312 U.S. 287, 317

Then the Court—and Justice Douglas with it—came a cropper. With only Justice Stone dissenting, the Court held, in 1940, in the *Gobitis* case[18] that Pennsylvania could expel from its public schools children of the Jehovah's Witnesses, who refused, because of their religious beliefs, to participate in flag saluting exercises. Religious freedom, Justice Frankfurter wrote for the Court, must give way to the state's attempt to promote "national unity" and secure "effective loyalty to the traditional ideals of democracy" by a compelled tribute to the flag, a "symbol of our national unity."[19] Two years later, in *Jones v. Opelika*,[20] the Court concluded that the sale of religious literature or the solicitation of contributions in connection with its distribution by Jehovah's Witnesses, while not subject to censorship, rendered the activity sufficiently commercial to justify a state license tax. This time Justices Douglas, Black, and Murphy joined Chief Justice Stone in dissent and also took the occasion to say that they had erred in the earlier flag salute case.[21]

In the following year *Opelika* was reversed on reargument,[22] and *Gobitis* was overruled by the *Barnette* case.[23] Justice Jackson, writing for the Court in the second flag salute case, said with his usual eloquence:

> If there is any fixed star in our constitutional constellation, it is that no official, high or petty, can prescribe what shall be orthodox in politics, nationalism, religion, or other matters of opinion or force citizens to confess by word or act their faith therein. If there are any circumstances which permit an exception they do not now occur to us.[24]

But the concurring opinion of Justice Black, in which Justice Douglas joined, perhaps got closer to the matter at hand:

> [W]e cannot say that a failure, because of religious scruples, to assume a particular physical position and to repeat the words of a patriotic formula creates a grave danger to the nation. . . .
>
> Words uttered under coercion are proof of loyalty to nothing but self-interest. . . .
>
> Neither our domestic tranquillity in peace nor our martial effort in war depend on compelling little children to participate in a ceremony which ends in nothing for them but a fear of spiritual condemnation.[25]

(1941); Carpenters & Joiner Local 213 v. Ritters Cafe, 315 U.S. 722, 729 (1942); Local 10, United Ass'n of Journeymen v. Graham Bros., 345 U.S. 192, 201 (1953); International Bhd. of Teamsters Local 295 v. Vogt, Inc., 354 U.S. 284, 295 (1957).
  18.   Minersville School Dist. v. Gobitis, 310 U.S. 586 (1940).
  19.   *Id.* at 596.
  20.   316 U.S. 584 (1942).
  21.   *Id.* at 623-24 (Black, J., dissenting).
  22.   Jones v. Opelika, 319 U.S. 103 (1943) (per curiam).
  23.   West Virginia State Bd. of Educ. v. Barnette, 319 U.S. 624, 642 (1943).
  24.   *Id.*
  25.   *Id.* at 644 (Black, J., concurring).

In any event, the rule of *Barnette* still lives and was recently put to good use when the Court held that the state of New Hampshire could not require a Jehovah's Witness citizen to display the state's motto, "Live Free or Die," on his automobile license plates.[26]

In a separate case,[27] Justice Douglas had written for the Court to explain why *Opelika* must be reversed and Jehovah's Witnesses must be free from license taxes even though they solicited contributions while distributing their literature:

> [T]he mere fact that the religious literature is "sold" by itinerant preachers rather than "donated" does not transform evangelism into a commercial enterprise. If it did, then the passing of the collection plate in church would make the church service a commercial project. The constitutional rights of those spreading their religious beliefs through the spoken and printed word are not to be gauged by standards governing retailers or wholesalers of books. . . . [A]n itinerant evangelist . . . does not become a mere book agent by selling the Bible or religious tracts to help defray his expenses or to sustain him. . . . It is one thing to impose a tax on the income or property of a preacher. It is quite another thing to exact a tax from him for the privilege of delivering a sermon.[28]

As the decisions I have mentioned indicate, most of the free expression cases coming to the Court in the first decade of Douglas's service involved Jehovah's Witnesses. But, in seeking first amendment protection, they did not always prevail. The Court, with Douglas joining the majority, held that the Witnesses were subject to reasonable state regulation in their use of streets for parades,[29] and, furthermore, that the state could prevent the minor children of Jehovah's Witnesses from distributing literature on the streets.[30]

II. THE CLEAR AND PRESENT DANGER TEST

Another group of cases arising during this early period returned to the "clear and present danger" test formulated by Brandeis and Holmes. These cases involved newspaper publishers, editors, and reporters, among others, who had been convicted of contempt of court for publishing comments about proceedings conducted in state courts. In each case Douglas voted with the Court to hold that, although a judge had power to punish disruptive conduct in his courtroom by contempt proceedings, such proceedings against out-of-court utterances violated the first amendment absent a showing that the utterances created a clear and present danger to fair judicial trials free from coer-

---

26. Wooley v. Maynard, 430 U.S. 705 (1977).
27. Murdock v. Pennsylvania, 319 U.S. 105 (1943).
28. *Id.* at 111-12.
29. Cox v. New Hampshire, 312 U.S. 569 (1941).
30. Prince v. Massachusetts, 321 U.S. 158 (1944).

cion or intimidation. In one case, no such danger was found in an editorial entitled "Probation for Gorillas?" which hailed the conviction of two labor union members for assaulting nonunion truck drivers and which said that the trial judge would "make a serious mistake if he grants probation."[31] In another, the requisite danger was held not to be presented by an editorial that protested the dismissal of an indictment in a rape case. The editorial failed to state that the prosecution had agreed that the indictment probably was defective or that the defendant was reindicted the next day. Additionally, the editorial inveighed against judges who sought out every technicality to protect defendants and nullify the efforts of the prosecution. Accompanying the editorial was a cartoon that "caricatured a court by a robed compliant figure as a judge on the bench tossing aside formal charges to hand a document marked 'Defendant dismissed,' to a powerful figure close at his left arm and of an intentionally drawn criminal type."[32]

The final case in this group, *Craig v. Harney*,[33] involved an action by a landlord in a county court, presided over by an elected lay judge, to evict from the plaintiff's business building a tenant who at the time was in the armed forces and whose affairs were being handled by an agent. At the close of the testimony the judge instructed the jury to return a verdict for the landlord. Instead, it returned one for the tenant. The judge repeated his instruction and the jury repeated its verdict. The same procedure was followed a third time and the jury finally returned a verdict for the landlord. The jury, however, stated that it acted under coercion from the court and against its conscience. Thereafter, the judge denied the tenant's motion for a new trial. Once again the Court found that no clear and present danger was presented by news stories and editorials which attacked the judge's decision. The pertinent articles characterized the judge's action as "arbitrary" and a "travesty on justice"; reported that others had labeled it a "gross miscarriage of justice"; said that the judge had properly brought down "the wrath of public opinion upon his head" and that people were aroused because a serviceman "seems to be getting a raw deal" but that there was "no way of knowing whether justice was done, because the first rule of justice, giving both sides an opportunity to be heard was repudiated"; and, finally, deplored the fact that the judge was a "layman" and not a "competent attorney" and that there could be no appeal to a court "familiar with proper procedure." Moreover, the articles failed to state that a rental check tendered in court on behalf of the tenant was post-dated and hence, in the opinion of the judge, not a valid tender.[34]

---

31. Bridges v. California, 314 U.S. 252, 272 (1941).
32. Pennekamp v. Florida, 328 U.S. 331, 338 (1946).
33. 331 U.S. 367 (1947).
34. *Id.* at 369-70, 374.

While conceding that the published comments were in one respect inaccurate, were also intemperate and unfair, and might cause the judge some trouble when he next stood for re-election, Douglas, in *Craig*, wrote for the Court that

[t]he law of contempt is not made for the protection of judges who may be sensitive to the winds of public opinion. Judges are supposed to be men of fortitude, able to thrive in a hardy climate . . . .[35]

. . . . Conceivably, a plan of reporting on a case could be so designed and executed as to poison the public mind, to cause a march on the courthouse, or otherwise so disturb the delicate balance in a highly wrought situation as to imperil the fair and orderly functioning of the judicial process. But it takes more imagination than we possess to find in this sketchy and one-sided report of a case any imminent or serious threat to a judge of reasonable fortitude.[36]

That was in 1947. Shortly thereafter, the clear and present danger test was put to a very different use. In 1948, in the *Dennis* case,[37] the national officers of the Communist Party of the United States were indicted under the federal Smith Act for conspiracy to advocate forcible overthrow of the government. They were convicted in 1949 after a nine month trial during which Judge Harold Medina had instructed the jury on his interpretation of the clear and present danger test. Judge Medina told the jury that, to convict, it must find that the defendants had conspired to advocate forcible overthrow with intent to cause such forcible overthrow "as speedily as circumstances would permit."[38] (Did anyone ever advocate action on anything any sooner than that?) The court of appeals upheld that conviction and, to demonstrate its understanding of the first amendment's limitations, Judge Learned Hand, for the court, purported to give a new precision to the clear and present danger test. It meant, he said, that the courts must ask "whether the gravity of the 'evil,' discounted by its improbability, justifies such invasion of free speech as is necessary to avoid the danger."[39]

In 1951, the Supreme Court, in *Dennis*, accepted Judge Hand's arithmetical formulation and his court's application of it and affirmed the appellate decision.[40] Justice Douglas dissented on grounds with which, I believe, many would now agree:

Communism in the world scene is no bogeyman; but Communism as a political faction or party in this country plainly is. Communism has been so thoroughly exposed in this country that it has been crippled as a political force. Free speech has destroyed

---

35. *Id.* at 376.
36. *Id.* at 375.
37. Dennis v. United States, 341 U.S. 494 (1951).
38. *Id.* at 512.
39. United States v. Dennis, 183 F.2d 201, 212 (2d Cir. 1950).
40. 341 U.S. 494 (1951).

it as an effective political party. . . . In days of trouble and confusion, when bread lines were long, when the unemployed walked the streets, when people were starving, the advocates of a short-cut by revolution might have a chance to gain adherents. But today there are no such conditions. The country is not in despair; the people know Soviet Communism; the doctrine of Soviet revolution is exposed in all of its ugliness and the American people want none of it.

How it can be said that there is a clear and present danger that this advocacy will succeed is, therefore, a mystery. . . . [I]n America [the defendants] are miserable merchants of unwanted ideas; their wares remain unsold. The fact that their ideas are abhorrent does not make them powerful. . . . To believe that [the defendants] and their following are placed in such critical positions as to endanger the Nation is to believe the incredible. . . . Only those held by fear and panic could think otherwise.[41]

Douglas persisted in this view in a subsequent Smith Act case in which the Court reversed a conviction because of the trial court's failure to give proper instructions to the jury on the necessity for proof that defendants had used inciting language.[42] And when, under another provision of the Smith Act, the Court in one case affirmed a conviction for knowing membership in the Communist party as an organization advocating forcible overthrow[43] and in another reversed for insufficiency of evidence,[44] Douglas dissented in the first case and concurred in the second on the ground that both convictions violated the first amendment. As he put it, dissenting in the case affirming the conviction:

We legalize today guilt by association, sending a man to prison when he committed no unlawful act. Today's break with tradition is a serious one. It borrows from the totalitarian philosophy. . . . The case is not saved by showing that [the defendant] was an active member. None of the activity constitutes a crime. . . . Not one single illegal act is charged to [the defendant]. That is why the essence of the crime covered by the indictment is merely belief—belief in the proletarian revolution, belief in the Communist creed. . . .

The creed truer to our faith was stated by the Bar Committee headed by Charles E. Hughes which in 1920 protested the refusal of the New York Assembly to seat five members of the Socialist Party: " . . . it is of the essence of the institutions of liberty that it be recognized that guilt is personal and cannot be attributed to the holding of opinion or to mere intent in the absence of overt acts . . . ."[45]

---

41. *Id.* at 588-89 (Douglas, J., dissenting).
42. Yates v. United States, 354 U.S. 298 (1957).
43. Scales v. United States, 367 U.S. 203 (1961).
44. Noto v. United States, 367 U.S. 290 (1961).
45. Scales v. United States, 367 U.S. 203, 263-68 (1961) (Douglas, J., dissenting).

A decade later the Court invalidated the conviction of a member of the Ku Klux Klan based on speech which it found did not present a clear and present danger.[46] Justice Douglas filed a concurring opinion, in which Justice Black joined, rejecting that test:

> Though I doubt if the "clear and present danger" test is congenial to the First Amendment in time of a declared war,[47] I am certain it is not reconcilable with the First Amendment in days of peace. . . .
>
> When one reads the opinions closely and sees when and how the . . . test has been applied, great misgivings are aroused. First, the threats were often loud but always puny and made serious only by judges so wedded to the *status quo* that critical analysis made them nervous. Second, the test was so twisted and perverted in *Dennis* as to make the trial of . . . teachers of Marxism an all-out political trial which was part and parcel of the Cold War that has eroded substantial parts of the First Amendment. . . .
>
> [Apart from cases] where speech is brigaded with action . . . and a prosecution can be launched for the overt acts caused . . . , speech is, I think, immune from prosecution.[48]

III. UNPROTECTED SPEECH

A. *Fighting Words*

Near the end of his second year on the Court, Douglas joined in a unanimous opinion holding that a particularly rambunctious Jehovah's Witness could be convicted for calling a police officer whom he encountered on a public street a "damned racketeer" and a "damned Fascist." Such "fighting words," words which "by their very utterance inflict injury or tend to incite an immediate breach of the peace," were held to be "of such slight social value as a step to truth that any benefit that may be derived from them is clearly outweighed by the social interest in order and morality."[49] Thus, the Court entered on the slippery slope of balancing the "social value" of speech against the "social interest in order and morality."

Justice Douglas has never expressly repudiated the "fighting words" doctrine, but he has otherwise very well resisted the slippery slope. Thus, he wrote for the Court in the *Terminiello* case[50] to invalidate the disorderly conduct conviction of one who had made an anti-Semitic speech. The defendant's words had provoked the throwing of rocks, bricks, bottles, and stinkbombs through the windows of the audi-

---

46. Brandenburg v. Ohio, 395 U.S. 444 (1969).
47. The reference to a "declared war" is to a long series of cases in which, over Douglas dissents, the Court refused to consider cases challenging the legality of our undeclared war in Vietnam. *See* V. COUNTRYMAN, THE JUDICIAL RECORD OF JUSTICE WILLIAM O. DOUGLAS 15 (1974).
48. 395 U.S. at 454, 456 (Douglas, J., concurring).
49. Chaplinsky v. New Hampshire, 315 U.S. 568, 572 (1942).
50. Terminiello v. Chicago, 337 U.S. 1 (1949).

torium in which he spoke, and during his speech he characterized those outside the auditorium as "slimy scum," "snakes," and "bedbugs." The decision did not reach the question whether those were "fighting words" since the conviction was under a city ordinance making it an offense to "invite dispute or to bring about a condition of unrest."[51] Douglas dissented when the Court later found a clear and present danger of riot in sustaining the disorderly conduct conviction of a speaker at an open-air meeting who characterized two city mayors and the president of the United States as "bums" and the American Legion as "a Nazi Gestapo." The speaker's words had precipitated some heckling from the crowd and a threat by one listener that he would remove the speaker from the platform if the police did not.[52] Douglas disagreed with the majority, finding neither "fighting words" nor incitement to riot.[53] "When a speaker mounts a platform," he said, "it is not unusual to find him resorting to exaggeration, to vilification of ideas and men, to the making of false charges. But those extravagances . . . do not justify penalizing the speaker by depriving him of the platform or by punishing him for his conduct."[54] He concluded that, instead of arresting the speaker, the police should have protected him from the crowd.

In a later case, Douglas dissented again when the Court upheld a state "group libel" law which provided criminal penalties for anyone who falsely attributed "depravity, criminality, unchastity, or lack of virtue to a class of citizens of any race, color, creed or religion." The majority found the statute valid as applied to a white segregationist whose circulars very clearly defamed blacks within the meaning of the statutory proscription.[55] The majority found that the defendant's utterances, like "fighting words," were "no essential part of any exposition of ideas and . . . of such slight social value as a step to truth that any benefit that may be derived from them is clearly outweighed by the social interest in order and morality."[56] Douglas protested:

> [R]ecently the Court in this and in other cases has engrafted the right of regulation onto the First Amendment by placing in the hands of the legislative branch the right to regulate "within reasonable limits" the right of free speech. . . .
>
>   . . . .
>
>   . . . Today a white man stands convicted for protesting in unseemly language against our decisions invalidating restrictive covenants. Tomorrow a Negro will be brought before a court for denouncing lynch law in heated terms. Farm laborers in the West

---

51. *Id.* at 6.
52. Feiner v. New York, 340 U.S. 315, 317 (1951).
53. *Id.* at 330 (Douglas, J., dissenting).
54. *Id.* at 331 (Douglas, J., dissenting).
55. Beauharnais v. Illinois, 343 U.S. 250 (1952).
56. *Id.* at 257.

who compete with field hands drifting up from Mexico; whites who feel the pressure of Orientals; a minority which finds employment going to members of the dominant religious group—all of these are caught in the mesh of today's decision. . . . Intemperate speech is a distinctive characteristic of man. Hotheads blow off and release destructive energy in the process. They shout and rave, exaggerating weaknesses, magnifying error, viewing with alarm. So it has been from the beginning; and so it will be throughout time. The Framers of the Constitution knew human nature as well as we do. They too had lived in dangerous days; they too knew the suffocating influence of orthodox and standardized thought. They weighed the compulsions for restrained speech and thought against the abuses of liberty. They chose liberty. That should be our choice today no matter how distasteful to us the pamphlet of [the defendant] may be.[57]

Only a few years ago, the Court upheld the disorderly conduct conviction of one who stopped to remonstrate with a policeman who was giving his friend a traffic ticket. The Court concluded that the speaker "was not engaged in activity protected by the First Amendment" but instead intended to cause public inconvenience and annoyance.[58] Douglas, in dissent, defended eloquently the speaker's right to confront the police authority boldly.

> Since when have we Americans been expected to bow submissively to authority and speak with awe and reverence to those who represent us? The constitutional theory is that we the people are the sovereigns, the state and federal officials only our agents. We who have the final word can speak softly or angrily. We can seek to challenge and annoy . . . . [A]t the constitutional level speech need not be a sedative; it can be disruptive.[59]

B. Commercial Speech

In another case decided near the end of his second year on the Court, Douglas concurred in a unanimous decision holding that the state could forbid the circulation of handbills on public streets by one who had acquired a former United States submarine and was using his handbills to advertise the boat and to solicit visitors for an admission fee.[60] The Court's opinion, by Justice Roberts, was cryptic; it stated the holding but did not explain it. "[T]he Constitution imposes no . . . restraint on government as respects purely commercial advertising."[61]

Seventeen years later, Douglas observed of that decision that it was "casual, almost offhand" and that "it has not survived reflec-

---

57. *Id.* at 285-87 (Douglas, J., dissenting).
58. Colten v. Kentucky, 407 U.S. 104, 109 (1972).
59. *Id.* at 122 (Douglas, J., dissenting).
60. Valentine v. Chrestensen, 316 U.S. 52 (1942).
61. *Id.* at 54.

tion."[62]   Later he again reaffirmed that his views on commercial speech had changed.[63]   Finally, very near the end of his service, he joined the Court when it changed its position on commercial speech. In *Bigelow v. Virginia*,[64] the Court held that the state of Virginia could not punish an editor for publishing a commercial advertisement for paid abortion services in New York.   Although the advertisement might sell some services legal in New York which would be illegal if performed in Virginia and although the defendant's motive in publishing it may have simply been financial gain, the Court found that the advertisement did communicate information of clear public interest. Indeed, after the Court's decisions that there was a constitutional right to abortion,[65] dissemination of such information took on an additional constitutional interest.   In *Bigelow*, the Court held that although there might be room for some legitimate regulation by the state, no state could any longer proceed on the assumption that "advertising, as such, was entitled to no First Amendment protection."[66]

Since Douglas's retirement, the Court has applied the doctrine of *Bigelow* to invalidate a state statute forbidding licensed pharmacists to advertise their prices for prescription drugs,[67] a state court rule which unduly restricted advertising by lawyers,[68] and the efforts of a town council to retard a flight of white homeowners from the community by forbidding "For Sale" signs on residential property.[69]   I hasten to add, however, that the limits of permissible regulation on commercial speech remain intensely undefined.[70]

C. *Obscenity*

Douglas has consistently refused to join the Court in yet another area where it has undertaken to balance the "social value" of speech against the "social interest" in morality.   In 1954 the Court invalidated a New York statute, which required a license to exhibit films and authorized the licensing authority to deny licenses for "immoral" films, because the statute was too vague and left too much discretion with the licensor.[71]   Douglas concurred,[72] but on the ground that even a more

62.   Cammarano v. United States, 358 U.S. 498, 514 (1959) (Douglas, J., concurring).
63.   Pittsburgh Press Co. v. Pittsburgh Comm'n on Human Relations, 413 U.S. 376 (1973) (Douglas, J., dissenting).
64.   421 U.S. 809 (1975).
65.   Roe v. Wade, 410 U.S. 113 (1973); Doe v. Bolton, 410 U.S. 179 (1973).
66.   421 U.S. at 825.
67.   Virginia State Bd. of Pharmacy v. Virginia Citizens Consumer Council, 425 U.S. 748 (1976).
68.   Bates v. State Bar, 433 U.S. 350 (1977).
69.   Linmark Assocs., Inc. v. Township of Willingboro, 431 U.S. 85 (1977).
70.   For a discussion of the constitutional issues involved in commercial speech cases see J. NOWAK, R. ROTUNDA & J. YOUNG, HANDBOOK ON CONSTITUTIONAL LAW 767-80 (1977); Rotunda, *The Commercial Speech Doctrine in the Supreme Court*, 1976 U. ILL. L.F. 1080.
71.   Superior Films, Inc. v. Department of Educ., 346 U.S. 587 (1954) (per curiam).
72.   *Id.* at 588 (Douglas, J., concurring).

precisely drawn licensing standard would impose an unacceptable censorship over motion pictures in the form of a prior restraint such as was condemned in *Near v. Minnesota*:[73]

> The First and the Fourteenth Amendments say that Congress and the states shall make "no law" which abridges freedom of speech or of the press. In order to sanction a system of censorship I would have to say that "no law" . . . is qualified to mean "some" laws. I cannot take that step.[74]

A few years later, in the *Roth* case,[75] the Court upheld convictions for mailing and selling "obscene" publications. The Court found that obscenity, which it then defined as that "which deals with sex in a manner appealing to prurient interest" and which is "utterly without redeeming social importance," was "not within the area of constitutionally protected speech or press."[76] Douglas again dissented in an opinion in which Justice Black concurred:

> I can understand (and at times even sympathize) [with] programs of civic groups and church groups to protect and defend the existing moral standards of the community. I can understand the motives of the Anthony Comstocks who would impose Victorian standards on the community. When speech alone is involved, I do not think that the government, consistently with the First Amendment, can become the sponsor of any of these movements. . . . Government should be concerned with antisocial conduct, not with utterances. . . . [I]f the First Amendment guarantee of freedom of speech and press is to mean anything in this field, it must allow protests even against the moral code that the standard of the day sets for the community. . . . [L]iterature should not be suppressed merely because it offends the moral code of the censor.[77]

Thereafter, Justices Black and Douglas adhered to their position that no censorship of obscenity was permissible, and thus were spared the burden of viewing the exhibits to determine whether they had been properly or improperly classified as obscene.[78] But, in the sixteen years following *Roth*, no majority of the Court could agree on what standard should be applied. As Justice Brennan once analyzed the confusion,[79] Chief Justice Warren and Justices Brennan and Fortas espoused a three level test: Material was obscene if (1) "the dominant theme of the material taken as a whole appeals to a prurient interest in

---

73. 283 U.S. 697, 713 (1931).
74. 346 U.S. at 589.
75. Roth v. United States, 354 U.S. 476 (1957).
76. *Id.* at 485-87.
77. *Id.* at 512-13 (Douglas, J., dissenting).
78. Justice Douglas announced in Paris Adult Theatre I v. Slaton, 413 U.S. 49, 71 (1973) (dissenting opinion), that "I never read or see the materials coming to the Court under charges of 'obscenity,' because I have thought that the First Amendment made it unconstitutional for me to act as a censor." Justice Black followed the same practice. Frank, *supra* note 6, at 603-04.
79. Paris Adult Theatre I v. Slaton, 418 U.S. 49, 81 (Brennan, J., dissenting).

sex;" (2) it is "patently offensive because it affronts contemporary community standards relating to the description or representation of sexual matters;" and (3) it is "utterly without redeeming social value."[80] Justices Clark and Harlan thought that the federal government could control only "hard core" pornography but that the states had more latitude and could ban any material "which, taken as a whole, has been reasonably found in state judicial proceedings to treat with sex in a fundamentally offensive manner, under rationally established criteria for judging such material."[81] Justice White regarded as obscene material whose "predominant theme appeals to the prurient interest in a manner exceeding customary limits of candor."[82] Justice Stewart regarded "hardcore pornography" as the limit of both federal and state power—and added that, though unable to define "hardcore" pornography, he knew it when he saw it.[83]

While seven members of the Court scrambled to match up enough standards to dispose of the obscenity cases which came before them, Douglas continued to protest that the Court was sitting as "the Nation's board of censors." He also added that he did not know "of any group in the country less qualified first, to know what obscenity is when they see it, and second, to have any considered judgment as to what the deleterious or beneficial impact may be on minds either young or old."[84] In one of his dissenting opinions in this area he elaborated on why he considered the matter so important.[85]

If "obscenity" can be carved out of the First Amendment, what other like exceptions can be created? Is "sacrilege" also beyond the pale? Are utterances or publications made with "malice" unprotected? How about "seditious" speech or articles? False, scandalous and malicious writings or utterances against the Congress or the President "with intent to defame" or to bring them "into contempt or disrepute" or to "excite" against them "the hatred of the good people" or "to stir up sedition," or to "excite" people to "resist, oppose or defeat" any law were once made a crime [under the Alien and Sedition Acts of 1798]. . . .

We forget today that under our Constitutional system neither Congress nor the States have any power to pass on the value, the propriety, the Americanism, the soundness of any idea or expression. It is that insulation from party or majoritarian control provided by the First Amendment—not our gross national product or mass production or pesticides or space ships or nuclear arsenal—that distinguishes our society from the other planetary re-

---

80. *Id.* at 81.
81. *Id.* at 80.
82. *Id.* at 82.
83. Jacobellis v. Ohio, 378 U.S. 184, 197 (1964) (Stewart, J., dissenting).
84. Ginsberg v. New York, 390 U.S. 629, 656 (1968) (Douglas, J., dissenting).
85. Byrne v. Karalexis, 396 U.S. 976 (1969) (Douglas, J., dissenting).

gimes.[86]

By 1973, Chief Justice Warren and Justices Black, Clark, Fortas, and Harlan were gone and, in the newly constituted Court, a majority of five (Chief Justice Burger and Justices White, Blackmun, Powell and Rehnquist) were able to formulate a standard on which they could agree. As they stated it in *Miller v. California*,[87] material was obscene if, first, "the average person, applying contemporary community standards, would find that the work, taken as a whole, appeals to the prurient interest," second, "the work, depicts or describes, in a patently offensive way, sexual conduct specifically defined by the applicable . . . law," and third, "the work, taken as a whole, lacks serious literary, artistic, political, or scientific value."[88] Additionally, because the majority believed that the first amendment should not be read "as requiring that the people of Maine or Mississippi accept public depiction of conduct found tolerable in Las Vegas or New York City,"[89] they emphasized that what appeals to the "prurient interest" and what is "patently offensive" were to be determined by "statewide standards" and not by "national standards."[90]

Only one year later, the same majority revised *Miller* somewhat to hold that in a federal case standards of the federal district, and not "statewide" standards, could be employed.[91] That same year, the Court held that state courts need not apply "statewide" standards but could instruct the jury to apply "community" standards without specifying any particular community.[92] Thus the way was opened for prosecutors, state and federal, to seek out the most puritanical locality in which a play or a movie is exhibited or a book or magazine is offered for sale and then to try, by the local standard, those who write, produce, or appear in the play or movie, those who distribute or exhibit the movie, or those who write, distribute, or sell the book or magazine. And there is some evidence that prosecutors are doing just that. The publisher of an allegedly obscene magazine is federally charged in Wichita, Kansas, with sending it through the mails. A New York actor has been convicted on federal charges in Memphis, Tennessee, for appearing in an allegedly obscene movie made in Florida.[93] And to compound matters, the United States Court of Appeals for the Second Circuit has recently held that, when the United States seizes allegedly obscene imported material, the test for obscenity is that of the point of

86. *Id.* at 981-82.
87. 413 U.S. 15 (1973).
88. *Id.* at 24.
89. *Id.* at 32.
90. *Id.* at 30, 37.
91. Hamling v. United States, 418 U.S. 87, 105-06 (1974).
92. Jenkins v. Georgia, 418 U.S. 153, 157 (1974).
93. *See* Dershowitz, *Screwing Around with the First Amendment*, PENTHOUSE, January 1977, at 106; Dershowitz, *Grim Repressive Power in "Local Standards" Rule*, Boston Globe, Apr. 15, 1977, at 20, col. 4.

seizure and not that of the residence of the would-be recipient.[94] Furthermore, the practice may not be confined to obscenity cases. For example, a criminal charge of "blasphemy" is now pending in Massachusetts against the New York publisher of *Lampoon* magazine.

D.   Libel and Slander

One form of speech long regarded as unprotected by the first amendment was that regulated by the traditional law of libel and slander—falsely defamatory speech. But in *New York Times Co. v. Sullivan*,[95] the Court held otherwise. In *New York Times*, an Alabama police commissioner had obtained a state court judgment for libel against the *Times* and the blacks and clergyman who had published an advertisement in the *Times* because the advertisement made falsely defamatory statements. The Supreme Court concluded, however, that the state could not award damages to a public official for libel unless the defamatory statement was made with "actual malice—that is, with knowledge that it was false or with reckless disregard of whether it was false or not."[96] Such a reading was necessary, the Court thought, because otherwise "would-be critics of official conduct may be deterred from voicing their criticism, even though it is believed to be true and even though it is in fact true, because of doubt whether it can be proved in court or fear and expense of having to do so."[97] The Court observed that the result of such fear would be to "dampen the vigor and limit the variety of public debate."[98] Justice Douglas joined in Justice Black's concurring opinion on the ground that the very concerns that led the Court to find a limited immunity for critics of public officials should have led to a finding of complete immunity.[99] The Court's rule, they thought, would still leave the would-be critics of public officials subject to the dampening effect of doubts whether they could prove that they acted without actual malice or of fear of the expense of having to do so. They persisted in that view as subsequent decisions applied the *Sullivan* rule not only to minor public officials including court clerks[100] and county recreation supervisors[101] but also to "public figures" such as candidates for public office,[102] the coach of the University of Geor-

---

94.   United States v. Various Articles of Obscene Merchandise, 562 F.2d 185, 190 (2d Cir. 1977).

95.   376 U.S. 254 (1964).

96.   *Id*. at 279-80.

97.   *Id*. at 279.

98.   *Id*.

99.   *Id*. at 293 (Black, J., concurring).

100.   Beckley Newspaper Corp. v. Hanks, 389 U.S. 81, 85 (1967) (Douglas, J., joining in the opinion of Black, J., concurring).

101.   Rosenblatt v. Baer, 383 U.S. 75, 88 (1966) (Douglas, J., concurring).

102.   Monitor Patriot Co. v. Roy, 401 U.S. 265, 277 (1971) (Douglas, J., joining in the opinion of Black, J., concurring); *see also* Patrick v. Field Research Co., 414 U.S. 922 (1973) (Douglas, J., dissenting from a denial of certiorari).

gia football team,[103] and a retired general who had injected himself into public affairs.[104] Finally, when the Court declined to give even limited immunity to a publisher who had defamed a private attorney, Douglas dissented, stating categorically that the first amendment should be read to forbid all sanctions for defamation.[105]

E. Privacy

A second area of state tort law that has been found to implicate protected first amendment interests is that of actions for breach of privacy. Traditionally, the laws of many states have given protection against nondefamatory speech, sometimes even if factually accurate, which invades the privacy of the subject. Such a law, applicable only to false speech, was involved in *Time, Inc. v. Hill*,[106] and was invoked by a family which found itself involuntarily injected into the news when it was held hostage by a number of escaped convicts. When a play was later produced, based on the family's experience but embellished to make it even more horrible, and when *Life* magazine published a review of the play, including its embellishments, the family sued the publisher of *Life* and obtained a judgment for damages for invasion of privacy. The Supreme Court overturned the judgment. The Court held that the Hill family had become "newsworthy," albeit unwillingly, that their experience was a matter of "public interest," and that, as a result, the rule of *New York Times Co. v. Sullivan* applied to prevent recovery from the publishers of *Life* unless it was shown that they acted with knowledge of the falsity which they had published or with reckless disregard for the truth.[107] Once again Justice Douglas concurred, but contended that the publisher's immunity should be complete.[108]

I confess to great misgivings about both the Court's and Justice Douglas's position in this case, particularly in view of the development of a constitutional right of privacy to which Douglas so greatly contributed. Douglas first indorsed the concept of a constitutional privacy interest in a dissenting opinion in the *Pollak* case[109] in 1952 when a majority of the Court denied the existence of a constitutional right of privacy on privately owned streetcars and buses. Consequently, the majority found the failure of the Public Utilities Commission of the District of Columbia to prevent the owner of the cars and buses from

---

103. Curtis Publishing Co. v. Butts, 388 U.S. 130, 170 (1967) (Douglas, J., joining the opinion of Black, J., concurring in part and dissenting in part).
104. Associated Press v. Walker, 388 U.S. 130, 170 (1967) (Douglas, J., joining the opinion of Black, J., concurring in part and dissenting in part).
105. Gertz v. Robert Welch, Inc., 418 U.S. 323, 360 (1974) (Douglas, J., dissenting).
106. 385 U.S. 374 (1966).
107. *Id.* at 387-88.
108. *Id.* at 401-02 (Douglas, J., concurring).
109. Public Utils. Comm'n v. Pollak, 343 U.S. 451, 467 (1952) (Douglas, J., dissenting).

subjecting his captive audience passengers to radio broadcasts did not deprive the riders of any constitutional right. Later, in the *Griswold* case,[110] Douglas wrote for the Court that a state law forbidding the dissemination of birth control information to married persons violated a constitutional right of privacy. Additionally, his position in the *Pollak* case was, it seems to me, largely vindicated by the Supreme Court's later decision in *Lehman v. City of Shaker Heights.*[111] In *Lehman*, the Court held that a city which operates a public rapid transit system and sells advertising space in its cars cannot be required to accept paid political advertising because the streetcar audience was a captive audience. Here, as in the cases in which the exercise of the constitutional rights of free speech and press come in conflict with the constitutional right to a fair trial,[112] the Court must accommodate two constitutional rights. Although the dimensions of the constitutional right of privacy have not yet been extended to the sort of privacy the Hill family sought to preserve, I am not satisfied with the accommodations made by the Court and by Justice Douglas in *Time, Inc. v. Hill*. My misgivings increased as I saw the rule of that case applied recently in a case very similar to *Time, Inc. v. Hill*, involving the invasion of the privacy of the family of the victim of a fatal accident[113] and extended in another case to shield a radio broadcasting company that obtained from public records and broadcast on its news program the name of a seventeen-year-old rape victim who did not survive the attack.[114] And I became certain that something was wrong when I read only last June, in a case for which Justice Douglas bears no responsibility, that a professional "human cannonball" can be given more protection by the state against the televising of his "entire act" than the state was allowed to give to the privacy of those involved in the earlier cases.[115]

IV. The Unprotected Rostrum

Many arguments have been made, some successfully, that some rostrums are not protected by the first amendment. Douglas voted with the Court to upset breach of the peace convictions based on peaceful demonstrations in the public areas before courthouses,[116] state capitols,[117] and city halls,[118] and a peaceful sit-in in a segregated county library to protest racial discrimination.[119] But when Justice Black

---

110. Griswold v. Connecticut, 381 U.S. 479 (1965).
111. 418 U.S. 298 (1974).
112. *See* text accompanying notes 30-33 *supra*.
113. Cantrell v. Forest City Publishing Co., 419 U.S. 245 (1974).
114. Cox Broadcasting Corp. v. Cohn, 420 U.S. 469 (1975).
115. Zacchini v. Scripps-Howard Broadcasting Co., 433 U.S. 562 (1977).
116. Cox v. Louisiana, 379 U.S. 536 (1965); Cox v. Louisiana, 379 U.S. 559 (1965). *See also* Cameron v. Johnson, 390 U.S. 611, 622 (1968) (Douglas, J., joining the dissent of Fortas, J.).
117. Edwards v. South Carolina, 372 U.S. 229 (1963).
118. Henry v. City of Rock Hill, 376 U.S. 776 (1964) (per curiam).
119. Brown v. Louisiana, 383 U.S. 131 (1966).

wrote for the Court to sustain a trespass conviction of those who protested before a county jail against racial segregation and the jailing of earlier demonstrators on the ground that jails are "built for security purposes" and not "open to the public," Douglas dissented:

> The jailhouse, like an executive mansion, a legislative chamber, a courthouse, or the statehouse itself . . . is one of the seats of government, whether it be the Tower of London, the Bastille, or a small county jail. And when it houses political prisoners or those who many think are unjustly held, it is an obvious center for protest . . . . Conventional methods of petitioning [the government] may be, and often have been, shut off to large groups of our citizens. Legislators may turn deaf ears; formal complaints may be routed endlessly through a bureaucratic maze; courts may let the wheels of justice grind very slowly. Those who do not control television and radio, those who cannot afford to advertise in newspapers or circulate elaborate pamphlets may have only a more limited type of access to public officials. Their methods should not be condemned as tactics of obstruction and harassment as long as the assembly and petition are peaceable, as they were here.[120]

Douglas agreed when the Court later reversed a disorderly conduct conviction of persons who peacefully demonstrated against segregation in public schools in Chicago by marching from city hall to the mayor's residence.[121] But he joined in Justice Black's concurring opinion, which suggested the basis for some limits.[122] Picketing was more than "speech," they noted, and narrowly drawn laws could be drafted to protect the mayor's right of privacy in his home from the conduct of picketers.[123]

Similarly, Douglas wrote for the Court to invalidate an ordinance which forbade the use of sound trucks without a license and which gave the licensing authority complete discretion to grant or deny a license.[124] He observed that "[a]ny abuses which loud-speakers create can be controlled by narrowly drawn statutes."[125] But when the Court later sustained the conviction of a sound truck user under an ordinance forbidding the use on the streets of any such truck "which emits . . . loud and raucous noises," Douglas dissented.[126] He noted that neither the charge against the defendant nor the instructions to the jury said anything about "loud and raucous noises." The effect of these failures, therefore, was to forbid all use of sound trucks—an even more flagrant violation of the first amendment than the licensing ordinance struck

---

120. Adderly v. Florida, 385 U.S. 39, 49-51 (1966) (Douglas, J., dissenting).
121. Gregory v. City of Chicago, 394 U.S. 111 (1969).
122. *Id.* at 113 (Black, J., concurring).
123. *Id.* at 124.
124. Saia v. New York, 334 U.S. 558 (1948).
125. *Id.* at 562.
126. Kovacs v. Cooper, 336 U.S. 77, 98 (1949) (Douglas, J., joining the dissent of Black, J.).

down in the previous case.[127]

In addition to such public areas as city streets, on some occasions even privately owned forums have been held subject to first amendment protection. For example, early in Douglas's tenure on the Court he joined in the decision in *Marsh v. Alabama*.[128] In *Marsh*, the Court held that the state could not impose criminal penalties on a Jehovah's Witness for distributing his literature on the streets in the business district of an entirely company-owned town in violation of a company rule against such distribution. The Court rejected an analogy to the right of a homeowner to regulate the conduct of his guests and announced that "[t]he more an owner, for his advantage, opens up his property for use by the public in general, the more do his rights become circumscribed by the . . . rights of those who use it."[129] The Court concluded that the state could not permit "a corporation to govern a community of citizens so as to restrict their fundamental liberties" by supplying a penal sanction for the company rule.[130]

Some two decades later, in a decision in which Douglas concurred, the Court applied the *Marsh* doctrine in *Amalgamated Food Employees Union v. Logan Valley Plaza, Inc.*[131] to hold that the first amendment protected peaceful picketing on a privately owned shopping center's parking lot which was adjacent to one of the stores in the center that the union picketers were trying to organize. Shortly thereafter, however, in *Lloyd Corp. v. Tanner*,[132] the Court declined to extend this ruling to protect persons who were distributing handbills to protest the draft and the war in Vietnam on the covered mall walkways of another shopping center. The Court distinguished the labor picketing case. In *Logan Valley* the picketers' message was "related to the shopping center's operations;" in *Lloyd*, it was not.[133] In *Logan Valley*, there was no other effective way to reach the store patrons for whom the picketers' message was intended; in *Lloyd* the handbillers could have as effectively distributed their handbills on the public streets.[134] Justice Douglas joined dissenters, rejecting both of these distinctions and contending that the rule of *Marsh v. Alabama* should apply.[135]

---

127. *Id.* at 101.
128. 326 U.S. 501 (1946).
129. *Id.* at 506.
130. *Id.* at 509.
131. 391 U.S. 308 (1968).
132. 407 U.S. 551 (1972).
133. *Id.* at 563.
134. *Id.* at 566.
135. *Id.* at 571 (Douglas, J., joining the dissent of Marshall, J.). After Douglas left the Court, it overruled *Logan Valley* entirely, Hudgens v. NLRB, 424 U.S. 507 (1976), and held that the United States could ban political speeches and leafletting on streets of a federal military reservation that were as open to the public as the streets of the company town in the *Marsh* case. *See* Greer v. Spock, 424 U.S. 828 (1976).

V. UNPROTECTED SPEAKERS

Certain classes of persons have long been subjected to special restrictions on their speech. One such class consists of public employees. The Hatch Act seeks to immunize federal employees in the executive branch from political pressure by forbidding them to take "an active part in political management or political campaigns" even during their off-duty hours.[136] In 1947 the Court upheld the application of this Act to a worker in the federal mint, who was threatened with discharge for being an officer of a political party, as a "reasonable" restriction on first amendment rights.[137] Douglas dissented. He thought that, at least as to industrial workers as distinguished from administrative personnel, the statute went too far by its "partial political sterilization."[138] This he thought true particularly since a law could be drawn which would focus on the real source of the evil—those who would use coercion on government employees for political purposes.

When the problem returned to the Court a few years ago, it reaffirmed its holding that Congress could prevent government employees from holding party office.[139] The Court also held that in other respects the Act was not unconsitutionally vague in its prohibitions because the Civil Service Commission had given meaning to it by developing on a case-by-case basis, and then embodying in its rules, thirteen categories of activities which its rules say the prohibitions "include but are not limited to."[140] Douglas again dissented, refusing to engage in this tortured endeavor, and contended that the entire statutory provision should be held unconstitutional.[141] He dissented again when the Court, in a companion case, upheld a very similar state statute applicable to state employees.[142]

A second class, subjected to even more onerous restrictions on freedom of speech, consists of those in the military service. *Parker v. Levy*[143] sustained the court martial conviction of an Army officer under the Uniform Code of Military Justice for "conduct unbecoming an officer and a gentleman" and conduct "to the prejudice of good order and discipline in the armed forces." The officer's offenses consisted of telling enlisted personnal that the United States involvement in the Vietnam war was wrong, that he would refuse to go to Vietnam if ordered to do so, and that blacks in particular should refuse to go because they were given the most hazardous duty and suffered the most

---

136. 5 U.S.C. § 7324(a) (1976).
137. United Public Workers v. Mitchell, 330 U.S. 75 (1947).
138. *Id.* at 126 (Douglas, J., dissenting).
139. Civil Serv. Comm'n v. National Ass'n of Letter Carriers, 413 U.S. 548 (1973).
140. *See* 5 C.F.R. § 733.122(b) (1977).
141. 413 U.S. at 600 (Douglas, J., dissenting).
142. Broadrick v. Oklahoma, 413 U.S. 601, 618 (1973) (Douglas, J., dissenting).
143. 417 U.S. 733 (1974).

casualties.[144]   The Court first drew elaborate distinctions between civilian society and "the military [which] is, by necessity, a specialized society separate from civilian society."[145]   Next, although the officer's punishment included three year's imprisonment, the Court rejected his contention that the applicable provisions of the Military Code were void for vagueness.[146] The Court concluded that Congress must be "permitted to legislate both with greater breadth and with greater flexibility" when prescribing rules for military society.   The Court recognized that speech was involved, but stated that

> [w]hile the members of the military are not excluded from the protection granted by the First Amendment, the different character of the military community and of the military mission requires a different application of those protections.   The fundamental necessity for obedience, and the consequent necessity for imposition of discipline, may render permissible within the military that which would be constitutionally impermissible outside it.[147]

Douglas dissented, refusing to read the invoked provisions of the Code as covering what the officer had said.[148]   He did not believe that the expression of one's views was either "unbecoming" or prejudicial to good order and discipline.   He also joined in another dissent, contending that those provisions were void for vagueness.[149]

In a later case in which the Court upheld the court-martial conviction of an enlisted man for attempting unsuccessfully to publish a similarly critical statement of the Vietnam War "with design to promote disloyalty and disaffection among the troops,"[150] Douglas again dissented:

> Secrecy and suppression of views which the Court today sanctions increases rather than repels the dangers of the world in which we live.   I think full dedication to the spirit of the First Amendment is the real solvent of the dangers and tensions of the day. That philosophy may be hostile to many military minds.   But it is time that the Nation made clear that the military is not a system apart but lives under a Constitution that allows discussion of the great issues of the day, not merely the trivial ones—subject to limitations as to time, place, or occasion but never as to control.[151]

Traditionally, a third underprotected group has consisted of students.   Again, countervailing notions of discipline and order intrude. But members of this group have recently made some gains in cases in

---

144.   *Id.* at 736-37.
145.   *Id.* at 743.
146.   *Id.* at 757.
147.   *Id.* at 758.
148.   *Id.* at 766 (Douglas, J., dissenting).
149.   *Id.* at 773 (Douglas, J., joining the dissent of Stewart, J.).
150.   Secretary of the Navy v. Avrech, 418 U.S. 676 (1974).
151.   *Id.* at 680 (Douglas, J., dissenting).

which Douglas concurred. *Tinker v. Des Moines School District*,[152] for example, held that public school children may not be disciplined for wearing black armbands in the school room to protest the Vietnam War. More recently, in *Papish v. University of Missouri Curators*,[153] the Court held that a state university could not expel a student for distributing on campus a newspaper that contained vulgar but not obscene language.

Teachers, as well as students, have been subjected to extraordinary restraints on expression, but they have found some first amendment protection in the rule of *New York Times Co. v. Sullivan*[154] when they criticize their employers.[155] And, since Douglas left the Court, teachers have established that the state cannot forbid all but authorized union representatives from appearing and speaking at public meetings of the board of education on matters subject to collective bargaining.[156]

Another group, and one of the most restricted in terms of ability to communicate, consists of the inmates of our prisons. In a 1974 decision, however, the Court invalidated prison regulations authorizing the censorship from prisoner mail of statements that "unduly complain" or "magnify grievances" or express "inflammatory political, racial, religious or other views" or that were "defamatory" or "otherwise inappropriate."[157] The Court recognized that mail censorship in prisons was appropriate if essential to the protection of some governmental interest other than suppression of expression. But, in this instance, the regulation was held to be related to nothing but suppression of expression. Note carefully, however, that rather than deciding that the prison inmates had free speech rights, the Court based its decision on the first amendment rights of those to whom the letters were addressed.[158] Douglas joined in a concurring opinion asserting that prisoners also had first amendment rights.[159] But he subsequently agreed with the Court that incoming mail could be opened—but not read—in the presence of the prisoner to allow inspection for contraband.[160]

---

152. 393 U.S. 503 (1969). *Cf.* New Rider v. Board of Educ., 414 U.S. 1097, 1097 (1973) (Douglas, J., dissenting) (hair style of Indian students constitutes speech under first amendment).
153. 410 U.S. 667 (1973).
154. 376 U.S. 254 (1964).
155. *See* Pickering v. Board of Educ., 391 U.S. 563 (1968). *Cf.* Arnett v. Kennedy, 416 U.S. 134, 203 (1974) (Douglas, J., dissenting) (federal employee's loss of job for discussing an issue in the public domain is an abridgement of free speech); Meinhold v. Taylor, 414 U.S. 943, 943 (1973) (Douglas, J., dissenting from denial of certiorari) (failure to renew school teacher's contract because he stated that school was bad for children raises first amendment issues).
156. City of Madison Joint School Dist. v. Wisconsin Employment Relations Comm'n, 429 U.S. 167 (1976).
157. Procunier v. Martinez, 416 U.S. 396 (1974).
158. *Id.* at 409.
159. *Id.* at 422 (Marshall, J., concurring).
160. Wolff v. McDonnell, 418 U.S. 539 (1974). *Cf.* Jones v. North Carolina Prisoners' Labor Union, 433 U.S. 119 (1977) (losing cost advantages of bulk mailings to inmates by prisoners' union did not implicate first amendment).

Later, when the Court announced that "a prison inmate retains those First Amendment rights that are not inconsistent with his status as a prisoner or with the legitimate penological objectives of the corrections system,"[161] but nevertheless sustained a state rule barring all media interviews with individual inmates, Douglas dissented.[162] He contended that barring such interviews was not required in the interest of prison discipline, inmate safety, or rehabilitation and was therefore an unconstitutional abridgement of the first amendment rights of the prisoners, the media, and the public.[163] He dissented again when the Court sustained a similar Federal Bureau of Prisons rule applicable to medium and maximum security prisons (three-quarters of all federal prisons) but not to minimum security prisons.[164]

VI. SPECIAL MEDIA PROBLEMS

In 1971, when the Supreme Court decided that the federal government was not entitled to an injunction to prevent newspapers from publishing the Pentagon Papers, each Justice filed a separate opinion.[165] Justice Douglas concurred in a broadly based opinion by Justice Black which took the position that the first amendment forbade all three branches of government from restraining freedom of the press in the name of "national security."[166] But Douglas also wrote an opinion in which Justice Black joined and which in part said:

> The dominant purpose of the First Amendment was to prohibit the widespread practice of governmental suppression of embarrassing information. It is common knowledge that the First Amendment was adopted against the widespread use of the common law of seditious libel to punish the dissemination of material that is embarrassing to the powers-that-be . . . . The present cases will, I think, go down in history as the most dramatic illustration of that principle. A debate of large proportions goes on in the Nation over our posture in Vietnam. That debate antedated the disclosure of the contents of the present documents. The latter are highly relevant to the debate in progress.[167]

Just as Douglas voted to invalidate a prior governmental restraint on publication in that case, he voted in a later case to invalidate governmental compulsion to publish. In *Miami Herald Publishing Co. v. Tornillo*,[168] the Court struck down a state "right to reply" law. The law had provided that any candidate for public office who was assailed in regard to his personal character or official record by any newspaper

---

161. Pell v. Procunier, 417 U.S. 817, 822 (1974).
162. *Id.* at 836 (Douglas, J., dissenting).
163. *Id.* at 837.
164. Saxbe v. Washington Post Co., 417 U.S. 843, 850 (1974) (Douglas, J., dissenting).
165. New York Times Co. v. United States, 403 U.S. 713 (1971).
166. *Id.* at 718-19 (Black, J.).
167. *Id.* at 723-24 (Douglas, J.).
168. 418 U.S. 241 (1974).

could compel the attacking newspaper to print his reply free of cost. Such compelled publication was held to be as unconstitutional as compelled nonpublication.

Justice Douglas did not participate in *Red Lion Broadcasting Co. v. FCC*[169] in which the Court upheld the FCC's "fairness doctrine." The fairness doctrine requires radio and television broadcasters to present discussion of public issues and to give each side of those issues fair coverage. In a later decision, however, the Court held that neither the Federal Communications Act nor the fairness doctrine required a broadcaster which had met its obligation to provide full and fair coverage of public issues to accept paid editorial advertisements from such organizations as the Democratic National Committee or a group opposed to the Vietnam War.[170] Douglas concurred but for different reasons.[171] He rejected both the fairness doctrine and the effort to compel broadcasting of editorial advertisements as a violation of the broadcasters' first amendment right to select their own programs:

The standards of TV, radio, newspapers, or magazines—whether of excellence or mediocrity—are beyond the reach of Government. Government—acting through courts—disciplines lawyers. Government makes criminal some acts of doctors and of engineers. But the First Amendment puts beyond the reach of Government federal regulation of news agencies save only business or financial practices which do not involve First Amendment rights.[172]

In the *Pittsburgh Press* case[173] the Court held that a city could forbid a newspaper to carry sex-designated "help-wanted" advertisements. The Court invoked the now discredited "commercial speech" doctrine,[174] pointed out that employment discrimination on the basis of sex was illegal in the city, and concluded that the newspaper could be forbidden to aid this illegal activity.[175] Douglas, who had already repudiated the "commercial speech" doctrine,[176] dissented:

I believe that Pittsburgh Press by reason of the First Amendment may publish what it pleases about any law without censorship or restraint by Government. The First Amendment does not require the press to reflect any ideological or political creed reflecting the dominant philosophy, whether transient or fixed. It may use its pages and facilities to denounce a law and urge its repeal or, at the other extreme, denounce those who do not respect its letter and spirit.

. . . .

---

169. 395 U.S. 367 (1969).
170. Columbia Broadcasting Sys. v. Democratic Nat'l Comm., 412 U.S. 94 (1973).
171. *Id.* at 148 (Douglas, J., concurring).
172. *Id.* at 155.
173. Pittsburgh Press Co. v. Pittsburgh Comm'n on Human Relations, 413 U.S. 376 (1973).
174. *See* text accompanying notes 60-70 *supra*.
175. 413 U.S. at 391.
176. *See* text accompanying notes 62-66 *supra*.

[T]here can be no valid law censoring the press or punishing it for publishing its views or the views of subscribers or customers who express their ideas in letters to the editor or in want ads or other commercial space.[177]

Douglas registered yet another dissent when the Court failed to find in the first amendment any privilege for reporters which would allow them to refuse to answer questions before a grand jury about sources of their news stories:[178]

Today's decision will impede the wide-open and robust dissemination of ideas and counterthought which a free press both fosters and protects and which is essential to the success of intelligent self-government. Forcing a reporter before a grand jury will have two retarding effects upon the ear and the pen of the press. Fear of exposure will cause dissidents to communicate less openly to trusted reporters. And, fear of accountability will cause editors and critics to write with more restrained pens.

. . . .

The press has a preferred position in our constitutional scheme, not to enable it to make money, not to set newsmen apart as a favored class, but to bring fulfillment to the public's right to know. The right to know is crucial to the governing powers of the people . . . . Knowledge is essential to informed decisions.[179]

VII. CONCLUSION

Obviously, Justice Douglas takes a very robust view of the first amendment. In doing so he frequently speaks in language that is both blunt and bold—language which pains the ears of some of my more fastidious colleagues.

Without attempting to exercise all of the leeway given me to defame public figures by *New York Times Co. v. Sullivan*, I have not hesitated to indicate when I thought Justice Douglas has been wrong. Having done that, however, I feel obligated to say that on issues of freedom of expression he has been more often right than any other Justice. Unfortunately, in my opinion, too many of his views on this subject have been expressed in dissenting opinions. Some of those dissenting opinions have later become the law. More have not.

We cannot expect to live in a perfect world, but for my part I would rather live in a society that protected the right of free expression as Douglas would protect it than in the present society. We could do without the law of defamation, although that would probably make the torts teachers unhappy. That point, and my misgivings about "fighting

---

177. 413 U.S. at 397-98 (Douglas, J., dissenting). *See also* Yale Broadcasting Co. v. FCC, 414 U.S. 941 (1973) (Douglas, J., dissenting from denial of certiorari).
178. Branzburg v. Hayes, 408 U.S. 665 (1972). *See also* Farr v. Pitchess, 409 U.S. 1243 (1973) (Douglas, J., Circuit Justice) (opinion in chambers).
179. 408 U.S. at 720-21.

words" and the invasion of privacy apart, we would, I believe, live in a society more free, more secure, and more pleasant if Justice Douglas's views had more often prevailed.

NATHANIEL NATHANSON

THE PHILOSOPHY OF MR. JUSTICE BRANDEIS AND CIVIL LIBERTIES TODAY†

Nathaniel L. Nathanson*

I. The Right To Be Let Alone

When I was in law school Mr. Justice Brandeis was at the height of his powers and his fame. His seventy-fifth birthday was celebrated by dedications and laudatory essays in many of the law reviews. In law schools, at least, "Justice Holmes and Brandeis dissenting" were household words. For most of us, their presence indicated with infallibility just where right and justice lay. Only very occasionally did they differ from one another, in which case we had to shoulder the painful responsibility of making up our own minds. In due course I will invite you to share a similar responsibility with me in trying to apply the philosophy of Mr. Justice Brandeis, if we can find it, to the problems of the present day.

Although we will be concerned primarily with the constitutional philosophy of Justice Brandeis, I think that the inquiry cannot be entirely divorced from the Justice's entire philosophy of life. That there was indeed such a philosophy no one familiar with his career can doubt. Yet the pattern of that philosophy is nowhere set forth in sparkling generalizations like those that garland the addresses of Mr. Justice Holmes and Judge Learned Hand. The public addresses of Justice Brandeis, almost all delivered before he joined the Court, dealt with concrete problems and how to solve them. Once on the Court, he hardly spoke publicly at all, except when he delivered his opinions from the bench. How then shall we set about the task of divining his personal philosophy? So much has been written about Justice Brandeis that we have a good deal of second-hand testimony on this score. We also have some first-hand testimony recently made available through

---

† *These remarks were originally delivered at the University of Illinois College of Law on November 16, 1978, as the first 1978-79 lecture of the David C. Baum Lectures on Civil Rights and Civil Liberties.*

* *Frederic P. Vose Professor of Law Emeritus, Northwestern University; Distinguished Visiting Professor of Law, University of San Diego. B.A. 1929, LL.B. 1932, Yale University; S.J.D. 1933, Harvard University; Law Clerk to Mr. Justice Brandeis, 1934-35.*

publication of four volumes of his personal letters.[1] I have found these especially fascinating for reasons that I hope will become evident as we go along.

A. Early Life and Career

I trust that you will forgive me if I begin with Brandeis as a law student. Apparently he fell in love with the law practically at first sight, and especially with the Harvard Law School. This is reflected in a letter to a Louisville lawyer friend who was destined to become his brother-in-law. He says,

> You have undoubtedly heard from other[s] of my work here, how well I am pleased with everything that pertains to the law.
> . . . .
> Law schools are splendid institutions. Aside from the instruction there received, being able continually to associate with young-men who have the same interest and ambition, who are determined to make as great progress as possible in their studies and devote all their time to the same—must alone be of inestimable advantages. Add to this the instruction of consummate lawyers, who devote their whole time to *you*, and a complete law-library of over fifteen thousand volumes and then compare the opportunities for learning which a student of the law has at Harvard Law School and in a law-office. After one has grasped the principles which underlie the structure of the Common Law, I doubt not, that one can learn very much in an office—That first year at law is, however, surely ill-spent in an office.[2]

Notice that he committed himself only as to the value of the first year. Nevertheless, on finishing that, he went on to a second year and then even to a third year of graduate work, although this was largely devoted to tutoring and other jobs, which enabled him to pay off a loan from his brother and even to begin the program of saving and investment which continued throughout his life. In his second year, writing to his sister, he says, "Law seems so interesting to me in all its aspects;—it is difficult for me to understand that any of the initiated should not burn with enthusiasm."[3]

After graduating in 1878 at the head of his class despite the handicap of weak eyes which required him to rely a great deal on readers, Brandeis tried practice for a year with a senior lawyer in St. Louis, where he found that the problems of an ordinary law practice were not

---

1. 1-5 LETTERS OF LOUIS D. BRANDEIS (M. Urofsky and D. Levy eds. 1971) [hereinafter cited as LETTERS].

2. 1 *id.* at 6. He also had a good word to say for the budding case method: "Some of our professors are trying to inculcate in us a great distrust of textbooks, and to prove to us the truth of the maxim—Melius est petere fontes quam sectari rivulos." [It is better to seek out the well-springs than to follow the rivulets.] *Id.* at 7.

3. *Id.* at 14.

always so fascinating. Then came an invitation to return to Boston to open a law office with a friend and classmate, Samuel Warren, whose scholastic record was second only to his own and whose family was also extremely well connected, both socially and in business. After carefully exploring the prospects, they took the plunge; and so began the firm of Warren and Brandeis. The letters of the next few years reveal nothing so much as a determination to succeed in the practice of law. This includes a vigorous social life, designed in part to attract clients and including membership in the Dedham Polo Club, where Brandeis did not play polo, but where he did ride enthusiastically, and in the Turn-verein, where, as he says in another letter to his sister, "I must go soon . . . and try and be captivating . . . and get some clients from their number."[4]

A little later in the same year, 1881, he reports to his brother that their prospects for the next year are not too good.

> We have only one lucrative litigation on hand, . . . and [it] will probably be settled before fall. . . . I don't expect my practice to amount to much for the next fifteen years but I do expect to have a high old time for the twenty five following. As the traveller said of Sparta:
>
> "Here alone it is a pleasure to grow old."[5]

Apparently he loved Boston, then the intellectual capital of the United States, where he already was hobnobbing with people like Oliver Wendell Holmes, Jr. and Ralph Waldo Emerson. But this is the last that we hear about a concern for lack of business. Instead, there is a slightly shocking note, dated January 30, 1884, in which (besides reporting he is "very busy") he says: "Have had a public career of late. Lectured on 'Taxation' Sunday[,] Spoke against 'Woman Suffrage' before the Legislative Com[mit]tee yesterday & appeared before the Insurance Com[mit]tee yesterday & today."[6]

In another letter to his brother, in 1886, comes the first intimation of a cause, although it is one in the regular course of his law business representing paper companies. He says,

> Your birthday we shall celebrate with another hearing on the rag question. The fight is now against the Boston Board of Health which is sustaining the grinding monopoly & fraud entitled—the Boston Disinfecting Co. . . .

---

4. *Id.* at 61. He also says: "Yesterday was a Sad Day. We buried irretrivably [*sic*] a half a dozen of the most beautiful and lucrative lawsuits—and all for the love of our clients. . . . The only consolation is that we get our opponent for a client." *Id.*

5. *Id.* at 64.

6. *Id.* at 66. Apparently he told the Legislative Committee that the vote was not a right but a privilege that imposed certain duties peculiar to the male sex. *Id.*, ed. n.1. I should add that by 1911 he had publicly changed his views. *Id.* I have no doubt that the switch occurred much earlier, if only because of his wife. In 1891 he had married a second cousin, Alice Goldmark, who was neither a shrinking violet nor lacking in social conscience.

. . . .

We have the evidence—both practical & scientific on our side—and the chances are quite good that political influence will not be potent enough to overcome that. Popular prejudice and ignorance may make us some trouble but we are in the right and must, in the end, come out successful. . . . It is only ignorance and dark dealing that we must fear.[7]

Nevertheless Brandeis and his clients lost both in the City Council and before the Massachusetts Supreme Court. His daughter is reported to have said that her father recollected this fight as the first time he realized how evil a monopoly could be.[8]

However this may be, Brandeis's real battles against monopoly, and to some extent his obsession with that evil, did not begin until his professional success was assured and his law firm established as one of the leading firms in Boston, under the name of Brandeis, Dunbar and Nutter. It was just about the turn of the century, 1897 to be exact, that Brandeis first began to indulge his penchant for public service. The opening gun was a letter to the Boston Evening Transcript opposing a bill to amend the charter of the Boston Elevated Railroad Company. This eventually developed into a battle of several years' duration, in which Brandeis acted not only as lawyer for the public interest but also as organizer of various citizen groups designed to educate the public and bring pressure on legislators. In some respects, Brandeis was the forerunner of our public interest law firms because he insisted on receiving no compensation for his services, even when the clients were willing and able to pay. Instead, when he was heavily engaged in nonpaying business, he paid an appropriate amount into the firm so that his younger partners would not suffer financially from this idiosyncrasy. We also have the word of one of his partners that this was on his own initiative, not on any suggestion of theirs.[9]

Brandeis was able to do this because he and Mrs. Brandeis lived with relative simplicity compared to their growing income. This does not mean that they denied themselves or their children comfort, education, or recreation. Brandeis always took a month's vacation, usually at the shore. He loved canoeing, sailing, and horseback riding, and his two girls shared these enthusiasms. But he also had a program of regular savings and investment in relatively safe securities, primarily railroad and public utility bonds. As he explained and also recommended to his brother, he did this deliberately so that he would not have to devote any time or energy to worrying about his investments; he especially abhorred stock market speculation. The result of this program of saving and investment was that he was a millionaire twice over when

---

7. *Id.* at 67-68.
8. *Id.* at 68, editor's note 2.
9. McClennen, *Louis D. Brandeis as a Lawyer*, 33 MASS. L.Q., No. 3, at 24 (1948).

he went on the Court in 1916, and had probably accumulated his first million about ten years earlier. Perhaps I should remind you that this was before there was an income tax.

This is as good a time as any to raise the question: *was* all this part of the grand design? Did Brandeis deliberately set out to accumulate a modest fortune so that he could then devote himself primarily to public causes? In a letter written in 1912 to a young man who had asked his advice on choosing a career so as to be of service to the country, Brandeis may have given a synopsis of his own life plan:

> Whatever you do, bear in mind that the fundamental requirement is that you should keep yourself free; that is, at all times be able to take such course as you think proper. In order to do this you will have to be free from financial necessities or obligations, and to that end lead a frugal life. When you make money in business remember that the only thing that you can properly buy with that money is freedom to do as seems to you from time to time right.[10]

As an example of his frugality, the Brandeis' combined bedroom and study, as I recall it, consisted of a bed, two chairs, a desk, and a bookcase. The books he was using to write an opinion were lined up on the window shelf.

There is some suggestion of this life plan in Mason's outstanding biography, especially in the subtitle, "A Free Man's Life."[11] Like most categorical answers to subtle questions, it is, I suspect, an oversimplification. Brandeis did not, like Athene, spring full grown from the brow of Zeus. Obviously he was endowed at birth with great intellectual capacity and perhaps he inherited, or had instilled into him at an early age from his parents and close relatives, a strength of character and moral sensitivity that both inspired and enabled him to devote himself to public causes and especially to the defense of the little man. But he was also a person of gradual growth and development. I think he devoted himself at the outset wholeheartedly and quite single-mindedly to the development of a successful law practice because that was the natural thing to do, especially at that time in our history. His father had been a successful and independent businessman; his brother was taking over and expanding that business; similarly, he wanted to develop a successful law firm of his own. Besides, he was an ambitious and competitive person as well as a sensitive and compassionate one. He prided himself on his abilities as a horseman and canoeist. He spoke lovingly of his horse Bob, Son of Battle, who, he said, was worthy of the name. Early in his career he enjoyed trial work, simply because of the challenge of combat. He even preferred a long trial to a short one because it really gave one a chance to test one's mettle. When

---

10. 2 LETTERS, *supra* note 1, at 709.
11. A. MASON, BRANDEIS, A FREE MAN'S LIFE (1946).

he spoke of the qualities of the men he admired, particularly of his leading business clients like William McElwain, the shoe manufacturer, and Edward Filene, the department store owner, he mentioned their courage as well as their intelligence, fairness,and public spirit. In his public interest battles, he marshalled his forces like a general, almost giving orders to his associates as if they were his lieutenants. He would write to Filene or McElwain, saying in effect: Our battle is approaching the critical stage; now is the time to make your influence felt, if you are going to help us at all.[12]

When I first read about these early battles, I had a hard time recognizing the protagonist as the same person with whom I had worked in October Term 1934. I had carried away with me the impression of a man of complete serenity and Olympian calm, dwelling in a rarefied atmosphere far above the madding crowd. But even after he had attained this pinnacle of apparent serenity and detachment, there could still be seen an occasional glint of battle in his eye—a kind of vicarious participation in someone else's war. I recall that after William O. Douglas had come to call on him—when Douglas was with the Securities and Exchange Commission and presumably just beginning his battles with Wall Street—the Justice said with a smile of satisfaction: "He's quite a fellah." In this respect, at least, it was not inappropriate that Douglas succeeded to the Brandeis chair on the Supreme Court.

Even in those tempestuous days when he seemed to glory in the fray, Brandeis insisted on certain ground rules: one, that he always "fought fair" and without indulging in personal attacks; and two, that he did not carry the battle beyond the point of diminishing returns. Thus, in the ultimate settlement with the Boston Gas Company, he embraced what he regarded as a fair and workable compromise even with respect to the unmitigated evil of watered stock—a compromise which some of his more doctrinaire cohorts attacked as a sell out. And in the sequel to the Ballinger investigation,[13] he gave the Taft administration's revised program for the handling of the natural resources of Alaska a clean bill of health in the face of bitter criticism from the more doctrinaire conservationists. Finally, in the climax to the second hearing on a general rate increase for the railroads, in which he regarded himself as impartial counsel to the Interstate Commerce Commission, despite his previous uncompromising attack on the proposed increase he recommended a partial increase for some of the railroads to the surprise and consternation of leading counsel for the shippers. This rather unusual mixture of resolute battler and impartial arbitrator led to the not so surprising result that he was sometimes in hot water with

---

12. At the height of the Ballinger investigation, his great conservation battle with the Taft administration, he wrote to his brother: "I am in excellent shape. Everybody seems to say: *'Was der lebt noch?'* ['Is he still alive?'], but for a man who would rather fight than eat, the surprise is unwarranted." 2 LETTERS, *supra* note 1, at 348.

13. *See* text accompanying note 18 *infra*.

both sides. This became particularly apparent during the protracted and controversial Committee hearings on his nomination to the Supreme Court, when his most articulate detractors included not only most of his previous opponents but also some of his former allies.[14]

B.   *The Brandeis Philosophy*

I appreciate that at this point, you might well ask what has all this got to do with civil rights or civil liberties? Perhaps the best answer I can give is that there must have been some connection between Brandeis's general philosophy and his libertarian philosophy, and some connection between his general philosophy and the way he chose to use his professional prowess once he was assured of professional success and his family of, at least, a modest competence. A shorthand description of the second connection is, I believe, simply noblesse oblige. Brandeis must have been aware that he was a superior person, perhaps also a fortunate person, not only in his natural endowments but also in the circumstances of his family upbringing and his associates. Besides his admiration and affection for his immediate family, he admired and was close to his uncle, Lewis Dembitz, a practicing lawyer but also a legal scholar of considerable distinction and a person of great culture and charm. In short, Brandeis felt an obligation to use his talents for something more than personal gain. I think it was fitting that Franklin Roosevelt—with his great penchant for coining pet names for his favorite people—always referred to Brandeis among intimates as Isaiah, although some of the earlier objects of Brandeisian invective might have found him more reminiscent of Jeremiah.

Turning now to the other connection—the link between his general philosophy and his libertarian philosophy—I think we get some clue if we look at the characteristics of his enemies and his allies in his fighting years. I have mentioned his first exposure to the municipal monopoly of rag disinfectants, but this was minor compared to the enemies of his own choosing, starting with the Boston Elevated and then gradually working up the scale through the Gas Company, the big life insurance companies, the New Haven Railroad and its controller, the House of Morgan, then all the large railroads and their bankers, then the Taft Administration, and finally his former client, the International Shoe Machinery Company, whose propaganda probably did more than any other single source to paint the Mephistofelian image of Brandeis that emerged during the confirmation hearings.

His complaint against the life insurance companies was that they were loading a disproportionate share of their costs on the so-called industrial insurance—insurance sold by house-to-house solicitors in poorer districts and paid for in small weekly cash installments—which

---

14. *See* TODD, JUSTICE ON TRIAL (1964).

was exceptionally profitable because it usually lapsed before maturity. Brandeis's remedy was to establish a competing system of Savings Banks Insurance whose cost was considerably less and which was less likely to lapse. [For Brandeis, this was a campaign to protect the little man from exploitation by the big man.] It was also a campaign of education in habits of thrift and managing one's own affairs. Its success in Massachusetts, at least, was one of his proudest accomplishments; the threat, if not the consummation, of its spread to other states had considerable effect in bringing down the cost of such insurance.[15]

The evils of monopoly, or the curse of bigness, as he later called it, was also a major theme in his battle against the New York, New Haven, and Hartford's attempt to gain control of all public transportation in New England. The capstone of this plan was to be the merger of the New Haven and the Boston and Maine Railroads. Both Brandeis's version of the seriousness of the problem and his developing philosophy are revealed in his address to the New England Dry Goods Association on February 11, 1908, in which he said,

> The proposed merger presents for the decision of the people of Massachusetts the most important question which has arisen in this Commonwealth since the Civil War.
>
> . . . .
>
> It has been suggested that we accept the proposed monopoly in transportation, but provide safeguards.
>
> This would be like surrendering liberty and substituting despotism with safeguards. There is no way in which to safeguard people from despotism except to prevent despotism. There is no way to safeguard the people from the evils of a private transportation monopoly except to prevent the monopoly. The objections to despotism and to monopoly are fundamental in human nature. They rest upon the innate and ineradicable selfishness of man. They rest upon the fact that absolute power inevitably leads to abuse. They rest upon the fact that progress flows only from struggle.[16]

Although Brandeis was not successful in blocking the Morgan-Mellon plan to monopolize transportation in New England, he lived to see the fulfillment of his worst prophecies in the financial collapse of the New Haven and Mr. Mellon's resulting resignation.[17] Even so, Brandeis,

---

15.　This is not just ancient history or limited to Massachusetts in significance. I am indebted to a colleague and former editor of the *University of Illinois Law Forum* for an excerpt from a current issue of *Consumer Reports* entitled "Insurance that Preys on the Poor." I can hardly begin to tell you how Brandeis would have loved this chart showing the comparative costs of New York Savings Bank Life Insurance and the five major sellers of industrial life insurance. See "Insurance that Preys on the Poor," CONSUMER REPORTS, November 1978, at 658.

16.　L. BRANDEIS, BUSINESS: A PROFESSION 262, 278 (1933).

17.　Anticipating this result by two years, Brandeis suggested to Norman Hapgood the following epitaph:

　　Mellon was a masterful man, resourceful, courageous, broad of view. He fired the imagi-

like Cassandra, was blamed by some for having caused the catastrophe he foretold.

Similarly, in the Ballinger investigation, Brandeis was concerned not only with the conservation issue and the breach of public trust, but also with the way in which Glavis, the little man at the bottom, was being sacrificed ruthlessly to protect the interests of the big man at the top.[18] It was probably the Ballinger investigation, with its concomitant attack upon President Taft, that accounted most directly for Taft's joining in the letter, signed by seven former Presidents of the American Bar Association, declaring that Brandeis was unfit for appointment to the United States Supreme Court. That bitterness did not persist during their service on the Supreme Court together; indeed Taft was sometimes quite lavish in his praise of Brandeis's contribution to the work of the Court, although he also expressed resentment at what he regarded as Brandeis's undue influence over Holmes, which gave Brandeis, as Taft saw it, two votes on crucial issues instead of one.

This attitude must have been especially present in Taft's mind in the great case of *Myers v. United States*,[19] involving the extent of the President's constitutional powers of removal. Taft wrote the majority opinion, sustaining unlimited presidential power, while Holmes, McReynolds, and Brandeis wrote dissenting opinions. Both Taft and Brandeis may have regarded this difference of opinion as a reprise of the Ballinger conflict, waged this time much more politely, in accordance with Marquis of Queensbury rules appropriate for the Supreme Court. Looming behind the elaborate marshalling of constitutional and legislative history was a fundamental philosophical difference with respect to American government and different assessments of the danger of an impotent executive as compared with the danger of a dictato-

---

nation of New England; but, being oblique of vision, merely distorted its judgment and silenced its conscience. For a while he trampled with impunity on laws human and divine; but as he was obsessed with the delusion that two and two make five, he fell at last the victim to the relentless rules of humble arithmetic.

Remember, O Stranger: "Arithmetic is the first of the sciences and the mother of safety."

2 LETTERS, *supra* note 1, at 500-01. *See also*, STAPLES AND MACON, FALL OF A RAILROAD EMPIRE (1947).

18.   As he summarized his own argument in a letter to Mark Sullivan, a friend and magazine editor:

[C]onservation means not only conserving the public property from wasteful use, but conserving the public property for the people. The struggle is essentially the struggle of the people against privilege,—the struggle of men against property. The whole movement is a movement to develop equality of opportunity. . . .

[T]his struggle was a struggle for equal justice; the same equal justice in the public service that the American is entitled to under the law. . . . What I endeavored to bring out was . . . that what we have to do is to protect the small man against the big; that there was no hesitation apparently in Ballinger and his associates going out of their way to destroy Glavis where his destruction appeared to be necessary for the exoneration of Ballinger; that the most extraordinary un-American act of condeming Glavis, not only without a hearing,—without his seeing the evidence produced against him, but without his ever having known that any charge had been preferred against him.

2 LETTERS, *supra* note 1, at 342-43.

19.   272 U.S. 52 (1926).

rial executive. The conclusion of the Brandeis opinion was reminiscent of his concluding argument in the Ballinger affair. He said in part:

> Checks and balances were established in order that this should be "a government of laws and not of men" . . . . The doctrine of separation of powers was adopted by the Convention of 1787, not to promote efficiency but to preclude the exercise of arbitrary power. The purpose was, not to avoid friction, but, by means of the inevitable friction incident to the distribution of governmental powers among three departments, to save the people from autocracy. . . . In America, as in England, the conviction prevailed then that the people must look to representative assemblies for protection of their liberties. And protection of the individual, even if he be an official, from the arbitrary or capricious exercise of power was then believed to be an essential of free government.[20]

In the light of the Ballinger investigation and the *Myers* case, there can be no doubt where Brandeis would have stood on the fundamental issues of Watergate. But on the exact issue of *Myers*, I am not so sure that he was altogether right. Personally I prefer the uncertain compromise of the *Humphrey's*[21] case in which Brandeis joined without comment.

Finally, in the break with the International Shoe Machinery Company, Brandeis's sympathies were with the shoe manufacturers, not only because some of them were his clients and friends, like McElwain, but also because they were the relatively little people standing up against the giant. He was also particularly outraged because the shoe machinery company had in effect put a potential competitor out of business by using its influence in financial circles to deny him the credit necessary for his survival. For Brandeis, freedom included free enterprise in a very personal way: the freedom to develop one's own business and at the same time to contribute to the welfare of his community. This is illustrated by the address he delivered at Brown University in 1912 entitled "Business—A Profession,"[22] an address that was in considerable part a tribute to his friends and clients, William McElwain and the Filenes.

Speaking of McElwain, Brandeis said,

> In 1902, the irregularity in the employment of the shoe worker was brought to his attention. This irregularity had been accepted by the manufacturers and workers alike as inevitable. . . . But with McElwain an evil recognized was a condition to be remedied; and he set his great mind to solving the problem. . . . Within a few years irregularity of employment had ceased in the McElwain factories; and before his death every one of his many thousand

---

20. 272 U.S. at 292-95 (Brandeis, J., dissenting).
21. Humphrey's Executor v. United States, 295 U.S. 602 (1935).
22. *See* L. BRANDEIS, *supra* note 16, at 1-12.

employees could find work three hundred and five days in the year.[23]

This is what Brandeis had in mind when he said he believed in free enterprise, rather than socialism.[24]

Brandeis's story about the Filenes was substantially similar, ending with this homily: "The Filenes thus have accepted and applied the principles of industrial democracy and social justice. But they have done more—they have demonstrated that the introduction of industrial democracy and social justice is at least consistent with marked financial success."[25]

I realize that this is not civil liberties in the ordinary sense of the word. But Brandeis never tired of asserting that political democracy could not survive without economic democracy. Because of this belief, he became a wholehearted supporter of the union movement, even though he was firmly opposed to the closed shop. Instead, he invented the preferential shop, which became the basis for settlement of what seemed to be intractable strife in the garment industry of New York and which in reality was close to what we would call the union shop. Furthermore, one of the reasons he hated the Steel Trust was its adamant opposition to collective bargaining. By economic democracy, however, he apparently had more in mind than simply collective bargaining with respect to hours and wages. As he put it in a short speech to the Filene Cooperative Association:

> One hundred years ago the civilized world did not believe that it was possible that the people could rule themselves . . . . America in the last century proved that democracy is a success.
>
> The civilized world today believes that in the industrial world self-government is impossible . . . . It rests with this century and perhaps with America to prove that as we have in the political world shown what self-government can do, we are to pursue the same lines in the industrial world.[26]

I do not know how far Brandeis would carry the concept of industrial democracy in a capitalist world, but I am told that new experiments in that direction are now being tried, both here and in Europe, in some instances with considerable success.

---

23. *Id.* at 5-7. As a matter of fact, it was Brandeis who alerted McElwain to the significance of employment irregularity when he was trying to settle a strike for McElwain.

24. When McElwain died Brandeis wrote to his brother that "he was in my opinion really the greatest man of my acquaintance." *See* A. MASON, *supra* note 10, at 147. And some time after McElwain's death, when the company encountered financial difficulties and was merged with the International Shoe Company, Brandeis commented sadly to Felix Frankfurter: "I interpret the . . . merger as a defeat for the McE[lwain]s. Probably debts overcame them." 4 LETTERS, *supra* note 1, at 559.

25. L. BRANDEIS, *supra* note 16, at 11-12.

26. L. BRANDEIS, THE CURSE OF BIGNESS 35 (O. Fraenkel ed. 1934).

C.   The Right to Privacy

Before he went on the Court, the closest Brandeis came to address-
ing a civil libertarian issue in the usual sense of the term was not in his
public causes, but rather in the famous article on "The Right to Privacy," which he and his partner Samuel Warren published in the
Harvard Law Review in 1890.[27] Even this was not prompted by a
strictly civil libertarian interest, but rather by Warren's indignation at
some newspaper publicity directed at his own family's social affairs.
The objective of the authors was to establish a general cause of action
for the redress of such grievances. For this purpose they adopted the
phrase, "the right to be let alone," first publicized by Judge Cooley in
his treatise on torts.[28] Their objective was to win a respectable place for
this right in the law of torts on its own merits and without reliance on
considerations of property or contract, which might apply only in special situations. They expressed their central thesis in these words:

> [T]he protection afforded to thoughts, sentiments, and emotions,
> expressed through the medium of writing or of the arts, so far as it
> consists in preventing publication, is merely an instance . . . of the
> more general right of the individual to be let alone. It is like the
> right not be assaulted or beaten, the right not to be imprisoned, the
> right not to be maliciously prosecuted, the right not to be defamed.
> In each of these rights, as indeed in all other rights recognized by
> the law, there inheres the quality of being owned or possessed—
> and (as that is the distinguishable attribute of property) there may
> be some propriety in speaking of those rights as property. But,
> obviously, they bear little resemblance to what is ordinarily com-
> prehended under that term. The principle that protects personal
> writings and all other personal productions, not against theft and
> physical appropriation, but against publication in any form, is in
> reality not the principle of private property, but that of an invio-
> late personality.[29]

I am told by scholars who should know that this article is considered by many the most influential law review article that was ever published; apparently much of it is now hornbook law.[30] Its main
contemporary interest lies not in the thesis itself, but in the thorough-
ness, boldness, and ingenuity of its development. I was also interested
in the extent to which the authors anticipated the qualifications that

---

27.   Warren & Brandeis, *The Right to Privacy*, 4 HARV. L. REV. 193 (1890).
28.   T. COOLEY, TORTS 29 (2d ed. 1888).
29.   Warren & Brandeis, *supra* note 27, at 205.
30.   *See, e.g.*, W. PROSSER, HANDBOOK ON THE LAW OF TORTS 802-04 (4th ed. 1971). Also
see Bloustein, *The First Amendment and Privacy: The Supreme Court Justice and the Philosopher*,
28 RUTGERS L. REV. 41 (1974); Kalven, *Privacy in Tort Law—Were Warren and Brandeis Wrong?*,
31 LAW & CONTEMP. PROB. 326 (1966); Woito & McNulty, *The Privacy Disclosure Tort and the
First Amendment: Should the Community Decide Newsworthiness?*, 64 IOWA L. REV. 185 (1979).
For another view of the right to be let alone, see Griswold, *The Right to be Let Alone*, 55 Nw. U.L.
REV. 216 (1960).

had to be developed, once the central doctrine won acceptance. I soon found that they were not unaware of the possibility of conflict with other rights or privileges, such as the right of the public to know or the privileges associated with certain types of communication according to the law of libel and slander. One example that they gave was this:

> To publish of a modest and retiring individual that he suffers from an impediment in his speech or that he cannot spell correctly is an unwarranted, if not unexampled, infringement of his rights, while to state and comment on the same characteristics found in a would-be congressman could not be regarded as beyond the pale of propriety.[31]

Just how the authors would have felt about some of the lengths to which the current doctrine of public figure has been carried is an interesting subject for speculation. I am inclined to think that Brandeis himself would have agreed with the court's somewhat reluctant conclusion in *Sidis v. F.-R. Publishing Corp.*,[32] holding that the notoriety of a former whiz kid, who later chose to live a life of complete obscurity, had created a public interest in his subsequent career. I reach this conclusion because, as Professor Freund has eloquently demonstrated,[33] Brandeis was not a sentimentalist; he would not permit hard cases to make bad law. I have no doubt that the Justice would have gotten considerable satisfaction from the success of Ralph Nader's suit against General Motors for violation of his privacy by subjecting him to an elaborate system of surveillance with the hope of discrediting or intimidating him and thus undermining the effect of his book entitled *Unsafe at Any Speed*.[34] Brandeis might have identified especially with this application of the right of privacy, both because Nader has come about as close as any one in our time to fulfilling Brandeis's role of the "People's Attorney" in his crusading days, and also because America's growing dependence on the automobile industry was one of the Justice's greatest aversions.

I hesitate to speculate on how the Justice would have voted in the more difficult case of *Time, Inc. v. Hill*,[35] involving a suit by the victims of a famous robbery on account of the republication three years later of the purported but inaccurate details of the event. In this connection, it is interesting to note that shortly after the publication of the privacy article, Brandeis wrote to his wife-to-be that he was thinking of writing another article on "The Duty of Publicity," a subject in which he was really more interested.[36] Brandeis would have agreed no doubt with

---

31. Warren & Brandeis, *supra* note 27, at 215.
32. 113 F.2d 806 (2d Cir. 1940).
33. P. FREUND, ON UNDERSTANDING THE SUPREME COURT 45, 66-68 (1949).
34. *See* Nader v. General Motors Corp., 25 N.Y.2d 560, 255 N.E.2d 765 (1970).
35. 385 U.S. 374 (1967).
36. *See* 1 LETTERS, *supra* note 1, at 100. Brandeis explained:
You know I have talked to you about the wickedness of people shielding wrongdoers & passing them off (or at least allowing them to pass themselves off) as honest men. . . .

the general spirit of our modern Information and Sunshine Acts. (One of his favorite phrases was that "sunlight is the best disinfectant.") Yet I say this with some hesitation because in his own operations, the Justice insisted on the utmost confidentiality; one of his strongest admonitions to a beginning law clerk was never to discuss with anyone—not even the other law clerks—what he was working on. Of course, that was before all the Justices and the law clerks had their offices in the Supreme Court building; I sometimes wonder how that injunction would have survived the present collegiality of the Court's junior staff.

D.   Olmstead *and the Fourth Amendment*

Many years after the privacy article, Brandeis returned to the theme of "the right to be let alone" in his dissent, partly joined by Mr. Justice Holmes, in *Olmstead v. United States.*[37] The principal issue was whether evidence obtained through telephone wiretaps was properly admitted into evidence to help establish a violation of the *National Prohibition Act.*[38] The majority of the Court, in an opinion written by Chief Justice Taft, held that admission was proper because no federal statute then prohibited wiretapping and because neither the fourth nor the fifth amendment was violated.[39]

The Brandeis dissent breathes the same spirit that infused his early article on privacy and his 1916 address to the Chicago Bar Association, entitled "The Living Law."[40] Beginning with Chief Justice Marshall's oft-quoted sentence, "We must never forget that it is a *constitution* we are expounding,"[41] Brandeis traces the development of Congressional powers "over objects of which the Fathers could not have dreamed. . . . Clauses guaranteeing to the individual protection against specific abuses of power must have a similar capacity of adaptation to a changing world."[42] The opinion continues:

If the broad light of day could be let in upon men's actions, it would purify them as the sun disinfects.
Id.

37.   277 U.S. 438 (1928).

38.   National Prohibition Act, ch. 85, 41 Stat. 305 (1919) (amended 1921, 1929) (repealed 1935).

39.   As the Chief Justice explained it, the key issue was the fourth amendment, not the fifth:
The Amendment itself shows that search is to be of material things—the person, the house, his papers or his effects. The description of the warrant necessary to make the proceeding lawful is that it must specify the place to be searched and the person or *things* to be seized.
. . . .
. . . The language of the Amendment cannot be extended and expanded to include telephone wires reaching to the whole world from the defendant's house or office. The intervening wires are not part of his house or office any more than are the highways along which they are stretched.
277 U.S. at 464-65.

40.   Address before the Chicago Bar Association (Jan. 3, 1916), *reprinted in* L. BRANDEIS, *supra* note 16, at 344-63.

41.   *See* McCulloch v. Maryland, 17 U.S. (4 Wheat.) 315, 407 (1819).

42.   277 U.S. at 472 (Brandeis, J., dissenting).

Moreover, "in the application of a constitution, our contemplation cannot be only of what has been but what may be." The progress of science in furnishing the government with means of espionage is not likely to stop with wire-tapping. Ways may some day be developed by which the Government, without removing papers from secret drawers, can reproduce them in court, and by which it will be enabled to expose to a jury the most intimate occurrences of the home. Advances in the psychic and related sciences may bring means of exploring unexpressed beliefs, thoughts and emotions. "That places the liberty of every man in the hands of every petty officer" was said by James Otis of much lesser intrusions than these. To Lord Camden, a far slighter intrusion seemed "subversive of all the comforts of society." Can it be that the Constitution affords no protection against such invasions of individual security?[43]

After reciting examples of fourth amendment protection Brandeis concludes:

The Makers of our Constitution undertook to secure conditions favorable to the pursuit of happiness. They recognized the significance of man's spiritual nature, of his feelings and of his intellect. They knew that only a part of the pain, pleasure and satisfactions of life are to be found in material things. They sought to protect Americans in their beliefs, their thoughts, their emotions and their sensations. They conferred, as against the government, the right to be let alone—the most comprehensive of rights and the right most valued by civilized men. To protect that right, every unjustifiable intrusion by the government upon the privacy of the individual, whatever the means employed, must be deemed a violation of the Fourth Amendment. And the use, as evidence in a criminal proceeding, of facts ascertained by such intrusion must be deemed a violation of the Fifth.[44]

Of course, the *Olmstead* decision has since been overruled explicitly in *Katz v. United States*,[45] a case involving the attachment, by federal agents acting without a warrant, of an electronic listening and recording device to a public telehpone booth, so as to record the conversation being conducted in the booth by a suspected professional gambler. The only complete dissenter was Mr. Justice Black, whose opinion was more of an answer to the Brandeis dissent in *Olmstead* than to Justice Stewart's opinion for the Court in *Katz*.[46] Brandeis

---

43. *Id.* at 474.
44. *Id.* at 478-79. The Justice further explained:

Experience should teach us to be most on our guard to protect liberty when the government's purposes are beneficent. Men born to freedom are naturally alert to repel invasion of their liberty by evil-minded rulers. The greatest dangers to liberty lurk in insidious encroachment by men of zeal, well-meaning, but without understanding.

Id. at 479.
45. 389 U.S. 347 (1967).
46. Justice Black said, for example:

would not have been shaken by Justice Black's argument. He would probably have said to Justice Black something like what he said to me when I once had the temerity to try to persuade him to change his vote: "I do not think you are right on the law, but even if you were, I would still be resolute."

I will resist the temptation to get involved in a discussion of the weight to be given to the specific intention of the framers in determining contemporary constitutional questions, a subject recently stirred in academia by Mr. Raoul Berger.[47] I would rather direct your attention to a difference of opinion within the majority itself in *Katz*. Justice White, in a concurring opinion, expressed the view: "We should not require the warrant procedure . . . if the President of the United States or his chief legal officer, the Attorney General has considered the requirements of national security and authorized electronic surveillance as reasonable."[48] Justice Douglas, for Justice Brennan and himself, responded that "spies and saboteurs are as entitled to the protection of the Fourth Amendment as suspected gamblers like petitioner," and that the President and Attorney General cannot "assume both the position of adversary-and-prosecutor and disinterested, neutral magistrate."[49] I have no doubt that Justice Brandeis would have agreed with Justices Douglas and Brennan.

The issue was settled, at least in part, in *United States v. United States District Court*,[50] when the Court, in an opinion by Mr. Justice Powell, held that electronic surveillance, approved by the Attorney General to protect the nation from domestic organizations, violated the fourth amendment. Although there was no dissent, there was some division in the Court as to whether it was necessary to reach the constitutional question.[51]

Tapping telephone wires, of course, was an unknown possibility at the time the Fourth Amendment was adopted. But eavesdropping (and wiretapping is nothing more than eavesdropping by telephone) was . . . "an ancient practice which at common law was condemned as a nuisance. 4 Blackstone, Commentaries 168. In those days the eavesdropper listened by naked ear under the eaves of houses or their windows, or beyond their walls seeking out private discourse." . . . There can be no doubt that the Framers were aware of this practice, and if they had desired to outlaw or restrict the use of evidence obtained by eavesdropping, I believe that they would have used the appropriate language to do so in the Fourth Amendment. They certainly would not have left such a task to the ingenuity of language-stretching judges. No one, it seems to me, can read the debates on the Bill of Rights without reaching the conclusion that its Framers and critics well knew the meaning of the words they used, what they would be understood to mean by others, their scope and their limitations. Under these circumstances it strikes me as a charge against their scholarship, their common sense and their candor to give Fourth Amendment's language the eavesdropping meaning the Court imputes to it today.

Id. at 366 (Black, J., dissenting) (quoting Berger v. New York, 388 U.S. 41, 45 (1967)).

47. *See* R. BERGER, GOVERNMENT BY JUDICIARY (1978). Also see Nathanson, Book Review, 56 TEX. L. REV. 579 (1978).

48. 389 U.S. at 364 (White, J., concurring).

49. *Id.* at 360 (Douglas, J., concurring).

50. 407 U.S. 297 (1972).

51. Justice White thought the conclusion could and should have been reached solely on

Justice Powell, in a carefully balanced opinion, accorded considerable weight to considerations of national security; nevertheless he concluded that fourth amendment values should prevail. National security interests, he thought, could be safeguarded adequately in ordinary circumstances by in camera proceedings before a magistrate authorized to issue a warrant for such surveillance.[52] He was also careful to emphasize that the particular case involved only domestic security and that there was no occasion to express an opinion with respect to intelligence activities of foreign powers and their agents.[53] He left open, however, the possibility that Congress might establish special procedures for security cases, different from those prescribed for ordinary cases.[54] Justice Douglas, although joining in Justice Powell's opinion, added an opinion of his own to emphasize the dangers of abuse inherent in such surveillance, saying, "We have as much or more to fear from the erosion of our sense of privacy and independence by the omnipresent electronic ear of the Government as we do from the likelihood that fomenters of domestic upheavel will modify our form of governing."[55] Justice Brandeis would, I believe, have been quite content with Justice Powell's opinion.

Before leaving the fourth amendment, I should at least mention the decision this past term in *Marshall v. Barlow's, Inc.*,[56] holding that an inspector for the Occupational Safety and Health Administration must obtain a search warrant instead of following the statutory procedure of first demanding entrance to a factory site for inspection purposes and then securing a compulsory court order if entrance is denied. Here the choice between the procedures established by the statute and those required by the Court is such a fine one that I am myself inclined to the dissenting view, expressed by Mr. Justice Stevens, that the judgment of Congress should have prevailed.[57] The majority view, insisting on the warrant requirement yet indicating that a warrant may issue simply on a showing that the proposed search was pursuant to a reasonable administrative program of regular inspection,[58] seems to add nothing of substance to the statutory requirement. It also trivializes the constitutional requirement that "no warrants shall issue but upon probable cause, supported by oath or affirmation, and particularly describing the place to be searched and the persons or things to be seized."[59] Having stated my preference—more as a teacher of administrative law

---

statutory grounds, and Chief Justice Burger concurred only in the result, without further explanation. *Id.* at 324, 335.

52. *Id.* at 320-21.
53. *Id.* at 322 n.20.
54. *Id.* at 323.
55. *Id.* at 333 (Douglas, J., concurring).
56. 436 U.S. 307 (1978).
57. *Id.* at 338-39 (Stevens, J., dissenting).
58. *Id.* at 320-21.
59. U.S. CONST. amend IV.

than a Brandeis disciple—I could add without fear of successful contradiction that the Justice would have felt the same way. But in truth, I would have more confidence in postulating that, however Justice Brandeis would have voted, he would have accepted either result without bothering to register a dissent. Despite their reputation as the great dissenters, Holmes and Brandeis husbanded their fire and did not dissent every time they were outvoted.

It is even more important to notice that the *Olmstead* case also involved the possible application of the exclusionary rule, irrespective of the scope of the fourth amendment protection, because the wiretap was clearly carried out in violation of state law. As Brandeis summarized his position:

> Independently of the constitutional question, I am of the opinion that the judgment should be reversed. By the laws of Washington, wire-tapping is a crime. . . . To prove its case, the Government was obliged to lay bare the crimes committed by its officers on its behalf. A federal court should not permit such a prosecution to continue.[60]

It was this part of the Brandeis dissent in which Mr. Justice Holmes joined, rather than in the part concerning the fourth amendment.[61] It also seems not at all unlikely that this was the part about which Brandeis cared most. This is suggested both by his whole philosophy of good government and by the concluding paragraph of the opinion:

> Decency, security and liberty alike demand that government officials shall be subjected to the same rules of conduct that are commands to the citizen. In a government of laws, existence of the government will be imperilled if it fails to observe the law scrupulously. Our Government is the potent, the omnipresent teacher. For good or for ill, it teaches the whole people by its example. Crime is contagious. If the Government becomes a lawbreaker, it breeds contempt for law; it invites every man to become a law unto himself; it invites anarchy. To declare that . . . the end justifies the means—to declare that the Government may commit crimes in order to secure the conviction of a private criminal—would bring terrible retribution. Against that pernicious doctrine this Court should resolutely set its face.[62]

In the light of that statement, can we have any doubt where Brandeis would stand in the current debate on the value of the exclusionary rule—a debate stirred in part at least by Chief Justice Burger's critique of the rule in his dissenting opinion in *Bivens v. Six Unknown Named Agents*?[63] Curiously enough, when I first wrote that sentence I was pretty sure that I knew what the answer was: Of course the Justice

---

60. 277 U.S. at 479-80 (Brandeis, J., dissenting).
61. *Id.* at 469-70 (Holmes, J., dissenting).
62. *Id.* at 485 (Brandeis, J., dissenting).
63. 403 U.S. 388, 411-27 (1971) (Burger, C.J., dissenting).

would still be resolute. Now, after studying and thinking about the question a little more, I am not so sure. This is not so much because Chief Justice Burger quoted the famous, incredulous statement of Judge Cardozo, speaking for a unanimous New York Court of Appeals: "The criminal is to go free because the constable has blundered."[64] Brandeis must have been aware that this was the attitude not only of the New York Court of Appeals, but also of his own State of Massachusetts and many other states. Presumably his conviction was not shaken by the disagreement. He might have been more concerned, however, by the more recent doubts and concerns expressed by scholars and judges, including Judge Henry Friendly, one of the most distinguished of his surviving law clerks. But he would have noticed that Judge Friendly's disagreement is carefully qualified as indicated by the following passage:

> There is still solid sense in Chief Judge Cardozo's doubt whether the criminal should "go free because the constable has blundered", if only we would have the grace to read him as meaning exactly what he said. The beneficent aim of the exclusionary rule to deter police misconduct can be sufficiently accomplished by a practice, such as that in Scotland, outlawing evidence obtained by flagrant or deliberate violation of rights. It is no sufficient objection that such a rule would require courts to make still another determination; rather, the recognition of a penumbral zone where mistake will not call for the drastic remedy of exclusion would relieve them of exceedingly difficult decisions whether an officer overstepped the sometimes almost imperceptible line between a valid arrest or search and an invalid one. Even if there were an added burden, most judges would prefer to discharge it than have to perform the distasteful duty of allowing a dangerous criminal to go free because of a slight and unintentional miscalculation by the police.[65]

Obviously this qualified criticism would not apply to *Olmstead* where the police conduct was clearly in violation of state law.

Brandeis would also notice that the empirical evidence on the beneficial effectiveness of the exclusionary rule is at best inconclusive. There are some authorities who believe that it is the best deterrent to unlawful police behavior, and others who believe that it is substantially ineffective.[66] Above all, if the Justice were to reconsider his position, he would want to know as much as possible about the facts. As he once said in a dissenting opinion in a case involving regulation of the

---

64. *Id.* at 413 (quoting People v. Defore, 242 N.Y. 13, 21, 150 N.E. 585, 587 (1926)).
65. Friendly, *The Bill of Rights as a Code of Criminal Procedure*, 53 CALIF. L. REV. 929, 951-53 (1965).
66. *See generally* Amsterdam, *Prospectives on the Fourth Amendment*, 58 MINN. L. REV. 429-39 (1974); Kamisar, *A Defense of the Exclusionary Rule*, 15 CRIM. L. BULL. 5 (1979); La Fave, *Improving Police Performance through the Exclusionary Rule*, 30 MO. L. REV. 391, 566 (1965); Oaks, *Studying the Exclusionary Rule in Search and Seizure*, 37 U. CHI. L. REV. 665 (1967).

weights of bread, "Sometimes, if we would guide by the light of reason, we must let our minds be bold. But in this case we have merely to acquaint ourselves with the art of breadmaking and the usages of the trade . . . ."[67] I am not suggesting that the efficacy of the exclusionary rule is as factually determinable as the art of breadmaking, but once the question were reopened, I have no doubt the Justice would want to know as much as possible about the modern problem of crime and the state of the art of law enforcement.

Finally, I think there are some other aspects of the surrounding law to take into account before making up our minds about the viability of the *Olmstead* dissent in modern times. Brandeis was writing before the great era of the constitutionalizing of the law of criminal procedure; before the incorporation of most of the Bill of Rights into the due process clause; before *Wolf v. Colorado*,[68] holding that the core of the fourth amendment is implicit in the concept of ordered liberty and therefore enforceable against the states through the due process clause; and before *Mapp v. Ohio*,[69] holding that this enforceability included the exclusionary rule. How Brandeis would have reacted to these decisions is a much harder question.[70] Remember that the Brandeis dissent in *New State Ice Company* also included this famous sentence: "It is one of the happy incidents of the federal system that a single courageous state may, if its citizens choose, serve as a laboratory; and try novel social and economic experiments without risk to the rest of the country."[71] In other words, Brandeis was a true believer in the virtues of federalism—that is, of real local self-government. He might have believed profoundly in the wisdom of the exclusionary rule and yet refused to compel its adoption by the states under the authority of the due process clause, just as he believed profoundly in the virtues of competiton and yet refused to enforce it against the states under the guise of due process in *New State Ice Company*.

One other modern aspect of the law relating to the exclusionary rule should have been taken into account before summing up the balance sheet on *Olmstead* in modern dress. At the time Brandeis wrote his dissent, there was no effective remedy against federal police officers violating the fourth amendment other than the exclusionary rule, and not much of a remedy against state officers. Since then, we have had the decision in *Monroe v. Pape*,[72] upholding a federal cause of action for unlawful search against state officers under section 1983;[73] the deci-

---

67. Jay Burns Baking Co. v. Bryan, 264 U.S. 504, 520 (1923) (Brandeis, J., dissenting).
68. 338 U.S. 25 (1949).
69. 367 U.S. 643 (1961).
70. Mr. Justice Frankfurter, Brandeis's surrogate on the Court, if he had one, wrote the opinion for the Court in *Wolf*, but dissented in *Mapp*.
71. 285 U.S. at 311 (Brandeis, J., dissenting).
72. 365 U.S. 167 (1971).
73. 42 U.S.C. § 1983 (1977).

sion in *Bivens*,[74] creating a similar federal cause of action against federal officers; and just this past term, the decision in *Monell v. Department of Social Services*,[75] holding that New York City may be liable for unlawful actions of its officers when authorized or condoned by the City.

I mention all of these somewhat peripheral considerations simply to emphasize what a dangerous game we play when we undertake to apply literally the wisdom of yesteryear to the problems of our time. That is why I am no longer sure as I thought I was when I first asked the question: If Brandeis could advise us today, would he still be resolute in defense of the exclusionary rule? Nevertheless, having been foolish enough to ask the question, I suppose I must have the temerity to answer it. The short answer is: Yes, I think he would be, subject perhaps to the qualification that Judge Friendly has suggested.

II. THE RIGHT OF SELF-DEVELOPMENT

A. Due Process

In speaking of the right to privacy, I have so far confined myself to the earlier strict meaning of the term, in the context of either a possible tort action or the protections of the fourth and fifth amendments. Since then, its usages have ballooned in a way that might have surprised even Brandeis. Consider, for example, Mr. Justice Douglas's development of the concept of privacy in *Griswold v. Connecticut*[76] as a penumbra emanating from nearly the whole of the Bill of Rights, with particular emphasis on the first, fourth, fifth, and even ninth amendments. This new use of the term, as well as the strained application of the concept to the right of abortion, seems to belong more under the general title that I have chosen for this lecture, The Right of Self-Development, or what Professor Freund has called the "theme of personhood."[77]

The *Griswold* case involved the application of a Connecticut statute prohibiting the use of birth control devices to a physician who prescribed them for use by a married couple. Mr. Justice Douglas, in his opinion for the Court, emphasizes the marital aspects of the relationship as well as its privacy saying:

> We deal with a right of privacy older than the Bill of Rights— older than our political parties, older than our school system. Marriage is a coming together for better or worse, hopefully enduring and intimate, to the degree of being sacred. It is an association that promotes a way of life, not causes, a harmony in living, not political faiths, a bilateral loyalty, not commercial or social projects. Yet it is an association for as noble a purpose as any

---

74. Bivens v. Six Unknown Named Agents, 403 U.S. 388 (1971).
75. 436 U.S. 658 (1978).
76. Griswold v. Connecticut, 381 U.S. 479 (1965).
77. Address by Professor Freund, 52 ALI PROCEEDINGS 568, 574 (1975).

involved in our prior decisions.[78]

Apart from its rhetoric, this passage suggests the intellectual framework into which Justice Douglas was putting the *Griswold* case. In his mind it was comparable to— but even stronger than—the case of *NAACP v. Alabama*,[79] in which the Court had protected the membership records of the NAACP from compulsory disclosure by the state, in the absence of a showing of some substantial public interest to be served by such disclosure. There, the opinion for the Court by Mr. Justice Harlan based its holding upon the due process clause of the fourteenth amendment, assuming that "freedom to engage in association for the advancement of beliefs and ideas"[80] was at stake. In other words, this was the kind of freedom protected by the first amendment, and incorporated into the liberty protected by the due process clause of the fourteenth amendment as one of "the specific pledges of particular amendments . . . found to be implicit in the concept of ordered liberty."[81] Such, at least, was the reasoning of Mr. Justice Harlan in the *NAACP* case. Whether it was also the reasoning of Justice Douglas in *Griswold* is more problematic. On its face, Justice Douglas's opinion seems to be suggesting that, if the privacy of association for political purposes is protected by the first amendment, so too must privacy of association for marital purposes by similarly protected. The analogy is, I believe, less than compelling.

Justice Harlan's concurring opinion in *Griswold*,[82] incorporating by reference his previous dissenting opinion in *Poe v. Ullman*,[83] is, I believe, more direct and satisfying. He too postulates a right to privacy in marital relationships—particularly the intimacies of sexual relationships—but he finds that right directly in the liberty protected by the due process clause of the fourteenth amendment.[84] According to Justice Harlan's understanding of the due process clause

> it is not the particular enumeration of rights in the first eight Amendments which spells out the reach of Fourteenth Amendment due process, but rather . . . those concepts which are considered to embrace those rights "which are . . . *fundamental*; which belong . . . to the citizens of all free governments" for "the purposes [of securing] which men enter into society."
>
> Due process has not been reduced to any formula; its content cannot be determined by reference to any code. The best that can be said is that through the course of this Court's decisions it has

---

78. 381 U.S. at 486.
79. 357 U.S. 449 (1958).
80. *Id.* at 460.
81. Palko v. Connecticut, 302 U.S. 319, 325 (1937).
82. 381 U.S. 479, 499 (1965) (Harlan, J., concurring).
83. 367 U.S. 497, 522 (1961) (Harlan, J., dissenting).
84. He puts it most succinctly when he says: "I believe that a statute making it a criminal offense for *married couples* to use contraceptives is an intolerable and unjustifiable invasion of privacy in the conduct of the most intimate concerns of an individual's personal life." *Id.* at 539.

represented the balance which our Nation, built upon postulates of respect for the liberty of the individual, has struck between that liberty and the demands of organized society.[85]

I have always thought that the foregoing passage and others like it from the dissenting opinion of Justice Harlan in *Poe v. Ullman* provide a more satisfactory rationale for the decision in *Griswold* than the rationalizations of Justice Douglas's opinion for the Court. Naturally enough, I am also inclined to believe that Brandeis would have taken a similar view. Apart from this purely subjective reaction, I think there is some objective evidence to support my guess. The Douglas opinion was, in my view, a labored attempt to avoid direct reliance upon the due process clause alone—a reliance that would necessarily accord due process a substantive, as well as procedural, content. It was also an attempt to avoid the impact of Justice Black's dissenting opinion insisting that the Court's decision was simply another instance of reading the personal prejudices of the judges into the due process clause—an exercise no more entitled to respect than the discredited freedom of contract cases stretching from *Lochner v. New York*[86] to *New State Ice Company v. Liebmann*.[87] Brandeis, on the other hand, would not have been intimidated by this line of attack. Despite his own personal doubt, expressed in his concurring opinion in *Whitney v. California*,[88] that the due process clause was originally intended to have any substantive content at all, and even though many of his great dissents were directed against the abuse of the due process clause as a protector of substantive rights, Brandeis did not hesitate to give it substantive content when his own sense of justice, or rather injustice, was deeply offended.

Consider, for example, Brandeis's opinion for the Court in *Nashville, Chatanooga and St. Louis Railway v. Walters*,[89] holding that the state supreme court had erred in refusing to consider as relevant to the due process question proof of special facts designed to establish that it was arbitrary and unreasonable to require a railroad to bear half the cost of constructing an underpass required by the state. The special facts presented by the railroad to sustain this position were that the underpass was prescribed as part of a national system of federal aid to

---

85. 367 U.S. at 541-42.
   Justice Harlan went on to say:
   the supplying of content to this Constitutional concept has of necessity been a rational process, it certainly has not been one where judges have felt free to roam where unguided speculation might take them. The balance of which I speak is the balance struck by this country, having regard to what history teaches are the traditions from which it developed as well as the traditions from which it broke. That tradition is a living thing. A decision of this Court which radically departs from it could not long survive, while a decision which builds on what has survived is likely to be sound. No formula could serve as a substitute, in this area, for judgment and restraint.
   Id. at 542.
86. 198 U.S. 45 (1905).
87. 285 U.S. 262 (1932).
88. 274 U.S. 357, 372 (1927) (Brandeis, J., concurring).
89. 294 U.S. 405 (1935).

highways for the furtherance of motor vehicle traffic, much of which consisted of motor carriers in direct competition with the railroad; that the increase in such traffic would greatly decrease rail traffic and deplete the revenue of the railroad company; and that the amount of taxes paid by the railroads of the state, part of which was devoted to the upkeep of public highways used by motor carriers, was disproportionately higher than the amount paid by motor carriers. Surely if the spectacle of a railroad being forced to contribute to the success of a competing mode of transportation was sufficient to offend the Justice's sense of injustice and so qualify for the protection of property under the due process clause, the same could be said for the liberty of married couples to determine for themselves whether to practice birth control. Whether the Justice would have followed the Court in its next step, in effect extending the same freedom to unmarried persons, is a somewhat harder question.[90] There is evidence that in sexual morals the Justice was an archconservative, but I think there is also reason to believe that he would have distinguished constitutionally between moral questions involving only consenting adults and those involving harm to third parties.

My principal point is that Brandeis would have been more comfortable with the Harlan opinions in *Poe v. Ullman* and *Griswold* than with that of Douglas in *Griswold*, because the Harlan approach was more consistent with the law Brandeis helped to make when he joined the opinions for the Court in *Meyer v. Nebraska*,[91] and *Pierce v. Society of Sisters*,[92] and when he wrote the opinion in the *Nashville* case.[93] It is also relevant that, in his procedural due process opinions, the Justice did not hesitate to accord a higher degree of protection to personal rights as distinguished from property rights.[94] Finally, I believe that Brandeis would have had more intellectual respect for Justice Harlan's willingness to admit and to struggle candidly with the elements of judgment involved in his approach than for the attempts of some members of the Court to paper over those elements with a parade of absolutes.

I suppose that the most controversial application of the constitutional doctrine of privacy in the extended sense is to be found in the abortion cases, and surely it would be cowardly to avoid subjecting that application to the Brandeisian telescope and microscope—if I may be excused for stealing a Hughes metaphor. You may recall that Justice Blackmun, in his opinion for the Court in *Roe v. Wade*,[95] after summa-

---

90. *See* Eisenstadt v. Baird, 405 U.S. 438 (1972).
91. 262 U.S. 390 (1923) (invalidating prohibition against teaching of German language in private elementary schools).
92. 268 U.S. 510 (1925) (invalidating statute prohibiting private elementary schools).
93. *See* notes 90-91 *supra*.
94. *See, e.g.*, St. Joseph Stockyards Co. v. United States, 298 U.S. 38 (1936); Crowell v. Benson, 285 U.S. 22 (1932); Ng Fung Ho v. White, 259 U.S. 276 (1922).
95. 410 U.S. 113 (1973).

rizing the constitutional background, states quite categorically:

> This right of privacy, whether it be founded in the Fourteenth Amendment's concept of personal liberty and restrictions upon state action, as we feel it is, or as the District Court determined in the Ninth Amendment's reservation of rights to the people, is broad enough to encompass a woman's decision whether or not to terminate her pregnancy.[96]

I need hardly tell you that this was not the end, but the beginning of the crucial inquiry. Just as Holmes and Brandeis would have agreed that "freedom of contract" was part of the "liberty" protected by the due process clause of the fourteenth amendment, without committing themselves to the result of the *Lochner* case and its progeny, so too they could agree that the decision of the pregnant mother to abort or not to abort was part of the same liberty, without committing themselves to the result in *Roe v. Wade*. The crucial question in each case is not what is liberty, but what is due process of law.

We all know that a respectable body of scholarly opinion holds the view that the decision in *Roe v. Wade*, giving the mother alone the absolute right to insist upon an abortion within the first six months of pregnancy, was indeed a replay of *Lochner* in modern dress.[97] I do not entirely share that view, and perhaps I should take a moment to tell you why, so that you will at least understand my bias. I do not especially sympathize with the claim that it is exclusively the pregnant woman's right to determine whether she shall continue to bear and give birth to a child, irrespective of the interests of the father, the unborn child, or society as a whole. Neither do I especially sympathize with the "right to life" enthusiasts who insist that the right of the unborn child to fulfill its destiny of birth, if physically possible, is determinative. Rather I incline to the view that it is the obligation of society to make a rational judgment with appropriate regard for the interests of the mother, the father (if known), the child, and society as a whole.

If you think that this is too mushy a resolution to deserve serious consideration, I will give you a few examples where I am perfectly clear as to what the result should be. I will start with the clearest case I can think of—the case of the girl who becomes pregnant as a result of rape by her drunken stepfather.[98] From there I can go gradually down the ladder of certainty, stopping, for example, with the case of the irresponsible girl of 12 years old who quite voluntarily, but ignorantly, engages in promiscuous sexual relations and then becomes pregnant, without

---

96. *Id.* at 153.
97. *See, e.g.*, Ely, *The Wages of Crying Wolf: A Comment on Roe v. Wade*, 82 YALE L.J. 920 (1973).
98. This might be called the "Peyton Place Case" in honor of the heroine of that novel who was subsequently relieved of her pregnancy by her friend, the Catholic doctor, in a Catholic hospital, operating in the dead of night under the pretense that he was performing an emergency appendectomy.

any idea of who the father is; or the case of the married couple with ten children, the father unemployed and ill, the mother unskilled except in household duties, who rather unexpectedly and adventitiously have sexual relations which result in pregnancy. In all of these situations, abortion would have been unlawful under the Texas statute involved in *Roe v. Wade*. Yet in every one of them, is it not apparent that the interest most in need of protection is that of the unborn child? And, in the absence of anyone better qualified to represent that interest, should it not be represented by the parents to be, assuming that they can be identified and are responsible individuals? I appreciate that in all of these situations and a myriad of others, the considerations pointing toward abortion may be over-balanced by profound religious convictions, but surely it should be the religious convictions of the parents or their surrogates, not those of a majority of the state legislature that should be determinative. I also believe that a Brandeis brief—in the tradition of the famous Brandeis brief in *Muller v. Oregon*[99]— could be written to establish the pernicious effects of the abortion statutes in all the situations I have stated, even though the brief in *Muller* was written to sustain, not to undermine, the maximum hours law involved there.[100]

Perhaps I should add another word about the abortion cases. I realize that much of the technique of decision in those cases might be regarded as antithetical to the well-known Brandeis philosophy of judicial self-restraint, so well delineated in Professor Freund's essays about the Justice.[101] It might be suggested, for example, that none of the horrendous examples that I chose was presented by the cases before the Court. This may be true, but it is also pertinent to note that the effect of anti-abortion statutes was to close legitimate avenues of medical relief to all these cases which did not come within the exceptions explicitly authorized by the statute. It would hardly do justice to insist that the victim of rape must find a doctor willing to violate the statute, in order to challenge its validity; or even to insist that the victim must show she cannot get a doctor to help her, in order to qualify for injunctive or declaratory relief. In fact, this last position was substantially that taken by the Court in *Poe v. Ullman*, in refusing to rule on the validity of the Connecticut birth control act, against a background of substantial nonenforcement and widespread violation of the statute. Widespread violation was hardly the effect of anti-abortion statutes in legitimate medical circles. Consequently, whatever might be thought of the merits of the *Poe v. Ullman* principle, it should surely not be applied as strictly in the abortion situation. How far it should be relaxed is a much harder question. I incline to the view that, in a situa-

---

99.   208 U.S. 412 (1908).
100.   For a synopsis of Brandeis's brief, see 52 L. Ed. 553 (1926).
101.   P. FREUND, *supra* note 33, at 57-59. *See also* Brandeis's concurring opinion in *Ashwander v. Tennessee Valley Authority* (1936).

tion involving important personal rights that cannot stand still for
ultimate vindication, a showing that the plaintiffs do not come within
the specific exemptions of the statute should be sufficient to test the
validity of the statute on its face and with respect to the most extreme
of its possible applications. Whether Justice Brandeis would agree with
me that far, I frankly doubt; he might be so faithful to his principles of
judicial self-restraint as to insist on seeing each of my postulated hard
cases presented in reality before ruling on the validity of the statute as
so applied. Certainly he would have difficulty with the broad legislative sweep of Justice Blackmun's opinion, outlining the appropriate
scope of future legislation. Whether this is a desirable kind of constitutional adjudication opens a whole vista of problems of judicial philosophy that I hesitate to embark upon within the ambit of these lectures.

B.   Freedom of Speech

Now I come to what might have been my starting point if I had
been talking about Justice Holmes, and not Justice Brandeis, and civil
liberties—namely, the first amendment, freedom of speech, and the
clear and present danger test. Of course, Brandeis participated in all
the World War I cases made famous primarily by the opinions of Justice Holmes—some opinions for the Court and some dissenting opinions. In most of these, Brandeis simply followed Holmes's lead, joining
in the opinions of the Court when Holmes wrote them and concurring
in Holmes's dissents. These included the opinion for a unanimous
Court in *Shenck v. United States*,[102] in which the clear and present danger test was first enunciated, but applied to sustain a conviction under
the Espionage Act of 1917 for circulating a pamphlet intended to ob-
struct the recruiting service. This was followed by similar Holmes
opinions for the Court sustaining similar convictions in *Frohwerk v.
United States*[103] and *Debs v. United States*.[104] Shortly thereafter came
the great Holmes dissent in *Abrams v. United States*[105] and several
years later, the Holmes dissent in *Gitlow v. New York*,[106] both of which
Brandeis also joined. I must leave to others the pleasure of analyzing
these opinions and exploring the question whether these opinions are
consistent with one another or whether Holmes and Brandeis changed
their minds while paying lipservice to the same principle. In two of the
World War I Espionage Act cases, however, Brandeis did write dissenting opinions for both himself and Justice Holmes: *Schaefer v. United
States*[107] and *Pierce v. United States*.[108] It was as though Holmes, hav-

---

102.   249 U.S. 47 (1919).
103.   249 U.S. 204 (1919).
104.   249 U.S. 211 (1919).
105.   250 U.S. 616 (1919).
106.   268 U.S. 652 (1925).
107.   251 U.S. 466 (1920).
108.   252 U.S. 239 (1920).

ing stated the general principle, left it to his junior to develop the details.

In *Schaefer,* Brandeis first quoted the principles of *Shenck* that the Court must determine "whether the words . . . create a clear and present danger that they will bring about the substantive evils that Congress has a right to prevent."[109] Then he added his own exegesis saying:

> This is a rule of reason. Correctly applied it will preserve the right of free speech both from suppression by tyrannous, well-meaning majorities and from abuse by irresponsible, fanatical minorities. Like many other rules for human conduct, it can be applied correctly only by the exercise of good judgment; and to the exercise of good judgment, calmness is, in times of deep feeling and on subjects which excite passion, as essential as fearlessness and honesty.[110]

But it was not until the famous concurring opinion in *Whitney v. California*[111] that Brandeis seized the opportunity to develop fully his own philosophy of the clear and present danger test. In order to examine that philosophy, it is necessary to quote a few familiar passages.

> Those who won our independence believed that the final end of the State was to make men free to develop their faculties; and that in its government the deliberative forces should prevail over the arbitrary. They valued liberty both as an end and as a means. They believed liberty to be the secret of happiness and courage to be the secret of liberty. They believed that freedom to think as you will and to speak as you think are means indispensable to the discovery and spread of political truth; that without free speech and assembly discussion would be futile; that with them, discussion affords ordinarily adequate protection against the dissemination of noxious doctrine; that the greatest menace to freedom is an inert people; that public discussion is a political duty; and that this should be a fundamental principle of the American government. They recognized the risks to which all human institutions are subject. But they knew that order cannot be secured merely through fear of punishment for its infraction; that it is hazardous to dis-

---

109. 251 U.S. at 482 (Brandeis, J., dissenting).
110. *Id.* at 482-83.
  Brandeis's opinions dealing with anti-war propaganda during World War I should not be construed as indicating any lack of support by Brandeis for our participation in that War. As a matter of fact, he was so intimately involved in advising Wilson with respect to industrial organization on the home front that Wilson asked him whether he could take a leave of absence from the Court to assume active direction of the labor front. When he replied that he could not do that, but offered to resign from the Court instead, Wilson wisely refused the offer, saying in effect: "We had to work too hard to get you there in the first place, to let you step down now." He was also obviously proud that his brother was working at a dollar a year in Washington. At the same time, Brandeis was involved behind the scenes in helping to organize a Jewish medical unit and a Jewish fighting unit for Palestine. *See* MASON, *supra* note 11, at 518-26.
111. 274 U.S. 357 (1926).

courage thought, hope and imagination; that fear breeds repression; that repression breeds hate; that hate menaces stable government; that the path of safety lies in the opportunity to discuss freely supposed grievances and proposed remedies; and that the fitting remedy for evil counsels is good ones. Believing in the power of reason as applied through public discussion, they eschewed silence coerced by law—the argument of force in its worst form. Recognizing the occasional tyrannies of governing majorities, they amended the Constitution so that free speech and assembly should be guaranteed.

Those who won our independence by revolution were not cowards. They did not fear political change. They did not exalt order at the cost of liberty. To courageous, self-reliant men, with confidence in the power of free and fearless reasoning applied through the processes of popular government, no danger flowing from speech can be deemed clear and present, unless the incidence of the evil apprehended is so imminent that it may befall before there is opportunity for full discussion. If there be time to expose through discussion the falsehood and fallacies, to avert the evil by the processes of education, the remedy to be applied is more speech, not enforced silence. Only an emergency can justify repression. Such must be the rule if authority is to be reconciled with freedom. Such, in my opinion, is the command of the Constitution. It is therefore always open to Americans to challenge a law abridging free speech and assembly by showing that there was no emergency justifying it.[112]

These passages seem to indicate that, although *Whitney*, strictly speaking, was a fourteenth amendment case and not a first amendment case, Brandeis did not hesitate to rely directly on the language of the first amendment. In addition, the emphasis is on the role of freedom of speech in a participatory democracy—freedom of speech is not merely a right; "public discussion is a political duty." Finally, to justify interference with such a right and duty, not only must the danger be imminent, it must be "relatively serious."[113]

---

112. *Id.* at 375-76, 377 (Brandeis, J., concurring).
113. *Id.* at 377-78.
    Curiously enough, this was not a dissenting but a concurring opinion because Miss Whitney did not specifically claim that there was no clear and present danger of serious evil, and because "there was other testimony which tended to establish the existence of a conspiracy on the part of the Industrial Workers of the World to commit present serious crimes, and likewise to show that such a conspiracy would be furthered by the activity of the society of which Miss Whitney was a member." *Id.* at 379. The point is also made that, because the case came up on review from a state court, "power of review is limited to . . . the particular claims duly made below." *Id.* at 380. Thus we are denied the opportunity of examining the *Whitney* case as an example of how Holmes and Brandeis would have applied the clear and present danger test to the actual situation. We are told only that they are "unable to assent to the suggestion in the opinion of the Court that assembling with a political party, formed to advocate the desirability of a proletarian revolution by mass action necessarily far in the future, is not a right within the protection of the Fourteenth Amendment." *Id.* at 379.

The clear and present danger test seemed to reach its heyday during the decade following Brandeis's retirement from the Court. It was applied, however, in situations far removed from the seditious utterances or political organization cases which gave it birth. These cases involved, for example, ordinances to prevent the littering of public streets;[114] license requirements of solicitation of charitable contributions;[115] registration of union leaders;[116] and imposition of contempt of court penalties for newspaper comments interfering with the administration of justice.[117]

Not until the decision in *Dennis v. United States*[118] did the Court again come face to face with the kind of seditious utterance and organization case which gave birth to the clear and present danger doctrine. The result was that the doctrine was watered down to apply to a situation where the danger was admittedly neither "clear" nor "present," as those words are ordinarily understood. The statute involved, the Smith Act, was basically a federal version of the same type of state statutes that were involved in the *Gitlow* and *Whitney* cases—a statute making it a crime to teach the duty, desirability, necessity, or propriety of overthrowing or destroying any government in the United States by force or violence, or to organize a party to teach that doctrine. By a vote of six-to-two, with Justices Black and Douglas dissenting, the Court sustained the validity of the statute and affirmed convictions of a member of the leaders of the Communist Party. However, there was no majority agreement upon an opinion for the Court, and we are left at sea if we search for the principle or ratio decidendi of the case.

The plurality opinion, delivered by Chief Justice Vinson, purported to adopt the "clear and present danger" test, but did so together with an interpretation first formulated by Judge Learned Hand writing for the court of appeals in affirming the convictions.[119] Justice Frank-

---

114. Schneider v. State, 308 U.S. 147 (1939).
115. Cantwell v. Connecticut, 310 U.S. 296 (1940).
116. Thomas v. Collins, 323 U.S. 516 (1945).
117. Craig v. Harvey, 331 U.S. 367 (1947).
   Professor Paul Freund, commenting upon this variety of uses, said:
   The truth is that the clear and present danger test is an oversimplified judgment unless it takes account also of a number of other factors: the relative seriousness of the danger in comparison with the value of the occasion for speech or political activity; the availability of more moderate controls than those which the state has imposed; and perhaps the specific intent with which the speech or activity is launched. No matter how rapidly we utter the phrase "clear and present danger", or how closely we hyphenate the words, they are not a substitute for the weighing of values. They tend to convey a delusion of certitude when what is most certain is the complexity of the strands in the web of freedoms which the judge must disentangle.
P. FREUND, *supra* note 33, at 27-28.
118. 341 U.S. 494 (1951).
119. Judge Hand's words were: "In each case [we] must ask whether the gravity of the 'evil', discounted by its improbability, justifies such invasion of free speech as is necessary to avoid the danger." United States v. Dennis, 183 F.2d 201, 212 (1950). The application of that test was summarized by Chief Justice Vinson in these words:
   The formation by the petitioners of such a highly organized conspiracy with rigidly disci-

furter, concurring, emphasized the respect that was due legislative judgment regarding the extent of the danger.[120] But, in determining the extent of that respect, he added: "We may take judicial notice that the Communist doctrines which these defendants have conspired to advocate are in the ascendancy in powerful nations who cannot be acquitted of unfriendliness to the institutions of this country."[121] In essence, Justice Frankfurter's test is not, I think, significantly different from the Hand-Vinson version of the clear and present danger test, although he was determined not to use the same words.

Justice Jackson's concurring opinion took the position that the clear and present danger test had no application to the case because that test was developed in cases "all arising before the era of World War II revealed the subtlety and efficacy of modernized revolutionary techniques used by totalitarian parties."[122] He would save the test "for application as a rule of reason in the kind of case for which it was devised."[123] This was not such a case because the Communist Party in America and elsewhere had become a well-organized conspiracy to accomplish its ultimate objective of undermining the Government of the United States. Justice Jackson's version of the case had a great deal of popular appeal. It conformed to the general image of the Communist Party built up at the trial and by the House Un-American Activities Committee hearing.[124]

I think the most pertinent answer to Justice Jackson was presented in the dissenting opinion of Justice Douglas.[125] He pointed out that the defendants were not being tried for conspiring to overthrow the Government, to commit acts of sabotage, to filch government documents, to plant bombs, or the like. That might be the popular image of the Communist Party and it might to some extent conform to the facts, but that was not the gravamen of the charge, nor was evidence introduced to support it. The alleged conspiracy was to teach the desirability and duty of overthrowing the government by force or violence, as defined in

---

plined members subject to call when the leaders, these petitioners, felt that the time had come for action, coupled with the inflammable nature of world conditions, similar uprisings in other countries, and the touch-and-go nature of our relations with countries with whom petitioners were in the very least ideologically attuned, convince us that their convictions were justified on this score.
341 U.S. at 510-11.

120. 341 U.S. at 550-51 (Frankfurter, J., concurring). He was unwilling to accept Judge Hand's rewriting of the clear and present danger test because it seemed "to make the validity of legislation depend on a judicial reading of events still in the womb of time—a forecast, that is, of the outcome of forces at best appreciated only with knowledge of the top most secrets of nations is to charge the judiciary with duties beyond its equipment." *Id.* at 551.

121. *Id.* at 547.

122. *Id.* at 567 (Jackson, J., concurring).

123. *Id.* at 568.

124. *See* Nathanson, *The Communist Threat and the Clear and Present Danger Test*, 63 HARV. L. REV. 1167 (1950), and Nathanson, *Freedom of Association and the Quest for Internal Security: Conspiracy from Dennis to Dr. Spock*, 65 Nw. L. REV. 153 (1970).

125. 341 U.S. at 581 (Douglas, J., dissenting).

the Smith Act. Had the government wished to charge a different kind of conspiracy, it could have done so and found a statute much older than the Smith Act to conform to Justice Jackson's version of the facts. I found Justice Douglas's dissent convincing at the time, and it still seems so to me. I believe that Brandeis would have been of the same opinion. His tough-mindedness and his insistence on looking closely at the facts would have exposed the difference between Jackson's general view of the Party and what was going on in this particular trial. If the Government really wished to convict the defendants of conspiring to overthrow the United States government, or even conspiring to interfere with the enforcement of its laws, Brandeis might have required the Government to make that charge and to assume the much more difficult burden of proving it.

The *Dennis* decision has never been overruled, yet its effects were practically undermined by Justice Harlan's opinion for the Court in *Yates v. United States.*[126] In abstract terms, Justice Harlan's opinion was not significantly different from that of Chief Justice Vinson in *Dennis*. He emphasized that, to pass constitutional muster, the statute must forbid not merely advocacy of the doctrine of the desirability of overthrowing the government of the United States, but also advocacy of action to accomplish that end, even if that action was to be deferred considerably. The problem was how the Government might prove the advocacy of action rather than the advocacy of doctrine. The test of the pudding was in the eating. On examination of the record, Justice Harlan found plenty of advocacy of doctrine, but precious little advocacy of action. Apparently, the requirements of proof were so stringent as to make further enforcement of the Smith Act impracticable. The Government abandoned further prosecution of Communist Party leaders, and the Smith Act became a dead letter. For the practical preservation of civil liberties, this was presumably a happy conclusion. For those of us primarily in search of governing principles, it tells very little.

The next step in the evolution of the clear and present danger test is almost equally opaque. It is the per curiam opinion of the Court, coupled with concurring opinions by Justices Black and Douglas, in *Brandenburg v. Ohio.*[127] The Ohio statute involved[128] was substantially the same as the statutes involved in *Whitney* and essentially similar to the statute involved in *Gitlow* and *Dennis*. The particular prosecution was directed against a speaker at a Ku Klux Klan meeting where a cross was burned; the speech was imperfectly recorded but it plainly included derogatory and threatening remarks directed at Negroes and Jews. The Court's opinion was directed entirely to the invalidity of the

126. 354 U.S. 298 (1957).
127. 395 U.S. 444 (1969).
128. Law of July 1, 1955, § 2923.13, 126 Laws of Ohio 580 (repealed 1974).

statute on its face. The decision in *Whitney*, the Court said, had been discredited thoroughly by later decisions, such as *Dennis* and *Yates*.

These later decisions have fashioned the principle that the constitutional guarantees of free speech and free press do not permit a State to forbid or proscribe advocacy of the use of force or of law violation except where such advocacy is directed to inciting or producing imminent lawless action and is likely to incite or produce such action.[129]

This particular sentence is a considerable addition to the language of Justice Harlan's opinion in *Yates*, which did not specify that the action advocated must be both imminent and lawless, but only spoke of advocating particular actions designed to accomplish, step by step, the eventual unlawful end. Nevertheless, this key sentence did not provoke any dissents. Instead, the reference to *Dennis* stirred Justices Black and Douglas to announce that they would have no further truck with the clear and present danger test. It had been tried and found wanting, as demonstrated in *Dennis* and similar cases. For them, "the line between what is permissible and not subject to control and what may be made impermissible and subject to regulation is the line between ideas and overt acts."[130]

I think there is no doubt that *Brandenburg* does not go so far as to embrace the line suggested by the Douglas concurring opinion—and previous opinions of Justice Black.[131] The more tantalizing question is whether it really disowns the clear and present danger test. Professor Gunther[132] suggests that it provides a new amalgam consisting partly of the original *Schenck* doctrine, but mostly of the ideas first expressed by Judge Learned Hand as a district judge in the *New Masses* case.[133] Professor Gunther's particular emphasis is on the *Brandenburg* requirement that the advocacy must be directed to inciting or producing imminent lawless action. It is not enough that the advocacy might have that effect, or is likely to have that effect; the language must be deliberately chosen to produce that effect. This, in Professor Gunther's view, is a substantial improvement over the way Holmes originally phrased the clear and present danger test. Professor Gunther bases his analysis not only on the published opinions of Hand and Holmes, but also on a quite lengthy correspondence in which Hand tried to persuade Holmes that the clear and present danger test, as it was first announced, did not provide adequate protection for freedom of speech.[134] Professor Gun-

---

129.   395 U.S. at 447 (*per curiam*).
130.   395 U.S. at 456 (Douglas, J., concurring).
131.   *See, e.g.*, Beauharnais v. Illinois, 343 U.S. 250, 267-76 (1952) (Black, J., dissenting); Dennis v. United States, 341 U.S. 494, 579-81 (1951) (Black, J., dissenting).
132.   *See* Gunther, *Learned Hand and the Origins of Modern First Amendment Doctrine: Some Fragments of History*, 27 STAN. L. REV. 719 (1975).
133.   New Masses Publishing Co. v. Patten, 244 F. 535 (S.D.N.Y.), *rev'd*, 246 F. 24 (2d Cir. 1917).
134.   *See* Gunther, *supra* note 132, at 754-55.

ther also suggests that the *Brandenburg* restatement of the general idea
of the clear and present danger test is thoroughly consistent with the
Brandeis elaboration of it in the *Whitney* concurring opinion, especially
in this passage in *Whitney*:

> But even advocacy of violation, however reprehensible morally, is
> not a justification for denying free speech where the advocacy falls
> short of incitement and there is nothing to indicate that the advo-
> cacy would be immediately acted on. The wide difference between
> advocacy and incitement, between preparation and attempt, be-
> tween assembly and conspiracy, must be borne in mind. In order
> to support a finding of clear and present danger it must be shown
> either that immediate serious violence was to be expected or was
> advocated, or that the past conduct furnished reason to believe
> that such advocacy was then contemplated.[135]

Thus, the shorthand of *Brandenburg* may be regarded as entirely consistent with the concurring opinion in *Whitney*, irrespective of whether
the label of clear and present danger is used.

Brandenburg was a curious case for another reason: it involved
activities which had little to do with the statute under which the prosecution was brought. This naturally suggests the question whether the
prosecution would have fared any better if it had been brought under a
statute or ordinance really designed to outlaw meetings that promote
Jew baiting and Black baiting. If you suspect that I am leading up to
the controversy sparked by a projected Nazi march in Skokie, Illinois,
you would be quite right. The Skokie controversy generated two separate pieces of litigation: one involving a suit by the Village of Skokie to
enjoin the Nazis from holding a projected demonstration,[136] and the
other involving a suit by a Nazi Party leader to enjoin enforcement of
an ordinance prohibiting the march.[137] For present purposes I will
concentrate on the second case. Perhaps I should confess at the outset
that this is a case about which I am myself deeply conflicted, but for the
present as least I will keep my conflicts to myself. My immediate concern is how to apply the Brandeis philosophy to this heartbreaking
problem.

To me, it seems clear that none of the Holmes-Brandeis freedom
of speech opinions plainly dictate, even under the clear and present
danger test, what the result should be in the Skokie case. Brandeis
himself referred to that test as a kind of rule of reason, apparently com-
paring it to the antitrust laws. It called for judgment, albeit a calm and
dispassionate one. Furthermore, there might be areas of speech in
which even the clear and present danger test had no application. In all
probability, one of those areas was obscenity. Although Holmes and

---

135.   274 U.S. 357, 376 (Brandeis, J., concurring).
136.   Village of Skokie v. National Socialist Party of America, 69 Ill. 2d 605, 373 N.E.2d 21, 14
Ill. Dec. 890 (1978).
137.   Collin v. Smith, 578 F.2d 1197 (7th Cir. 1978).

Brandeis had no occasion to struggle with the definition of obscenity as an exception to freedom of speech, I am confident that Brandeis himself would have had no doubt as to the appropriateness of the obscenity exception and would have had little sympathy with the Black-Douglas, and later Brennan, attempt to nullify it. Whether or not he would have had some sympathy for the argument that racial and religious slurs—especially the Nazi symbol, in the light of history—are the equivalent of an obscenity is a harder question. In the *Whitney* concurring opinion, one can find some indications that Brandeis regarded freedom of speech primarily as an instrument of participatory democracy—that he recognized, even in the fulminations of the International Workers of the World, some possible contribution to what he called the "discovery and spread of political truth."[138] Consequently, he might well have been sympathetic to the argument that racial and religious slurs, like obscenity, make no contribution to such discovery. I think, too, that he would have had no hesitation in accepting the "fighting words" exception to freedom of speech.[139] I have already had occasion to say that he was a very proud man. He would have sympathized fully with the right of others to resent, and even to resent forcefully, direct personal insult. Consequently, I would assume that he would have recognized the right of the state to prohibit such insults as a means of maintaining the peace and order of the community. But even that concept might not excuse all types of suppression. Brandeis joined in the Chief Justice Hughes opinion for the Court in *Near v. Minnesota*,[140] setting aside, as a violation of freedom of the press, an injunction prohibiting the continued publication of malicious, scandalous, and defamatory newspaper articles, with anti-semitic overtones.

So much for general impressions. Of course a vast amount of first amendment constitutional law has grown up since Brandeis left the Court. Most notable and relevant are the decisions in *Beauharnais v. Illinois*[141] and *New York Times v. Sullivan*.[142] The Illinois statute sustained in the *Beauharnais* case provided the model in substantive terms for the Skokie ordinance struck down in the *Collin* case.[143] It made it a criminal offense to publish or exhibit material which "portrays depravity, criminality, unchastity, or lack of virtue of citizens of any race, color or creed or religion," and exposes such citizens to "contempt, derision or obloquy" or is productive of "breach of the peace or riots."[144] Justice Frankfurter, writing for a majority of five, sustained the statute, and found support in both the fighting words doctrine and the general

---

138. 274 U.S. at 375 (Brandeis, J., concurring).
139. *See* Chaplinsky v. New Hampshire, 315 U.S. 568 (1942).
140. 283 U.S. 697 (1931).
141. 343 U.S. 250 (1952).
142. 376 U.S. 254 (1964).
143. *See* text accompanying note 137 *supra*.
144. Law of June 29, 1917, § 224a, 1917 Ill. Laws 362 (repealed 1962).

law of libel. But most of all, he found support in the history of race relations in Illinois and in the rationality of the legislative judgment. In that analysis he spoke only of the fourteenth amendment, and as Justice Black complained in his dissent, the first amendment was "not even accorded the respect of passing mention."[145] This does not mean, however, that Frankfurter was not perfectly aware that he was speaking of freedom of speech as part of the liberty included in the due process clause of the fourteenth amendment, just as Brandeis in the concurring opinion in *Whitney* spoke of the language of the first amendment as if it were included in the fourteenth.[146]

I am inclined to believe that Brandeis might well have agreed with Frankfurter's opinion in *Beauharnais*, both on the ground that this injury was indeed a moral one and to that extent as offensive as obscenity, and also on the ground that danger of violence was, on the basis of past experience, both clear and present. It may be that I am partly influenced in this belief because Frankfurter tells us in his diaries[147] that Brandeis completely agreed with his position in the Flag Salute cases,[148] a position which it seems to me much more difficult to defend than his position in *Beauharnais*.[149]

That leaves for consideration the opinion in *New York Times v. Sullivan*,[150] which the majority in the *Collin* case suggests may well have undercut the authority of *Beauharnais*.[151] There is a good deal of truth in this, since the Frankfurter opinion in *Beauharnais* relies considerably upon the recognized exception of the law of libel. But this is not entirely conclusive, because, as Judge Sprecher in his partially dissenting opinion in *Collin* points out, the principle of *New York Times* is limited to public figures, and it is at least arguable that the same principle is inapplicable to group libel statutes or ordinances like that in the Skokie case.[152] Indeed, I am inclined to the view that both Brandeis and Frankfurter might well have agreed with the result in the *New*

---

145. 343 U.S. 250, 268 (Black, J., dissenting).
146. Brandeis said in *Whitney*:
The right of free speech, the right to teach, and the right of assembly, are, of course, fundamental rights. . . . These may not be denied or abridged. But, although the rights of free speech and assembly are in their nature fundamental, they are not in their nature absolute. Their exercise is subject to restriction if the particular restriction proposed is required in order to protect the State from destruction or from serious injury, political, economic, or moral. 274 U.S. at 373 (Brandeis, J., concurring).
147. *See* F. FRANKFURTER, FROM THE DIARIES OF FELIX FRANKFURTER 255 (1975).
148. *See, e.g.*, Minersville School Dist. Bd. of Educ. v. Gobitis, 310 U.S. 586 (1940).
149. I think it should also be noted, that although the decision was five to four, the dissents of both Justice Reed and Justice Jackson were much more limited than the fundamental issue which is of most concern to us. Justice Reed was concerned that the statute was too vague, especially in the term "lack of virtue." Beauharnais v. Illinois, 343 U.S. 250, 277-84 (1952) (Reed, J., dissenting). Justice Jackson was concerned that it did not permit the defense of truth. Brandeis might have agreed with either of those, but surely not with the dissents of Black and Douglas. *Id.* at 287-305 (Jackson, J., dissenting).
150. 376 U.S. 254 (1964).
151. *See* Collin v. Smith, 578 F.2d 1197, 1205 (7th Cir. 1978).
152. *Id.* at 1218 (Sprecher, J., concurring in part and dissenting in part).

York Times case and still have adhered to the general position of the *Beauharnais* case. Whether this would have also led them to resolve the Skokie case in favor of the village is still another question, but it would have certainly given the village a much better chance of success. However, it should also be noted that *Beauharnais* was a criminal prosecution for past violation, whereas *Collin* involved a kind of prior restraint—the denial of a permit.

C. Brandeis and Zionism

I cannot close this attempt to recapture the philosophy of Justice Brandeis without some attention to his philosophy as a Jew, and especially as a Zionist Jew.[153] I feel this way partly because of my own experience with the Justice and partly because of what I have learned from Professor Paul Freund. Toward the close of my year with the Justice, I received a call from a friend who was then the relatively new Rabbi of the Temple in New Haven which I had attended as a boy. My friend wanted to meet the Justice. I arranged the interview partly by explaining to the Justice that the Rabbi's congregation was predominately non-Zionist but that he himself was young and open to persuasion. There followed the longest interview I ever participated in with the Justice.[154] Both the Rabbi and I got the full treatment, culminating with what the Justice foresaw as the eventual triumph of Zionism and the rebirth and the mutual enrichment of two great civilizations, the Jewish culture and the Arab culture. Professor Freund tells of a similar experience when Brandeis administered the oath of office to a Louisville friend who had been appointed Ambassador to Great Britain. After the swearing in, the Justice inquired whether the Ambassador had had any occasion to learn about Palestine. When the Ambassador said, "No," there followed an hour's exposition about the past and future of Palestine. I have no doubt that it was substantially the same as the lecture delivered to the Rabbi and me.[155]

Brandeis became a Zionist when it was not the fashionable thing to be among successful and apparently assimilated American Jews.[156]

---

153. Zionism is used here as shorthand for the general philosophy favoring the reestablishment of a national homeland for the Jewish people.

154. I recall Mrs. Brandeis called on the phone three times to remind the Justice that it was time for their daily walk.

155. I also have no doubt that the Justice deliberately arranged for both Paul and me to be there so that we would also get the benefit of his sermon.

156. Many people were surprised by Brandeis's rather late and sudden conversion to Zionism. Apparently he grew up in a family that had no particular religious affiliation. I do not know what Mrs. Brandeis's religious upbringing was, but they were married by her brother-in-law, Dr. Felix Adler, a founder of the Ethical Culture Society. Brandeis's uncle, Lewis Dembitz, was a practicing Jew, but there is no indication that this relationship, although intellectually significant, had any particular religious significance for Brandeis.

During the years that Brandeis was building a successful law practice and a reputation as the People's Attorney, there was no indication of any interest in the Jewish religion or in Jewish community activities, except for occasional financial contributions. How then can we explain the

But neither was it fashionable in the early 1900's to be a public interest lawyer. In each case, Brandeis found his way on his own. Brandeis's public speeches give us some hint of what really caught his sympathy, sparked his imagination, and generated his tremendous drive for effective action. First of all, his sympathy was caught by the terrible plight of the Jews in Russia and other East European countries, especially during and immediately after World War I. But it was not only their physical suffering that moved him; it was their degradation, their apparent loss of self respect, and their treatment as second class citizens, if indeed they were citizens at all. What moved him most of all was that some people were doing something about it, and that these oppressed

---

fact that suddenly in 1912 Brandeis emerged as a full-fledged Zionist, and within a few years became the acknowledged leader of the American Zionist movement—at a time when Zionism was literally the impossible dream? The answer to this conundrum is given partly in the Brandeis letters and partly in the account of Jacob de Hass who was the catalyst who precipitated this amazing change.

In 1910, de Hass was the Editor of the Jewish Advocate in Boston. A representative of the Massachusetts Saving Bank Insurance Plan called on him to arrange some favorable publicity directed at Jewish workers. When de Hass indicated he would like to meet the author of the Plan, an interview was arranged and, in the course of it, de Hass asked Brandeis if he was related to a lawyer in Louisville named Louis Dembitz. When Brandeis explained that this was his uncle, de Hass remarked that Dembitz was "indeed a noble Jew." Brandeis asked why he used that term. De Hass explained that Dembitz was an active Zionist. Brandeis then began to ask about Zionism. There followed a series of interviews in which de Hass not only poured out the whole story of Zionism, but also became Brandeis's guide to an intensive course of reading. About two years later, according to de Hass, Brandeis was scheduled to address the monthly dinner of the Century Club, an association of Boston Jewish professional men. He was expected to talk about his fight with the New Haven Railroad, then approaching its climax, but announced that he had decided to talk instead about something more important to his audience—his new interest in Zionism. The word soon spread in Zionist circles that Brandeis had joined the ranks, and gradually he became more involved in making speeches, raising funds, and developing the organization. *See* J. DE HASS, LOUIS DEMBITZ BRANDEIS 52 (1929).

In 1914, he became chairman of what was called the Provisional Executive Committee for General Zionist Affairs. From 1914 until 1916, when he went on the Court, he was the titular and functional head of the American Zionist movement. As a present on his sixtieth birthday in 1916, he received an album containing 10,000 signatures. From 1916 until 1921, he was the spiritual and intellectual leader of the movement and honorary president of the organization, although the active offices were held and the public work was done by his lieutenants, such as Circuit Judge Julian W. Mack, Rabbi Stephen S. Wise, and Professor Felix Frankfurter. In this period he also played an influential role behind the scenes in the formulation of the Balfour Declaration, the first international recognition of a Jewish right to a national homeland in Palestine. From 1921 until 1931, there was a hiatus in this formal leadership due to internal organizational struggles, but the Justice's own interest and support for the Zionist ideal never wavered.

The memoirs of David Ben Gurion tell us that he came to the United States in 1933 especially to see Justice Brandeis and to talk to him about the importance of developing the Negev and particularly a port on the Red Sea now Eilat. Brandeis asked how much it would cost to establish the first Jewish settlement on that spot. Ben Gurion explained it would probably cost about $100,000. He had barely finished speaking when Brandeis handed him a draft, saying: "Here are your hundred thousand dollars." Ben Gurion protested that he had come to him for moral support, not money. Brandeis answered: "I want to have the privilege of being the first one to help lay the foundation on that spot." Looking back on these incidents, it occurred to me that if Zionism meant that much to the Justice, it might be worth a few minutes of our time to try to figure out why. *See also* E. RABINOWITZ, JUSTICE LOUIS D. BRANDEIS: THE ZIONIST CHAPTER OF HIS LIFE, at 129-30 (1968).

and apparently degraded people were finding a way to help themselves. This is best expressed in his own words:

> The rebirth of the Jewish nation is no longer a mere dream. It is in process of accomplishment in a most practical way, and the story is a most wonderful one. A generation ago a few Jewish emigrants from Russia and from Roumania, instead of proceeding westward to this hospitable country where they might easily have secured material prosperity, turned eastward for the purpose of settling in the land of their fathers.
>
> To the worldly-wise these efforts at colonization appeared very foolish. Nature and man presented obstacles in Palestine which appeared almost insuperable; and the colonists were in fact ill-equipped for their task, save in their spirit of devotion and self-sacrifice. The land, harassed by centuries of misrule, was treeless and apparently sterile; and it was infested with malaria. The Government offered them no security, either as to life or property. The colonists themselves were not only unfamiliar with the character of the country, but were ignorant of the farmer's life which they proposed to lead; for the Jews of Russia and Roumania had been generally denied the opportunity of owning or working land. Furthermore, these colonists were not inured to the physical hardships to which the life of a pioneer is necessarily subjected. To these hardships and to malaria many succumbed. Those who survived were long confronted with failure. But at last success came. Within a generation these Jewish Pilgrim Fathers and those who followed them, had succeeded in establishing these two fundamental propositions:
>
> *First*: That Palestine is fit for the modern Jew.
>
> *Second*: That the modern Jew is fit for Palestine.[157]

The reference to the Pilgrim Fathers was no accident. Brandeis regarded himself as a citizen of Massachusetts, as well as a citizen of the United States. As a citizen of Massachusetts, he identified with the Pilgrim Fathers just as he identified with the Founding Fathers in his constitutional opinions. So too, Brandeis identified with the Jewish people and particularly with the Jewish Pilgrims, who were recreating a new-old land in Palestine. He was proud of what they were doing. He was excited by what Aaron Aronson was accomplishing in developing new strains of wheat that would be grown in Palestine, and by the work of Ebenzer Ben Jehuda in developing the new-old language of Hebrew.[158] He was anxious not only that this great experiment should

---

157. *See* L. BRANDEIS, BRANDEIS ON ZIONISM 26-27 (1942).
158. *See id.* at 39, 51.
    He also took pride in the fact that the Jews were no longer hiring Arabs to defend their settlements, but were training their young men to do it themselves. I remember once asking him if he was disturbed by reports of Arab attacks on Jewish settlements. He answered calmly: "No, the Jews know how to shoot straight." I remember too that when we were working on the Farmers

succeed, but that it should also reflect the highest ideals of the Jewish religion and tradition.

D. Conclusion

We have been looking for the key to the Justice's overall philosophy—a key that must fit his latter day love affair with Zionism as well as his early love for the law, his hatred of monopoly, his devotion to freedom, and his conception of justice. Professor Freund, in his great essay entitled "Portrait of A Liberal Judge," finds the key in what he calls a "morality of mind."[159] I would not dare to try to improve on that, but I must add, as we say in the trade, a footnote to link it with our own particular concern.

Obviously Brandeis had a highly developed sense of injustice, to borrow a phrase made famous by Edmund Cahn,[160] especially injustice perpetrated against others. He also had a drive to do something about it—a compulsion, if you will, to protect the weak against overreaching by the strong, and a determination to find lasting solutions for human problems within a framework that paid equal respect to everyone's human dignity. In that framework, civil liberty played no small part, but it was not a panacea, nor could it be cheaply purchased. Rather, it came heavily freighted with duty and responsibility.

One of Brandeis's favorite sayings was "Responsibility is the great developer of men."[161] He used it in reference not only to the responsibilities of office and the responsibilities of business, but also with respect to the responsibilities of citizenship. In his version of participatory democracy, everyone shared that responsibility and had a duty to make a contribution appropriate to his ability and means. He refused to accept the excuse that some people had neither the means nor the ability. For the most part, he insisted, the innate differences in people are not so great. I have called this lecture The Right of Self-Development, but the Justice would have preferred to call it The Right and the Duty of Self-Development. If we want Brandeis on our side in the fight for civil liberties and civil rights, we must take him on his own terms. We must remember that every right brings with it a reciprocal duty: the duty to use it wisely and well, to the best of one's ability, and for the common good. It is a stern code to live by, yet Brandeis found both joy and serenity in it. Would that we could all follow in his footsteps.

Bankruptcy Act opinion and especially the footnotes which concerned the problem of farm tenancy, he said to me: "Our people in Palestine have found a better way."

159. P. FREUND, *supra* note 33, at 45, 48-49. *See also* P. Freund, *Mr. Justice Brandeis*, 70 HARV. L. REV. 769 (1957), *reprinted in* P. FREUND ON LAW AND JUSTICE, at 119-45 (1967). M. UROFSKY, A MIND OF ONE PIECE (1971).

160. E. CAHN, THE SENSE OF INJUSTICE (1949).

161. *See* St. Joseph Stockyards Co. v. United States, 298 U.S. 38, 92 (1936) (Brandeis J., concurring). *See also* 5 LETTERS *supra* note 1, at 45-46.

LOUIS H. POLLAK

WILEY BLOUNT RUTLEDGE: PROFILE OF A JUDGE†

Louis H. Pollak *

I.

Wiley Blount Rutledge was a teacher of law for fifteen years—at the University of Colorado (which was his *alma mater*), at Washington University, and at the University of Iowa. He was a federal judge for ten years—four years on the Court of Appeals for the District of Columbia, and six years on the Supreme Court. And then, in the summer of 1949, at the age of fifty-five and at the height of his powers, he was dead. Like Cardozo, Rutledge was a Justice too short a time to have had a pervasive impact across the full sweep of the Court's jurisprudence. But—again like Cardozo—Rutledge had in his too-brief tenure achieved general recognition as one who was sure to become a Justice of decisive and enduring influence, time alone permitting. Death prevented Cardozo from becoming a Justice of the rank of his brother Brandeis. And death prevented Rutledge from becoming a Justice of the rank of his brethren Frankfurter and Black. But, just as Brandeis knew the true stature of Cardozo, so Frankfurter and Black—who differed on all things, except on fundamentals (as Black said of his and Frankfurter's differences, they "were far less about the ultimate aims of our Constitution than they were about the most appropriate way for our Court to aid in achieving those aims"[1])—were in accord in valuing

---

† This article is an expansion of a lecture originally delivered at the University of Illinois College of Law on March 8, 1979, as the second 1978-79 David C. Baum Lecture on Civil Rights and Civil Liberties.

* United States District Judge, Eastern District of Pennsylvania; A.B. 1943, Harvard College; LL.B. 1948, Yale University.

I am grateful to Dean Cribbet and his colleagues for the privilege of joining the resplendent roster of prior Baum Lecturers in doing honor to the late Professor Baum. I am also very gratified that the preparation of the lecture provided an occasion for giving public witness to my affection and admiration for Justice Rutledge. I was privileged to serve as one of the Justice's two law clerks in the 1948 Term. My partner in clerkship was Philip W. Tone, now an eminent Judge of the United States Court of Appeals for the Seventh Circuit. I hope that Judge Tone will find this lecture to be a faithful assessment of the qualities of mind and spirit of the Justice whom we served in his last year.

The delivery of this Baum Lecture brought me an additional fortuitous dividend: by coming to Champaign-Urbana at the right time, I had the opportunity to wish a happy sixtieth birthday to my brother-in-law, Dr. Edwin L. Goldwasser, the distinguished physicist and Vice Chancellor for Research at the University of Illinois. Many of the qualities which characterized Justice Rutledge are also found in Dr. Goldwasser, and help to account for his achievements as scientist and educator.

1. Black, *Mr. Justice Frankfurter*, 78 HARV. L. REV. 1521 (1965).

Rutledge.

A year after Rutledge's death, Black wrote about "this gentle but courageous man" a sentence of memorable valediction: "The only thing of which he was ever afraid was that he might agree to an unjust result."[2] Frankfurter had occasion to judge Rutledge before he ever met him. Some weeks after Cardozo's death, in the summer of 1938, the Frankfurters (he was then still a law teacher) were invited to Hyde Park for an annual and informal visit of old friends. But President Roosevelt was plainly ill at ease. Finally, the President took Frankfurter off to his study, and there told his friend that it would be politically impossible to appoint him to Cardozo's seat. "I've given very definite promises to Senators and party people that the next appointment to the Court would be someone west of the Mississippi." Frankfurter, relating the conversation in later years, recalled that it "was very embarrassing to me, and moreover I wanted to get through with it and relieve the President of the United States of something that had evidently been troubling to him. I said, 'I perfectly understand. It never occurred to me that you should appoint me, and there is every reason in the world why you should appoint somebody west of the Mississippi.' "[3] Whereupon, the President asked Frankfurter about various western candidates, all of them judges. Frankfurter had views on some of them, and undertook to appraise the work of the others and report to the President in due course. Frankfurter later recalled:

I went back to Cambridge, worked on these memoranda, reported to FDR, and that was that. I awaited whom he would name from among the judges he canvassed with me. I attended to my knitting, and nothing further happened until during Christmas week. It was a day or two after Christmas, maybe two days after that I had a phone call. The phone rang, long distance, and there was the President of the United States, and he said that another suggestion had been made to him, and he wanted to know what I thought of it: Dean Wiley Rutledge of the Law School of the University of Iowa, what did I think of him? I said, "I do not know him. I've never met him, and therefore I have no opinion, but if you want me to find out from people in whose judgment I have confidence, what they think about it, it's very easy for me to do so because all the law professors are now meeting in Chicago."

It was the meeting of the American Association of Law Schools, and he said, "I wish you would."

I then got on the phone and got hold of T. R. Powell in Chicago, who was one of our delegation, (that is of the Harvard Law School) that year, and I told him absolutely nothing about the inquiry of FDR and the Supreme Court, but I put to him the questions on which I wanted light on Wiley Rutledge which would

2. Black, *Mr. Justice Rutledge*, 25 IND. L.J. 423 (1950).
3. FELIX FRANKFURTER REMINISCES 280 (H. Phillips ed. 1960).

reveal the intellectual and moral content of the man. He knew Rutledge somewhat. I said, "You ask fellows like Lloyd Garrison and so on—just wrestle around and call me back collect and tell me what the result of your inquiries are."

He knew that it was something important. Men who had the kind of relations he and I had understood each other without spelling it out, and in due course Powell called me back and gave me a very detailed report, detailed estimate, assessment as to why he liked Rutledge's qualities and potentialities on the basis of which I wrote a memorandum to the President the upshot of which was that if I had to act on the information my net of inquiry had fished up I would think that Rutledge was qualified for the Court and would be a properly appointed man.[4]

What would Thomas Reed Powell have learned from Lloyd Garrison (then the Dean of the Wisconsin Law School) and the other law professors which would have persuaded Frankfurter to advise the President that Rutledge would be "a properly appointed man"? The record would have shown a law teacher and dean who had become a respected figure in the civic and legal life of St. Louis and of Iowa City notwithstanding his public espousal of positions—for example, support for the Court-packing plan—which were by no means accepted ingredients of the establishment value structure. And the record of Rutledge within the academy, the record of his influence on students and faculty colleagues, would have confirmed the public image. One may credit the retrospective testimony of Willard Wirtz, who was later to become a major public figure in his own right, but who in the 'thirties was a junior colleague of Rutledge's:

What is the heritage teachers have from Wiley Rutledge?

If this question can be answered, if there is an essence here which can be captured in awkward words, the key is a simple fact we all know. Wiley Rutledge, above almost all others, loved and respected his fellow men. This was the quality of his great personal attraction and it was the core of his reputed liberalism. It was probably this which was also the magic of his teaching.

. . . .

Wiley Rutledge was proud of the law schools and of the profession for which they train. But he spoke out repeatedly against the impersonalness of legal education and against the reflections of that same quality in the profession itself. He protested the hollowness of curricula and courses in which the value elements inherent in sound legal concepts emerge only incidentally. He pointed out the inevitability of false emphasis resulting from the climaxing of each semester with a series of examinations which reveal only clinical accomplishment. We train artisans, he said, while a demo-

---

4. *Id.* at 281-82.

cratic society pleads for architects.[5]

And so it is clear that Frankfurter was on sound ground in advising the President of the United States that Rutledge was well qualified. But if Frankfurter entertained thoughts that his report might lead to Rutledge's selection, such conjectures were fated to be ill-founded; and this for the reason that Frankfurter had no way of figuring on how two other actors would play their parts.

One was Rutledge himself, whom Frankfurter knew only by hearsay. When Rutledge learned—at about the same time as the President's phone call to Frankfurter—that Senator Gillette of Iowa had recommended to the President that Rutledge be named to succeed Cardozo, Rutledge wrote his Senator and asked that the recommendation be withdrawn. Rutledge was grateful for the Senator's confidence, but insisted that his name not be pressed as against that of Frankfurter who was, in Rutledge's view, preeminently qualified for elevation to the Court.[6]

The other person whose behavior Frankfurter had failed to anticipate was somebody he thought he knew very well—the President of the United States. As Frankfurter later remembered it:

> On Tuesday, January 4 . . . while I was dressing, while I was in my B.V.D.'s, the door bell rang at 192 Brattle Street, and my wife was going down. We had a guest for dinner, Professor Robert Morse Lovett of the University of Chicago who is a very, very punctual man. It was seven o'clock. My wife all dressed was going down, and here I was in my B.V.D.'s. She said, "Please hurry! You're always late."
>
> Just then while I had this conjugal injunction the telephone rang. I went to the telephone. My study was right across the hall, opposite our bedroom. The telephone rang, and there was the ebullient, the exuberant, resilient warmth-enveloping voice of the President of the United States, "Hello. How are you?"
>
> "I'm fine. How are you?"

---

5. *In Memory of Wiley Blount Rutledge*, Proceedings of the Bar and Officers of the Supreme Court of the United States, April 10, 1951, 20-22. Wirtz stresses that the key to Rutledge's teaching was:

> treating his students as human beings, getting to know them as individuals. He did this, seemingly oblivious to the other demands upon his time, by opening his office door and his home, inviting the students in singly and in groups of two or three, and then sitting and talking with them. The conversation would be personal at first, as teacher and student found out what underlay the other's reactions. Then it would broaden out, proceeding with an awareness of assumptions, predilections and biases. Now the human heart of the subject matter of the day's lecture could be taken up intelligently, and that of the morning's headlines. The subject would become not just a particular case or a news story but how a decent, honest, intelligent man approaches any subject coming within the professional competence and obligation of the lawyer. For an hour or so law would be taught as it was a hundred years ago when the neophyte learned his profession in the office of an established member of the bar. "Reading law" they called it. But it was so much more than that. It was the transmission of a tradition of professional service, the handing on perhaps less of information than of a spirit and a whole quality of professional competence and responsibility.

6. Brant, *Mr. Justice Rutledge—The Man*, 25 IND. L.J. 424, 435 (1950).

"How's Marion?"

"Fine."

"You know, I told you I don't want to appoint you to the Supreme Court of the United States."

I said, "Yes." I no more expected the denouement of this conversation. You know, he was given to teasing. Some people said that it was an innocently sadistic streak in him. He just had to have an outlet for fun. "I told you I can't appoint you to the Supreme Court."

"Yes, you told me that."

"I mean this. I mean this. I don't want to appoint you to the Supreme Court."

Here I was in my B.V.D.'s, and I knew Marion would be as sore as she could be. She had said I'm always late which is indeed substantially true. "I mean it. I don't want to appoint you. I just don't want to appoint you."

I said, "Yes, you told me that. You've made that perfectly clear. I understand that."

I was getting bored, really, when he whipped around on the telephone and said, "But unless you give me an unsurmountable objection I'm going to send your name in for the Court tomorrow at twelve o'clock"—just like that, and I remember saying, and it is natural to remember this very vividly—"All I can say is that I wish my mother were alive."[7]

So Frankfurter was nominated, confirmed, and appointed, as he should have been. Two months later Rutledge's name was once again prominently mentioned for a vacancy on the Court. This time it was the Brandeis seat. Rumor had it that the front-runner was William O. Douglas—like Rutledge, a law teacher, but one who had emerged into the real world of high place in government, namely, the chairmanship of the SEC. On March 13, 1939, Rutledge wrote his friend Clarence Morris (the eminent torts scholar who was then teaching at Texas and was later to teach at Pennsylvania) predicting that Douglas would be named, "possibly today or tomorrow. In addition to his obviously superior qualifications and strong support within the administration, I suspect 1940 has its part to play." And the President did in fact send Douglas's name to the Senate on March 15. The next day, the President nominated Rutledge to a vacancy on the Court of Appeals for the District of Columbia.

Rutledge served on the court of appeals for four years. The court's docket was a varied one. Besides conducting the regular business of a federal court of appeals, the "App. D.C." was growing into the special role which, a generation later, is taken for granted—that of chief judicial monitor of the executive departments and independent

---

7. FELIX FRANKFURTER REMINISCES, *supra* note 3, at 282-83.

regulatory agencies whose numbers and functions had burgeoned during Franklin Roosevelt's first and second administrations. In addition,
the App. D.C. was still performing a function of which it has since been
substantially relieved, that of highest court of the District on most questions of local law. In effect it was simultaneously a federal appellate
court, a high court of administrative appeal, and a state supreme court.

In personal terms, the Judges (or Justices, as they were called) of
the App. D.C. were a close-knit group, but they were people of widely
varying outlooks. Most akin to Rutledge in jurisprudential approach
was Henry Edgerton, also a former law teacher, who had been a paci-
fist in World War I. Another good friend, a stalwart Democrat but
hardly a passionate New Dealer, Fred M. Vinson, had served the administration loyally as a Kentucky Congressman, and would in due
course be called on by Roosevelt to leave the bench to head the Office
of War Mobilization, and then would be called on by Truman to serve
as Secretary of the Treasury, and thereafter to return to judicial duty,
and to colleagueship with Rutledge, as Chief Justice in succession to
Harlan Fiske Stone. Justin Miller had been a law school dean both at
Southern California and at Duke, and had come to Washington under
Roosevelt as an Assistant Attorney General. Harold Stephens, a practitioner who, like Miller, had served in Roosevelt's Justice Department,
turned out to be a judge of adamantine and literalist principle. Presid-
ing over the group was the sole Republican, Chief Justice D. Lawrence
Groner. It is said that Groner made it part of his administrative responsibilities to ensure that Edgerton and Rutledge rarely sat on the
same three-judge panel on cases raising issues of public policy which
Groner deemed controversial.[8] If this be so, it must in any event be
said that much can be forgiven a judge whose humor lightens the judicial process as Groner's could.[9]

---

8.   Brant, *supra* note 6, at 437.
9.   Illustrative is Beach v. United States, 144 F.2d 533 (1944), in which Groner overturned
the Mann Act conviction of Carmen Beach. Beach had taken a young woman, employed in her
District of Columbia dress shop and residing in her District of Columbia apartment, four blocks
in a taxi to the Hamilton Hotel to engage in prostitution. In concluding that statutes of more
recent vintage than the Mann Act, designed for the particular governance of the District, covered
the subject matter so intricately that the Mann Act's reference to transportation "in the District of
Columbia . . . for the purpose of prostitution" should be treated as superseded, Groner wrote:

> One section of the present law prohibits the offence itself; another, the offence of operating a
> house of prostitution; another, the act of procuring a person to live in prostitution; or procur-
> ing a person for acts of prostitution; or procuring a person for the immoral enjoyment of a
> third person; another, for inviting or inducing a person to go with him or her for purposes of
> prostitution anywhere in the District, or to a residence, or to any other house or building
> (including a hotel), or to accompany or follow him or her to any place whatever within the
> District, including parks or elsewhere, for purposes of prostitution; and finally the Pandering
> Act itself, which makes it a felony for any person in the District of Columbia to induce any
> female to reside in a house of prostitution, to engage in prostitution, or to reside with any
> other person for the purpose of prostitution. So complete is the coverage that about the only
> place in which the act can be done without running athwart the local law is in an anchored
> balloon.

Rutledge's work on the App. D.C. was a substantial apprentice-ship for the work which lay ahead on the Supreme Court. He wrote with care, and at length, on a wide range of topics. He was a judge reverential of the democratic legal order, and of the legal institutions which give it strength, texture, and vitality. Most revealing, perhaps, was the frequent division between Rutledge and Stephens.

A good example is *Frene v. Louisville Cement Co.*,[10] a damage ac-tion brought by plaintiff against a Kentucky cement manufacturing company in the District Court for the District of Columbia, in which the claim was that defendant's product "Brixment"—a water-proofed mortar—did not conform to the representations which led plaintiff to purchase it for use in putting up his Washington home. The suit was begun by personal service in the District on one Lovewell, a resident of Maryland. Lovewell was an employee of defendant whose job was to solicit orders for defendant's products in the District, Maryland, and Virginia, and who frequently—as was true with respect to plaintiff's house—would visit the construction sites where one of defendant's products was being used. The question for the appellate court was whether the trial judge had properly dismissed the case for lack of ju-risdiction over the defendant. Speaking for himself and Edgerton, Rut-ledge reversed. Rutledge persuasively demonstrated the artificiality of the then-prevailing rule, embodied in cases such as *Green v. Chicago, Burlington & Quincy Ry. Co.*,[11] that "mere solicitation" within the fo-rum state (or District of Columbia) was not a sufficient quantum of corporate activity to render a corporate defendant "present" and hence amenable to judicial jurisdiction in that forum. And then Rutledge went on to hold that in any event the case before the court was not in tension with *Green* and like cases because on its facts it slipped safely into the category of "solicitation plus" which was adequate to sustain jurisdiction. Stephens, in dissent, declared that "the decision of the Court is a repudiation of . . . *Green v. Chicago, Burlington & Quincy Ry. Co.* and denies to the appellee a disposition of the instant case according to the law as declared by . . . the Supreme Court."[12] Edger-ton, joining with Rutledge, explained why *Green* was dispositive:

> There a western railroad solicited western business, and in some instances collected its price, in Pennsylvania. The plaintiff sought to sue the road in Pennyslvania for personal injuries re-ceived in Colorado. If the man in the street were asked whether the sale of western transportation in Pennsylvania amounted to the

---

Id. at 535 (footnotes omitted). Thurman Arnold (Rutledge's successor on the App. D.C.) joined Groner. Edgerton dissented. The Supreme Court reversed. United States v. Beach, 324 U.S. 193 (1945). *See also* Note, *Interstate Immorality: The Mann Act and the Supreme Court*, 56 YALE L.J. 718, 720 n.16 (1947).

10.   134 F.2d 511 (D.C. Cir. 1943).
11.   205 U.S. 530 (1907).
12.   134 F.2d at 523.

doing of business there by a railroad whose tracks and trains were thousands of miles away, he would be likely to say no, or at least that the question was doubtful. But if he were told that appellee's agent in the District solicited District dealers to buy its product for District use, and solicited District consumers to buy it of District dealers, that appellee shipped it to the District and that its agent supervised its use there (though only in an advisory way) and discussed there its shortcomings and resulting complaints, he would not doubt that appellee was doing business there. Moreover, it is impossible to tell how far the decision in the *Green* case was due to reluctance to require the defendant and its witnesses to cross the continent and defend in the east a cause of action which arose in the west.[13]

Rutledge's and Edgerton's practical view of the question when a foreign corporation is sufficiently "present" within the forum to warrant being sued is, of course, the view which ultimately guided Chief Justice Stone, in *International Shoe Co. v. Washington*,[14] in bringing the law of *in personam* jurisdiction into the twentieth century.

Rutledge's practical view of the law did not always bring him to the "liberal" result. In *Ex parte Rosier*,[15] Rutledge was of the view that an inmate of St. Elizabeth's Hospital adjudicated of unsound mind in February 1940, and again in July of the same year, was not entitled as of right to a third hearing on his claim that he was sane when he petitioned for *habeas corpus* in October. The trial judge, so Rutledge concluded, could take judicial notice of the two very recent adjudications, could accept Superintendent Overholser's assurances that the renewed petition was framed by a litigious fellow inmate and that the petitioner's condition was in fact unchanged, and could deny the petition without a hearing. But Rutledge's practical view did not persuade Stephens and Vinson. Stephens, speaking for the court, was lengthy and magisterial:

> What the outcome of such a hearing as the appellant was entitled to under the provisions of the statutes relating to habeas corpus proceedings and under the due process clause of the Constitution might have been we do not of course assume to say. It might have been made to appear, and the trial court might have decided, that the appellant had regained his sanity and was entitled to discharge. It might have been determined that the assertions of Dr. Overholser that the appellant was still of unsound mind were correct; that is, the court might have reached, after a proper hearing, the same conclusion that it reached without a hearing. But that is of no moment. The determination actually reached by the trial court was reached without a proper hearing.

---

13.   *Id.* at 518.
14.   326 U.S. 310 (1945).
15.   133 F.2d 316 (D.C. Cir. 1942).

The necessity for hearing under the law of the land cannot be escaped. *"Qui aliquid statuerit parte inaudita altera, aequum licet dixerit, haud aequum fererit."* (He who decides anything, one party being unheard, though he should decide right, does wrong. . . .)

. . . .

. . . If the burden of work upon the trial court is too great—as there is much reason to believe in view of the large volume of business in this jurisdiction—the remedy is not by denying right of hearing to those who claim that they are restrained of their liberty without warrant of law; it is rather by Congressional action to enlarge the personnel of the courts. Administrative inconvenience, even occasional abuse of the facilities of the courts, is but a small price to pay for the precious right of access to the courts guaranteed under our system of government to all who claim to be wronged. It is in those forms of government against which we are now waging war that administrative convenience and "efficiency" are set ahead of the citizen's right to be heard in respect of his liberty.

For a court to fix a period which must expire, after the dismissal, on hearing, of a petition for a writ, before a second petition stating on its face a cause of action for release will be heard by a trial court, would be judicial violation of the constitutional provision that the privilege of the writ of habeas corpus shall not be suspended unless in cases of rebellion or invasion the public safety may require it.[16]

The obverse of Rutledge's pattern of disagreement with Stephens[17] was his pattern of agreement with Edgerton.[18] But on occasion Rut-

---

16. *Id.* at 327, 332.

17. For other instances, see Brown v. Brown, 134 F.2d 505 (D.C. Cir. 1942), McKenna v. Austin, 134 F.2d 659 (D.C. Cir. 1943), and Scharfeld v. Richardson, 133 F.2d 340 (D.C. Cir. 1942).

In the latter case, the issue was the validity of a civil jury verdict in the sum of $200 arising out of a fatal assault committed by Arthur Scharfeld's dog "Popo" on "Little Bits," a Pomeranian belonging to Emily Erck. The claim on appeal was that Little Bits, having no dog tag at the time of Popo's attack, fell outside the protection of the law, as contemplated by Section 918 of the District of Columbia Code, which specificed that 'Any dog wearing the tax tag . . . shall be permitted to run at large within the District of Columbia, and any dog wearing the tax tag . . . shall be regarded as personal property in all the Courts of said District, and any person injuring or destroying the same shall be liable to a civil action for damages. . . ." Vinson, declining to find that the tax tag statute abrogated the common law right of action, wrote an extended opinion of affirmance. Stephens wrote a more extended dissent. Rutledge joined Vinson's opinion "for the reasons stated therein and upon the following additional authority"—the "additional authority" turning out to be a poem attributed to "Miller, Justin, *Pooch Poems* 1," which ran as follows:

> This saga of Popo, malevolent pooch,
> And Erck's Pomeranian pet;
> Your etymological-legal approach
> To canons of dog etiquette,
> Persuade [sic] me that canines are property still
> Whether licensed, unlicensed or tagged;
> Not *ferae naturae*, or fair game to kill
> So long as there's a tail to be wagged.

Id. at 344.

18. When they sat together. *See* text at note 8 *supra*.

ledge and Edgerton parted company. The most significant example of this was *Busey v. District of Columbia*.[19] The *Busey* case arose from the following facts: Section 1736 of the District of Columbia license law provided that, "No person shall sell any article of merchandise, or anything whatever, excepting newspapers sold at large and not from a fixed location, upon the public streets, or from public space within the District of Columbia, without a license. . . ." David Busey and Orville J. Richey stood at the intersection of Park Road and 14th Street, N.W., selling, at five cents per copy, two publications of the Jehovah's Witnesses, *Watchtower* and *Consolation*. Neither Busey nor Richey had secured the license—five dollars for a short term, twenty-five dollars annually—contemplated by Section 1736. They were therefore arrested, charged, convicted, and fined five dollars each or, in lieu thereof, a day in jail. Busey and Richey took their case from the police court to the court of appeals. That court affirmed.

Edgerton, joined by Groner, swept away constitutional difficulties, concluding that

> a reasonable license fee, applicable to street sellers generally, and not intended or shown to restrict the expression of any views, is valid in its application to sellers of religious magazines. . . . Within wide limits, democracy and the Constitution require freedom of expression and freedom of legislation. We are asked to invade the second freedom in order, it is said, to protect the first. It is not for us to say whether the license law is good for the community. It is an Act of Congress. Though it covers some sales of religious literature, it conflicts with no defensible concept of the constitutional freedom of the press or of religion. We must therefore enforce it.[20]

Rutledge thought otherwise. First, he would have avoided the constitutional issue by classifying *Watchtower* and *Consolation* as "newspapers" and hence covered by the exemption Congress wrote into the Act. Failing that, he was prepared to meet the constitutional issue head on:

> The charge "for use of the public streets for business purposes" is proper for business use beyond the common right. It is a sort of rental or reimbursement for wear and tear from special use. But it has no valid bearing on the common right or use, more especially those of free speech, a free press, and freedom of religion or conscience.
>
> That these are part of street heritage means they cannot be impaired by any power capable to destroy them, notwithstanding their exercise may be regulated appropriately in accommodation

---

19.   129 F.2d 24 (D.C. Cir. 1942).

20.   *Id.* at 27-28.

to other uses. Taxation is not appropriate for such regulation. Once that wedge enters, it widens with every legislative stroke. Its chief effect toward securing public order, decorum and free movement of traffic is by suppressing public expression. Taxed speech is not free speech. It is silence for persons unable to pay the tax.

. . . .

This is no time to wear away further the freedoms of conscience and mind by nicely technical or doubtful construction. Everywhere they are fighting for life. War now has added its censorships. They, with other liberties, give ground in the struggle. They can be lost in time also by steady legal erosion wearing down broad principle into thin right. Jehovah's Witnesses have had to choose between their consciences and public education for their children. In my judgment, they should not have to give up also the right to disseminate their religious views in an orderly manner on the public streets, exercise it at the whim of public officials, or be taxed for doing so without their license. I think the judgment should be reversed.[21]

Busey was decided on April 15, 1942. On April 30, the Supreme Court heard arguments in cases arising in Opelika, Alabama, Casa Grande, Arizona, and Fort Smith, Arkansas, in each of which a municipal ordinance like the District of Columbia license act was being challenged by Jehovah's Witnesses. On June 8, the Court, speaking through Justice Reed, in a single opinion entitled *Jones v. Opelika*,[22] sustained the three ordinances. Chief Justice Stone and Justice Murphy each wrote an extended dissenting opinion. And Black and Douglas joined both dissents. The Murphy dissent expressly cited and relied on "Rutledge, J., dissenting in *Busey v. District of Columbia*."[23]

It will be recalled that in *Busey* Rutledge had taken particular note that the licensing requirement was not the only interference with their religion which Jehovah's Witnesses had to put up with. "Jehovah's Witnesses," Rutledge had observed, "have had to choose between their consciences and public education for their children." Rutledge's reference, although not spelled out by case name and citation, was of course to Frankfurter's opinion for the Court in 1940 in the celebrated *Gobitis* case.[24] There, by a vote of eight-to-one—Stone alone dissenting—the Court had rejected the claim of Jehovah's Witness parents that for their children to salute the American flag, as was required of children in the public schools of Minersville, Pennsylvania, was to contravene the Lord's mandate as set forth in *Exodus*:

---

21. *Id.* at 37-38.
22. 316 U.S. 584 (1942).
23. *Id.* at 614 n.4 (Murphy, J., dissenting).
24. Minersville School Dist. v. Gobitis, 310 U.S. 586 (1940).

Thou shalt have no other Gods before me:
Thou shalt not make unto thee any grave image,
or any likeness of anything that is in heaven above,
or that is in the earth beneath, or that is in the water under the earth:
Thou shalt not bow down thyself to them, nor serve them: . . .[25]
The connection between the *Gobitis* problem and the license problem was also apparent to Black, Douglas, and Murphy. Following the dissenting opinions in *Opelika*, they filed a separate statement:

> The opinion of the Court sanctions a device which in our opinion suppresses or tends to suppress the free exercise of a religion practiced by a minority group. This is but another step in the direction which *Minersville School District v. Gobitis*, 310 U.S. 586, took against the same religious minority, and is a logical extension of the principles upon which that decision rested. Since we joined in the opinion in the *Gobitis* case, we think this is an appropriate occasion to state that we now believe that it also was wrongly decided. Certainly our democratic form of government, functioning under the historic Bill of Rights, has a high responsibility to accommodate itself to the religious views of minorities, however unpopular and unorthodox those views may be. The First Amendment does not put the right freely to exercise religion in a subordinate position. We fear, however, that the opinions in these and in the *Gobitis* case do exactly that.[26]

An occasion to reexamine *Gobitis* was not far to seek. On October 6, 1942, a three-judge federal court in West Virginia enjoined enforcement, as against Jehovah's Witness children, of a state-wide requirement that public school pupils salute the flag. Judge John Parker wrote:

> Ordinarily we would feel constrained to follow an unreversed decision of the Supreme Court of the United States, whether we agreed with it or not. It is true that decisions are but evidences of the law and not the law itself; but the decisions of the Supreme Court must be accepted by the lower courts as binding upon them if any orderly administration of justice is to be attained. The developments with respect to the *Gobitis* case, however, are such that we do not feel that it is incumbent upon us to accept it as binding authority. Of the seven justices now members of the Supreme Court who participated in that decision, four have given public expression to the view that it is unsound. . . . Under such circumstances and believing, as we do, that the flag salute here required is violative of religious liberty when required of persons holding the religious views of plaintiffs, we feel that we would be recreant to our duty as judges, if through a blind following of a decision

---

25. *Exodus* 20:3-5.
26. 316 U.S. at 623-24.

which the Supreme Court itself has thus impaired as an authority, we should deny protection to rights which we regard as among the most sacred of those protected by constitutional guaranties.

. . . .

The salute to the flag is an expression of the homage of the soul. To force it upon one who has conscientious scruples against giving it, is petty tyranny unworthy of the spirit of this Republic and forbidden, we think, by the fundamental law.[27]

In assessing Judge Parker's readiness to disregard, in this instance, "an unreversed decision of the Supreme Court of the United States," one must note that Judge Parker had special reason for skepticism about the rewards which accrue to lower court judges who are at pains to engage in "blind following" of every one of the Justices' decisions. For it will be recalled that the chief reason why, a decade before, the Senate declined by one vote to confirm him for the place on the Court to which President Hoover had nominated him was that Judge Parker had, in reliance on applicable Supreme Court precedent, approved the entry of a labor injunction, thereby earning the politically fatal enmity of the nation's labor leaders.[28] At all events, it is plain from the quoted excerpts from his opinion that Judge Parker was voting his strong constitutional convictions. From his decree an appeal was taken, and probable jurisdiction in *West Virginia State Board of Education v. Barnette* was noted on January 4, 1943.[29]

Meanwhile, on October 3, 1942, three days before Judge Parker's decision in *Barnette*, an event occurred which was to touch Rutledge rather more directly. At the President's request, Justice Byrnes resigned from the Supreme Court to head the Office of War Mobilization. And so the stage was set for Franklin Roosevelt to choose his eighth, and last, Justice. From the biography of Rutledge written by my late Yale colleague, Fowler Harper, one learns that on the day Byrnes left the Court, Rutledge's great friend Irving Brant—the St. Louis newspaper editor and writer on law and politics who had been urging Roosevelt to name Rutledge to the Court ever since 1936—began a campaign of correspondence on Rutledge's behalf. And the first of the letters, which went to a St. Louis lawyer who was a close friend of Rutledge's and Brant's, contained the following report:

As nearly as I can learn, the present field of real possibilities includes Rutledge, Senator Barkley, Solicitor General Fahy, Judge Parker and Dean Acheson, with Rutledge leading on merit, Barkley in political support, and your old friend and ex-liberal Felix Frankfurter plugging for Fahy or Acheson, either of whom he

27. Barnette v. West Virginia State Bd. of Educ., 47 F. Supp. 251, 252-53, 255 (D.W. Va. 1942).
28. Judge Parker's nomination was also opposed by the NAACP, but labor's opposition was the decisive obstacle to his confirmation.
29. 317 U.S. 621.

thinks he can control.[30]

Brant's uncharacteristically myopic and graceless disparagement of Frankfurter as an "ex-liberal"[31] may reasonably be thought to count against the reliability of the balance of Brant's hearsay report. But the information later assembled by Professor Harper suggests that Brant's contemporaneous report was not wholly wide of the mark. The point of greatest interest is Rutledge's own reaction to this third occasion on which his name was prominently mentioned for the Court. In November, one of those to whom Brant had written to encourage grass-roots efforts favoring Rutledge, answered Brant as follows:

> Right after Justice Byrnes resigned, I wrote Wiley about the matter and expressed my desire to be of assistance. He replied at once and very emphatically discouraged any such assistance. He expressed his conviction that the appointment should go to a Republican and asked me to use such influence as I might have in favor of Judge John J. Parker of North Carolina, pointing out that a distinct injustice had been done Judge Parker by the Senate's failure to confirm his previous appointment. Wiley's thought as to the appointment of a Republican was that it would promote unity at a time when it was most needed. . . .[32]

This time, however, Rutledge's advice was not heeded. On January 11, 1943, the President nominated him to fill the place vacated by Byrnes. And on February 15, after confirmation by the Senate, Rut-

---

30. F. HARPER, JUSTICE RUTLEDGE AND THE BRIGHT CONSTELLATION 38 (1965).

31. Compare the moving words of Judge Friendly, in his memorial tribute to Frankfurter:

The Justice would not have wished anyone to assert today that all his choices in twenty-three years of judging represented the ultimate wisdom; he was happily conscious of human frailty, importantly including his own. But some of us do reserve the right to resent suggestions by valiants of the law reviews that the man who raised his voice on behalf of Tom Mooney during World War I and stood up for Sacco and Vanzetti in its aftermath was activated by timidity when he took a position increasingly unpopular in the academic circles whose good opinion he most valued.

In Memory of Felix Frankfurter, Supreme Court of the United States, Oct. 25, 1965, at 37-38.

A detailed and thoughtful demonstration that Frankfurter's *corpus juris* as a Justice complemented and reinforced the liberal jurisprudence of his lawyer-professor years is the subject of the Baum Lecture recently delivered by William T. Coleman, Jr., Board Chairman of the NAACP Legal Defense Fund and former Secretary of Transportation. *See* 1978 U. ILL. L.F. 279. (Coleman served as law clerk to Frankfurter, as did a number of others who have made important contributions to strengthening the democratic order through law:—e.g.; Louis Henkin, of Columbia, and the late Alexander M. Bickel, of Yale, two of the leading constitutional law scholars of this generation; Anthony Amsterdam, of Stanford, chief architect of the NAACP Legal Defense Fund's litigation campaign challenging capital punishment; Paul Bender, of Pennsylvania, one of the current editors of the path-breaking casebook written by Thomas I. Emerson and David Haber a generation ago, POLITICAL AND CIVIL RIGHTS IN THE UNITED STATES; former FTC Commissioner Philip Elman, who, while Assistant Solicitor General, was the principal author of the government's *amicus* brief in *Brown v. Board of Education*; Joseph L. Rauh, Jr., the nation's senior civil liberties lawyer and a founder of ADA; former Attorney General Elliot L. Richardson; and Albert J. Rosenthal, Albert M. Sacks and Harry H. Wellington, the deans of, respectively, the Columbia, Harvard and Yale Law Schools. Frankfurter's law clerks are an important part of his enduring liberal legacy).

As to the balance of the quoted excerpt from Brant's letter, Professor Harper observed that Frankfurter "had been Brant's first choice for Cardozo's seat" (as, of course, he had also been Rutledge's) and that neither Fahy nor Acheson was likely to be controllable by anyone. Harper, *supra* note 30, at 38-39.

32. *Id.* at 39-40.

ledge was sworn in as an Associate Justice of the Supreme Court. On the same day, the Court directed that *Jones v. Opelika* be set down for reargument.[33]

II.

A. The First Amendment

One month after Rutledge took his seat, the Court heard two days of reargument in *Jones v. Opelika*, and also heard argument in two new cases in which Jehovah's Witnesses were challenging an analogous licensing ordinance in force in Jeanette, Pennsylvania. Immediately thereafter, the Court heard argument in the flag salute case from West Virginia.

In May, the Court produced a spate of opinions on licensing ordinances, the predictable bottom line of which was that the previous term's five-to-four ruling in *Jones v. Opelika* was abandoned: the replacement of Byrnes with Rutledge had produced a five-to-four margin the other way.[34] A month later, the Court vindicated Judge Parker's perception that *Gobitis* had been "impaired." In *Barnette*,[35] Justice Jackson, for a six-Justice majority (the other five, as could be expected, being Stone, Black, Douglas, Murphy, and Rutledge) repudiated the eight-to-one *Gobitis* decision of three years before. Jackson's opinion not only reached the right result, but, in demolishing the position Frankfurter had announced for the Court in *Gobitis* and expanded upon in his *Barnette* dissent, reached a level of eloquence theretofore attained, in the First Amendment jurisprudence of the Supreme Court, only by the Holmes dissents in *Abrams*[36] and *Gitlow*,[37] and by the Brandeis concurrence in *Whitney*.[38] It may be churlish to add that, arguably, Jackson's eloquence in *Barnette* outstripped his analysis.[39]

Rutledge was rarely eloquent. The judicial beachheads he took were won, not by sleight-of-words, but on the merits. And in several instances the full force of his views was not recognized until years after his death. This was most emphatically true in the realm of the First Amendment.

A representative example is Rutledge's opinion in *Thomas v. Collins*.[40] Speaking for the Court, he upheld the right of R. J. Thomas,

---

33. 318 U.S. 796. Also on the same day, the retiring Justice of the court of appeals filed his last opinion in that court. American Nat'l Bank & Trust Co. v. United States, 134 F.2d 674 (D.C. Cir. 1943).

34. Murdock v. Pennsylvania, 319 U.S. 105 (1943); Douglas v. City of Jeanette, 319 U.S. 157 (1943). *Cf.* Martin v. Struthers, 319 U.S. 141 (1943) (in which Rutledge joined in Murphy's concurrence).

35. West Virginia Bd. of Educ. v. Barnette, 319 U.S. 624 (1943).

36. Abrams v. United States, 250 U.S. 616 (1919).

37. Gitlow v. New York, 268 U.S. 652 (1925).

38. Whitney v. California, 274 U.S. 357 (1927).

39. See Pollak, *Public Prayers in Public Schools*, 77 HARV. L. REV. 62, 71-73 (1963).

40. 323 U.S. 516 (1945).

then President of the United Auto Workers, to come to Houston in 1943 to make a speech supporting an organizing campaign of the oil workers without complying with a Texas statute requiring "[a]ll labor union organizers operating in the State of Texas" to secure "an organizer's card" from the Secretary of State "before soliciting any members for his organization." The fact that Thomas was a paid union official actively engaged in the industrial life of the nation and the several states did not per se, in Rutledge's view, put Thomas outside the pale of the First Amendment any more than (although Rutledge did not draw the analogy in detail) sales of *Watchtower* rendered Jehovah's Witnesses liable to the state's licensing authority. "This conjunction of liberties is not peculiar to religious activity and institutions alone. The First Amendment gives freedom of mind the same security as freedom of conscience. . . . And the rights of free speech and a free press are not confined to any field of human interest."[41] This proposition might seem platitudinous today, were it not for the recent renascence of the notion that free speech and free press are dominantly connected with, and hence perhaps should be jurisprudentially confined to, the promotion of political thought and expression.[42]

Thomas v. Collins, like some other Rutledge opinions, is too long and discursive for maximum impact. Yet it contains doctrinal pronouncements of major implication:

> [A]ny attempt to restrict [First Amendment] liberties must be justified by clear public interest, threatened not doubtfully or remotely, but by clear and present danger. The rational connection between the remedy provided and the evil to be curbed, which in other contexts might support legislation against attack on due process grounds, will not suffice. These rights rest on firmer foundation. Accordingly, whatever occasion would restrain orderly discussion and persuasion, at appropriate time and place, must have clear support in public danger, actual or impending. Only the gravest abuses, endangering paramount interests, give occasion for permissible limitation.[43]

For Rutledge, R. J. Thomas's appeal put into demanding focus the central meaning of judicial review by highlighting

> the duty our system places on this Court to say where the individual's freedom ends and the State's power begins. Choice on that border, now as always delicate, is perhaps more so where the usual presumption supporting legislation is balanced by the preferred place given in our scheme to the great, the indispensable democratic freedoms secured by the First Amendment.[44]

---

41. *Id.* at 531.
42. *See generally* Bork, *Neutral Principles and Some First Amendment Problems,* 47 IND. L.J. 1 (1971).
43. 323 U.S. at 530.
44. *Id.* at 529-30.

But Rutledge was clear that the ultimate and unavoidable responsibility for making that delicate choice lies with the Justices. "That judgment in the first instance is for the legislative body. But in our system where the line can constitutionally be placed presents a question this Court cannot escape answering independently, whatever the legislative judgment, in the light of our constitutional tradition."[45]

Four years later, Frankfurter was to expatiate at length upon judicial references to "the preferred position" of First Amendment liberties as examples of "a mischievous phrase."[46] After reviewing a number of earlier decisions, Frankfurter was finally at pains to acknowledge Rutledge's opinion in *Thomas v. Collins* as containing

> perhaps the strongest language dealing with the constitutional aspect of legislation touching utterance. But it was the opinion of only four members of the Court, since Mr. Justice Jackson, in a separate concurring opinion, referred to the opinion of Mr. Justice Rutledge only to say that he agreed that the case fell into "the category of a public speech, rather than that of practicing a vocation as a solicitor."[47]

And this observation led Frankfurter to his conclusion, namely that "the claim that any legislation is presumptively unconstitutional which touches the field of the First Amendment . . . has never commended itself to a majority of this Court."[48]

Rutledge, not bothering to take issue with the syntactical exegesis by which Frankfurter disconnected Jackson from Black, Douglas, Murphy, and himself (the other members of the *Thomas v. Collins* majority), responded simply that "I think my brother Frankfurter demonstrates the conclusion opposite to that which he draws, namely, that the First Amendment guaranties of the freedom of speech, press, assembly and religion occupy preferred position not only in the Bill of Rights but also in the repeated decisions of this Court."[49]

In retrospect, the debate of thirty years ago between Frankfurter and Rutledge about the preferredness of the First Amendment seems almost beside the point; for, without quibbles about the use of a particular phrase, mischievous or otherwise, the Justices have through a settled course of constitutional adjudication clearly established as authoritative Rutledge's sense of the gravity of the First Amendment's mandates. That would have been gratifying—and not surprising—to Rutledge, had he lived. He also would have been gratified—and not surprised—that Frankfurter would in later years write as firm a defense of the values of unfettered inquiry as ever Rutledge himself wrote, and Rutledge would have been the more gratified that Frankfurter also was

---

45. *Id.* at 531-32.
46. Kovacs v. Cooper, 336 U.S. 77, 90 (1949) (Frankfurter, J., concurring).
47. *Id.* at 94.
48. *Id.* at 94-95.
49. *Id.* at 106 (Rutledge, J., dissenting).

to acknowledge the decisive and independent revisory responsibility of the Justices and to do so in words which might have seemed to Rutledge to echo his own. Herewith, the penultimate paragraph in Frankfurter's concurring opinion in *Sweezy v. New Hampshire*,[50] where he joined his brethren in denying the authority of the state to compel an economics professor at a state university to respond to questions about his wife's and his connections with the Progressive Party:

> To be sure, this is a conclusion based on a judicial judgment in balancing two contending principles—the right of a citizen to political privacy, as protected by the Fourteenth Amendment, and the right of the State to self-protection. And striking the balance implies the exercise of judgment. This is the inescapable judicial task in giving substantive content, legally enforced, to the Due Process Clause, and it is a task ultimately committed to this Court. It must not be an exercise of whim or will. It must be an overriding judgment founded on something much deeper and more justifiable than personal preference. As far as it lies within human limitations, it must be an impersonal judgment. It must rest on fundamental presuppositions rooted in history to which widespread acceptance may fairly be attributed. Such a judgment must be arrived at in a spirit of humility when it counters the judgment of the State's highest court. But, in the end, judgment cannot be escaped—the judgment of this Court.[51]

If, in the free speech setting, Rutledge was commonly aligned with Black, Douglas, and Murphy, with Frankfurter as their principal antagonist, the tables were apt to be turned when the issue was one of establishment of religion. The paradigm case was *Everson*,[52] in which Black—joined by Douglas and Murphy, and also by Vinson and Reed—upheld New Jersey's subvention of bus transportation for students at parochial schools. The opinion was one of Black's least successful efforts, and warranted the sardonic Jackson riposte in dissent:

> In fact, the undertones of the opinion, advocating complete and uncompromising separation of Church from State, seem utterly discordant with its conclusion yielding support to their commingling in educational matters. The case which comes irresistibly to mind as the most fitting precedent is that of Julia who, according to Byron's reports, "whispering 'I will ne'er consent,'—consented."[53]

But it was Rutledge's dissent—massive and penetrating, and building inexorably on Madison's "Memorial and Remonstrance Against Religious Assessments"—which showed the fundamental untenability of the Court's position:

---

50. 354 U.S. 234 (1957).
51. *Id.* at 266-67.
52. Everson v. Board of Educ., 330 U.S. 1 (1947).
53. *Id.* at 19.

Two great drives are constantly in motion to abridge, in the name of education, the complete division of religion and civil authority which our forefathers made. One is to introduce religious education and observances into the public schools. The other, to obtain public funds for the aid and support of various private religious schools. See Johnson, The Legal Status of Church-State Relationships in the United States (1934); Thayer, Religion in Public Education (1947); Note (1941) 50 Yale L.J. 917. In my opinion both avenues were closed by the Constitution. Neither should be opened by this Court. The matter is not one of quantity, to be measured by the amount of money expended. Now as in Madison's day it is one of principle, to keep separate the separate spheres as the First Amendment drew them; to prevent the first experiment upon our liberties; and to keep the question from becoming entangled in corrosive precedents. We should not be less strict to keep strong and untarnished the one side of the shield of religious freedom than we have been of the other.[54]

The work begun by Rutledge in *Everson* in 1947 was carried forward a year later by Frankfurter, concurring in *McCollum*,[55] the first "released time" case. For the decade-and-a-half which followed, it was the historical and constitutional vision of these two Justices that gave such intellectual coherence as there was to judicial discourse in this vexed area. In 1962, Douglas, who in 1947 had agreed with Black in *Everson* and in 1952 had written for the Court in upholding New York's "released time" program in *Zorach v. Clauson*[56] over dissents by Black, Frankfurter, and Jackson, was forced by the first "school prayer" case to return to first principles. The heart of Douglas's concurrence in *Engel v. Vitale*,[57] joining the Court in invalidating the prayer promulgated by the New York Regents for the state's millions of public school children, was this:

My problem today would be uncomplicated but for *Everson v. Board of Education*, which allowed taxpayers' money to be used to pay "the bus fares of parochial school pupils as a part of a general program under which" the fares of pupils attending public and other schools were also paid. The *Everson* case seems in retrospect to be out of line with the First Amendment. Its result is appealing, as it allows aid to be given to needy children. Yet by the same token, public funds could be used to satisfy other needs of children in parochial schools—lunches, books, and tuition being obvious examples. Mr. Justice Rutledge stated in dissent what I think is durable First Amendment philosophy:

"The reasons underlying the Amendment's policy have

---

54. *Id.* at 63.
55. McCollum v. Board of Educ., 333 U.S. 203 (1948). *But cf.* Zorach v. Clauson, 343 U.S. 306 (1952) (in which Frankfurter dissented).
56. 343 U.S. 306 (1952).
57. 370 U.S. 421 (1962).

not vanished with time or diminished in force. Now as when it was adopted the price of religious freedom is double. It is that the church and religion shall live both within and upon that freedom. There cannot be freedom of religion, safeguarded by the state, and intervention by the church or its agencies in the state's domain or dependency on its largesse. Madison's Remonstrance, Par. 6,8. The great condition of religious liberty is that it be maintained free from sustenance, as also from other interferences, by the state. For when it comes to rest upon that secular foundation it vanishes with the resting. *Id.*, Par. 7,8. Public money devoted to payment of religious costs, education or other, brings the quest for more. It brings too the struggle of sect against sect for the larger share or for any. Here one by numbers alone will benefit most, there another. That is precisely the history of societies which have had an established religion and dissident groups. *Id.*, par. 8, 11. It is the very thing Jefferson and Madison experienced and sought to guard against, whether in its blunt or in its more screened forms. *Ibid.* The end of such strife cannot be other than to destroy the cherished liberty. The dominating group will achieve the dominant benefit; or all will embroil the state in their dissensions. *Id.*, Par. 11."[58]

And thus, fifteen years after *Everson* was decided, Rutledge gained a fifth vote.

Vintage jurisprudence, aged in the reports, gains strength over time. In February of this year, the Court of Appeals for the Third Circuit affirmed *per curiam* a district court judgment that the teaching in a public school of an elective course entitled "Science of Creative Intelligence—Transcendental Meditation" breached the First Amendment's establishment clause.[59] In a thoughtful and penetrating concurrence, Judge Adams rejected the argument, which drew heavily on recent writings of Professor Tribe and others, that some teaching might be regarded as "religion" for the purposes of the First Amendment's free exercise clause but not for the purposes of the establishment clause. Said Judge Adams:

Despite the distinguished scholars who advocate this approach, a stronger argument can be made for a unitary definition to prevail for both clauses. This would seem to be the preferable choice for several reasons. First, it is virtually required by the language of the first amendment. As Justice Rutledge put it over thirty years ago:

"Religion" appears only once in the Amendment. But the word governs two prohibitions and governs them alike. It does not have two meanings, one narrow to forbid "an estab-

---

58.   *Id.* at 443-44 (citations omitted).
59.   Malnak v. Yogi, 592 F.2d 197 (3d Cir. 1979).

lishment" and another, much broader, for securing "the free exercise thereof." "Thereof" brings down "religion" with its entire and exact content, no more and no less, from the first into the second guaranty, so that Congress and now the states are as broadly restricted concerning the one as they are regarding the other.[60]

B. Fair Process

Douglas's acknowledgment in 1962 that Rutledge had been right in *Everson* in 1947 was an event of jurisprudential consequence, but not one that had the definable impact of overturning a settled course of decisions. By contrast, Black's acknowledgement in 1961 that Rutledge had been right, twelve years before, in *Wolf v. Colorado*,[61] changed the Constitution.

It will be recalled that *Wolf*, which came before the Court in the 1948 Term, presented two questions. The first was whether the Fourteenth Amendment's due process clause imposed on the states the Fourth Amendment's prohibition on "unreasonable searches and seizures." The second was whether, if the answer to the first question was yes, state courts were required to bar from criminal trials evidence seized in violation of the prohibition, as federal courts are by virtue of the exclusionary rule announced sixty-five years ago in *Weeks v. United States.*[62]

For Black, the applicability to the states of the prohibition on unreasonable searches and seizures was plain, since in *Adamson v. California*,[63] three years before, he had staked out in a monumental dissent the legal-historical position that the Fourteenth Amendment imposed on the states every limitation that the Bill of Rights (amendments one through eight) imposed on the United States. Douglas had subscribed to that dissent. Murphy and Rutledge, dissenting separately in *Adamson*, had accepted the Bill of Rights as the minimum content of Fourteenth Amendment due process, but added the proviso that due process must be expansive enough to cope with degradations not specifically anticipated by the drafters of the Bill of Rights.

So in *Wolf* none of the four *Adamson* dissenters required persuasion on the applicability of the Fourth Amendment to the States. And the other five members of the Court, speaking through Frankfurter, accepted the Fourth Amendment's protection of privacy as "implicit in 'the concept of ordered liberty'," and hence, under *Palko v. Connecticut*,[64] part of the due process of law a state must accord to all within its jurisdiction.

---

60.   *Id.* at 211.
61.   338 U.S. 25 (1949).
62.   232 U.S. 383 (1914).
63.   332 U.S. 46 (1946).
64.   302 U.S. 319, 325 (1938).

But Frankfurter and those who joined his opinion—Vinson, Reed, Jackson, and Burton—could not take the second step of requiring the states to follow *Week's* exclusionary rule: "[W]e . . . hesitate to treat this remedy as an essential ingredient of the right."[65] Black, adhering to his *Adamson* insistence on the equivalence of the Bill of Rights and the first section of the Fourteenth Amendment, nonetheless voted with the majority to affirm the Colorado state court criminal conviction which was based on illegally seized evidence—and this because he agreed "with what appears to be a plain implication of the Court's opinion that the federal exclusionary rule is not a command of the Fourth Amendment but is a judicially created rule of evidence which Congress might negate."[66]

Douglas, Murphy, and Rutledge each filed a dissent. Coming on June 27, 1949, the last day of the 1948 Term, the Murphy and Rutledge dissents were among their last judicial utterances.

Rutledge began his dissent with a sentence in quotation marks: "Wisdom too often never comes, and so one ought not to reject it merely because it comes late." With this introductory flourish, Rutledge welcomed his brethren-of-the-majority's belated recognition that the Fourteenth Amendment prohibited state officials from executing "unreasonable searches and seizures." And in the next breath, he deplored the majority's failure to recognize that the exclusionary rule was the vital corollary of the prohibition without which, as the Court had said in *Weeks*—and Rutledge repeated—"the protection of the Fourth Amendment . . . might as well be stricken from the Constitution."[67]

The initial sentence—"Wisdom too often never comes, and so one ought not to reject it merely because it comes late"—was garnished with appropriate citation in the rough first draft of the Rutledge dissent that one of his law clerks had prepared. The citation was to an opinion dissenting from a *per curiam* opinion in an estate tax case filed five months earlier. The *per curiam* in *Henslee v. Union Planters National Bank*[68] was written by Rutledge and held that the case before the Court was controlled by a prior decision, *Merchants Bank v. Commissioner*,[69] in which Rutledge spoke for the Court and Douglas and Jackson dissented. In *Henslee*, Douglas and Jackson noted their dissent again. And Frankfurter filed a dissenting opinion which ran in its entirety as follows:

Wisdom too often never comes, and so one ought not to reject it merely because it comes late. Since I now realize that I should have joined the dissenters in the *Merchants Bank* case, I shall not compound error by pushing that decision still farther. I would af-

---

65. 338 U.S. at 29.
66. 338 U.S. at 39-40.
67. 232 U.S. at 393.
68. 335 U.S. 595 (1949).
69. 320 U.S. 256 (1943).

firm the judgment, substantially for the reasons given below.[70]
When Rutledge looked at the draft *Wolf* dissent submitted by his law
clerk, he said of the first sentence, "We can't do that to Felix." But the
remedy was not, as the law clerk had supposed, to excise the sentence
taken without a warrant from Frankfurter's earlier dissent; the remedy
was to leave the purloined sentence, clad in quotation marks but with
the citation excised, thereby covering up the theft and frustrating archi-
vists and annotators of constitutional doctrine to the last syllable of
recorded time.

But Rutledge's concerns in writing the *Wolf* dissent were not ar-
chival. They were personal: not needlessly to offend a cherished friend
and colleague. And they were also institutional: to write what must be
written to enlarge the possibility that on another day the majority of the
Justices might act upon a wisdom arrived at belatedly. And at the
same time Rutledge intended to protect the Constitution from future
assaults which he felt were invited both by Frankfurter's opinion for
the Court and by Black's concurrence:

> I also reject any intimation that Congress could validly enact
> legislation permitting the introduction in federal courts of evi-
> dence seized in violation of the Fourth Amendment. I had
> thought that issue settled by this Court's invalidation on dual
> grounds, in *Boyd v. United States*, of a federal statute which in
> effect required the production of evidence thought probative by
> Government counsel—the Court there holding the statute to be
> "obnoxious to the prohibition of the Fourth Amendment of the
> Constitution, as well as of the Fifth."[71]

Wolf remained the law until the closing days of the 1960 Term,
when the Court decided *Mapp v. Ohio*.[72] A plurality of four, speaking
through Justice Clark (Rutledge's successor), jettisoned *Wolf* and announced that the *Weeks* exclusionary rule henceforth applied to the
states. Those who subscribed to Clark's opinion were Douglas, who
had dissented in *Wolf*, and two others who, like Clark, had come to the
Court after *Wolf* was decided, Chief Justice Warren and Justice Brennan. The fifth vote to overturn *Wolf* was that of Black. The senior
Justice was at pains to explain his change of mind:

> Reflection on the problem . . . in the light of cases coming before
> the Court since *Wolf*, has led me to conclude that when the Fourth
> Amendment's ban against unreasonable searches and seizures is
> considered together with the Fifth Amendment's ban against com-
> pelled self-incrimination, a constitutional basis emerges which not
> only justifies but actually requires the exclusionary rule.
>
> The close interrelationship between the Fourth and Fifth
> Amendments, as they apply to this problem, has long been recog-

---

70. 335 U.S. at 600 (citations omitted).
71. 338 U.S. at 48 (citations omitted).
72. 367 U.S. 643 (1961).

nized and, indeed, was expressly made the ground for this Court's holding in *Boyd v. United States*. There the Court fully discussed this relationship and declared itself "unable to perceive that the seizure of a man's private books and papers to be used in evidence against him is substantially different from compelling him to be a witness against himself." It was upon this ground that Mr. Justice Rutledge largely relied in his dissenting opinion in the *Wolf* case. And, although I rejected the argument at that time, its force has, for me at least, become compelling with the more thorough under-standing of the problem brought on by recent cases.[73]

And thus it came about that Rutledge's commitment to fair proc-ess—protecting the privacy of home and office against lawless entry—was finally vindicated. Black had at long last been persuaded by the dissenting wisdom of his old friend, and persuaded too that "one ought not to reject [wisdom] merely because it comes late."[74]

C. *Political Questions and "The Politics of the People"*

"It is hostile to a democratic system to involve the judiciary in the politics of the people. And it is not less pernicious if such judicial inter-vention in an essentially political contest be dressed up in the abstract phrases of the law." So Frankfurter said for the Court in 1946, in *Cole-grove v. Green*,[75] rejecting an attempt to get a declaration of the uncon-stitutionality of dramatic differences in population between various Congressional districts in Illinois. For a decade and a half, *Colegrove* was widely understood to mean that a law suit challenging legislative malapportionment was beyond the compass of federal courts. Some-times Frankfurter's opinion was read as going to subject matter juris-diction, sometimes to justiciability, and sometimes to the merits of the claim that malapportionment offended the equal protection clause.[76] But, whichever reading was accepted, the result was the same: federal court litigation of this genre was foreclosed. Until *Baker v. Carr*.[77]

In *Baker v. Carr*, Justice Brennan led the Court, over Frank-furter's dissent,[78] to declare that the federal judicial power did extend to controversies of the kind apparently foreclosed by *Colegrove*. In reaching this result, Brennan painstakingly reconstructed what had ac-tually been decided in *Colegrove*: Only seven Justices had participated. Frankfurter, delivering the opinion of the Court, in fact had spoken only for himself and Reed and Burton. Black, joined by Douglas and Murphy, had vigorously dissented: in the dissenters' view, there was

---

73. *Id.* at 622 (citations omitted).
74. *See generally* Kamisar, *The exclusionary rule in historical perspective: the struggle to make the Fourth Amendment more than 'an empty blessing,'* 62 JUD. 337 (1979).
75. 328 U.S. 549, 553-54 (1946).
76. See South v. Peters, 339 U.S. 276 (1950). *Cf.* MacDougall v. Green, 335 U.S. 281 (1948).
77. 369 U.S. 186 (1962).
78. In which Justice Harlan joined; Harlan also filed a dissent in which Frankfurter joined.

jurisdiction, justiciability, and a straightforward cause of action under the equal protection clause. The decisive vote, and voice, was Rutledge's: the Court had authority to entertain the complaint; but the complaint, filed in the eleventh hour before a Congressional election, was wanting in equity.[79] And so, as Brennan perceived, *Colegrove*, rightly parsed, was authority *for* the Court's decision in *Baker v. Carr* that federal courts have authority and competence to entertain law suits challenging legislative malapportionment.

In Chief Justice Warren's view, his Brother Brennan's decision in *Baker v. Carr* was the most important decision rendered in Warren's Chief Justiceship. If one may, with all respect, offer the dissenting view that Warren's own decision in *Brown v. Board of Education* was of even greater consequence, *Baker v. Carr* was, nonetheless, a constitutional pronouncement of fundamental importance: "If the Court in *Baker v. Carr* had affirmed dismissal of the complaint, the Court would in effect have declared that the only power to arrest the pervasive systemic disorder of malapportionment lay in the hands of those who [throve] upon the malady. And this would have been an ominous declaration, for the malady [was] a grave one . . . . [W]hat [was] at stake [was] the central integrity of the governmental mechanisms the American people adopted as the means of carrying out the American experiment."[80]

---

79. *Accord*, Rutledge, J. concurring in MacDougall v. Green, 335 U.S. 1 (1948).

80. Pollak, *Judicial Power and "The Politics of the People,"* 72 YALE L.J. 81, 88 (1962). *Compare* Bickel, *The Durability of Colegrove v. Green,* 72 YALE L.J. 39 (1962). In retrospect, it is of interest to recall the view of *Colegrove v. Green* taken by the three-judge district court, in explanation of its order of dismissal, 64 F. Supp. 632, 633-35 (N.D. Ill. 1946):

Specifically the plaintiffs' grievance lies in the failure of the State of Illinois to so apportion the congressional districts as to give equality of voting power to the citizens of said state. It is alleged, and if not admitted, not denied, for example, that in one district a voter has the voting strength of eight voters in another district. Petitioners base their argument on the sound and elementary proposition that all the electors should have an equal voice and that none should be disfranchised. . . . Not only has the State of Illinois failed to redistrict the state according to population after the last census, but it has failed to do so for over forty years. Its action is apparently deliberate and defiant of both Federal and State Government and the principles upon which they are founded.

Defendants do not defend this action. Their defense is that this gross misrepresentation of Illinois citizens is due to certain legislators who, to retain political strength greater than they are entitled to, or would be entitled to, if equality in representation occurred, refuse to act or to grant relief to this existing disgraceful situation in Illinois.

. . . .

Our study of the opinion of the Supreme Court in the case of Wood v. Broom, 287 U.S. 1, 6, 53 S.Ct. 1, 77 L.Ed. 131, has resulted in our reaching a conclusion contrary to that which we would have reached but for that decision. We are an inferior court. We are bound by the decision of the Supreme Court, even though we do not agree with the decision or the reasons which support it. We have been unable to distinguish this case and as members of an inferior court, we must follow it. Only the Supreme Court can overrule that decision.

Although that decision was by a five to four vote of the members of the Supreme Court, the opinion of the four dissenters gives no comfort to the plaintiffs. While they would not dispose of the case on the ground that the Act of Congress there under consideration did not call for equality in population and therefore is not a necessary requisite to a valid apportionment, they are of the opinion that the appeal should be dismissed for want of equity. On the ground of lack of equity the four dissenting judges spoke before the enactment of the Declaratory Judgments Act. It in no way gave consideration to the Enforcement Act of 1870, 16 Stat. 140, or of the rights that arose thereunder. We might assume that the grounds for af-

III.

Rutledge was not doctrinaire. He was concerned with the practicalities of the law's processes—with making legal institutions effective to promote the reasonable expectations, the felt sense of worth, and the mutual respect of his fellow citizens. Law had to make sense to "the man in the street," the critic to whom Edgerton had deferred in his concurrence in Rutledge's holding that the Louisville Cement Company, through its Maryland resident agent Lovewell, sold enough Brixment in the District of Columbia to be suable there.[81] Prescribed legal remedies had to fulfill their promises—as, for example, Illinois's postconviction remedies signally failed to do until Rutledge used his remorseless intelligence to pierce the *coram nobis* curtain.[82]

The most thoughtful critique of Rutledge's judging was written a quarter of a century ago by a one-time Rutledge law clerk then in practice, who has since embarked in his own right on a judicial career which gives promise of enduring distinction—John Paul Stevens. In assessing the methodology of the teacher-turned-judge, Stevens made an important point about Rutledge's opinions. The length—the sometimes over-length—of Rutledge's opinions was a function of his insistence that judges should explain their decisions with precision and in detail in order fully to illuminate, for the benefit of all legitimately in-

---

firmance set forth in the dissenting opinion were rejected by the majority opinion, but we can hardly assume that the law as announced by the majority is not the law governing us.

The majority view holds squarely that Sec. 3, of the Act of August 8, 1911, 2 U.S.C.A. § 3, which required districts to be of contiguous and compact territory and contain as nearly as practical an equal number of inhabitants, is not effective today. Subsequent enactments by implication repealed Sec. 3 of the Act of 1911 and they do not contain any similar provision respecting equality in population of the districts.

In the absence of this decision we would assume that such requirement arose necessarily from the Constitution. Inequality in population of the districts is so contrary to the spirit of the Government and of the Constitution that we would assume it was a required condition to representation in the Congress of the United States. There is little or no difference between an unequal voice in election of members to Congress and a denial altogether of participation in the election of Congressmen. It is at most a matter of degree. The right to vote, however, is not one of those boasted guarantees of the Constitution, if it appears that one voter has eight times as many votes as another.

If the district defined by the state legislature provides that a Congressman shall be elected in one district with eight times as many citizens as in another district, we fail to see how they could not provide that such district should not have representation at all. Such is the inevitable result of a doctrine which denies equality as a basis for congressional representation.

However, we think it is our plain, clear duty to follow the decision of the Supreme Court in this case.

. . . .

This disposition of the pending suit does not end the plain obligation of the Illinois legislature to perform its duty. Justice demands that it act. As one of the greatest of the 48 commonwealths that comprise the Union, she can not afford to become a leader in a new rebellion. A defiance based on the alleged right to discriminate between voters or between districts would not be a sound basis to start another rebellion.

. . . .

It follows from what has been said that plaintiffs' suit must be and is hereby dismissed.

81. *See* text accompanying notes 10-14 *supra.*
82. *See* Marino v. Ragen, 332 U.S. 561, 563 (1947).

terested, the judicial perception of the problems which had given rise to litigation.[83] Rutledge recognized that lawyers, with clients to counsel and other litigation to initiate or defend against, had clear entitlements to learn what a court was up to. So did judges of other courts. And so, too, did the teachers and students of law who, in the pages of the law reviews, exercise ultimate appellate power. And so, most emphatically, did ordinary citizens—as the law clerks who served the Justice in his last year learned when the Justice said, after lengthy discussion of their proposed disposition of a pending case: "I understand your view of the matter. But I don't know how to say it in a way that would be understood by a man who owns a corner drug store."[84]

Of the opinions he wrote for the Court during his last year, Rutledge may well have felt that *F.C.C. v. WJR, The Goodwill Station*[85] was one of the least consequential. And so, in most of the respects by which Supreme Court opinions are graded, it was. And yet, in its provenance and execution, the opinion in important ways exemplifies those habits of wisdom which made this Justice a judge: the awareness that due process is both fair and sensible process; the commitment fully to carry out the judge's duty to listen with care and to respond with equal care in the endless seminar with the bar, litigants, and the larger American community, which is the stuff of judging; and the respect owed all other participants in the judicial process, including fellow judges.

F.C.C. v. WJR, The Goodwill Station came to the Supreme Court from the Court of Appeals for the District of Columbia, where Rutledge had served his four years' apprenticeship. The central question before the Court of Appeals was whether the Federal Communications Commission had erred in denying the petition of WJR, a Detroit radio station, to reconsider the FCC grant of a construction permit to build a new broadcast station in Tarboro, North Carolina. WJR alleged that the new station, which was to operate on the same assigned frequency as WJR's, would interfere with WJR's reception. The Commission, in declining to reconsider the grant of the construction permit, ruled that WJR was seeking protection from interference in a far wider radius (that is, for a far weaker signal) than was the standard of protection recognized by the Commission as a normal incident of a broadcast license of the category to which WJR's license belonged.

The case was argued before a panel of the Court of Appeals in March of 1947, and reargued before the full bench in June. In October of 1948, the Court of Appeals delivered its judgment remanding the

---

83. Stevens, *Mr. Justice Rutledge* in MR. JUSTICE 177, 181-83 (A. Dunham & P. Kurland eds. 1958).

84. One of the two opinions Rutledge handed down for the Court on June 27, 1949 (the last day of his last year) was S.E.C. v. Central-Illinois Corp., 338 U.S. 96 (1949). In announcing the decision, Rutledge summarized the case and its disposition, apologized for the length of the opinion, and specially requested that no one not a specialist in securities law try to read the opinion.

85. 337 U.S. 265 (1949).

case to the Commission for a hearing on WJR's petition for reconsideration of the Tarboro construction permit. The opinion for the three-judge majority was delivered by Justice Stephens, who was soon to become Chief Justice in succession to Chief Justice Groner. A dissent was filed by Justice Prettyman; Edgerton joined the Prettyman dissent.

Stephens's majority opinion did not say that the Commission was wrong as a matter of law in deciding that WJR had not alleged potential interference within a contour of signal strength recognized by the Commission as legally protected under WJR's license. That, according to the majority opinion, was up to the Commission to determine, in the first instance, in the hearing on the petition for reconsideration that the Commission was instructed to conduct. The core of Stephens's decision was that the Commission's rejection of WJR's petition for reconsideration was constitutionally flawed, for the reason that WJR was not accorded an opportunity to present *oral argument* in support of its petition:

> It is the view of the majority that due process of law, as guaranteed by the Fifth Amendment, requires a hearing, including an opportunity to make oral argument, on every question of law raised before a judicial or quasi-judicial tribunal, including questions raised by demurrer or as if on demurrer, except such questions of law as may be involved in interlocutory orders such as orders for the stay of proceedings *pendente lite*, for temporary injunctions and the like. A ruling upon a demurrer is obviously not interlocutory for if the demurrer is sustained the pleader's cause (or defense) is dismissed upon the merits; if the demurrer is overruled, the opposite party is put to a trial and the machinery of the tribunal is set in motion.[86]

What was the authority for this constitutional rule?

> It has been so long taken for granted by courts that the due process clause guarantee of hearing before decision includes hearing upon questions of law as well as upon questions of fact, and it has been so long taken for granted that hearings on questions of law include hearings on such questions arising under demurrers, and the practice of courts to grant such hearings has been of such long standing, that there is little authority concerning the requirements of due process in these respects. There has been no need for litigants to obtain rulings in support of the right of hearing on questions of law when opportunity to be heard on such questions has not been denied.[87]

The constitutional rule promulgated by Stephens was not only immense in its implication for the administrative process, but it bade fair to revolutionize the judicial process as well. It would appear that, under the iron sway of Stephens's due process clause, no trial court

---

86. WJR, The Goodwill Station, Inc. v. FCC, 174 F.2d 226, 233 (D.C. Cir. 1948).
87. *Id.*

could safely rule on a motion to dismiss, or a motion for summary judgment, without hearing oral argument. And, very likely, all appellate courts, including the Supreme Court, would have to hear arguments on all motions to dismiss appeals, or to deny *certiorari* petitions, for lack of jurisdiction. Wherefore, it was hardly surprising that the Federal Communications Commission sought, and the Supreme Court granted, *certiorari* to review the judgment of the Court of Appeals. Nor is it surprising that the Supreme Court reversed. What may occasion surprise is that the Justice writing for the Court felt impelled to spend nineteen pages of the United States Reports explaining the decision to reverse.

But the elaborateness of the Court's opinion is easily accounted for: *WJR*, having been decided in the Court of Appeals in October of 1948, was argued in the Supreme Court on April 22, 1949. Right after the Justices left the bench following the argument, Rutledge came into the room in his chambers which housed his two law clerks: "You probably noticed the whispering among the brethren. Most of them wanted to reverse from the bench, but Fred"—referring to Chief Justice Vinson—"and I wouldn't let them do that. You know, Fred and I served with Harold Stephens on the Court of Appeals; and he and I know him better than the other fellows do. Harold would have been very upset, after all the work he did, if this Court had summarily reversed. So Fred asked me to write an opinion, letting Harold down as gently as possible, and so of course I said I would."

When the law clerk to whom the case was assigned produced a draft nine pages in length, Rutledge opined that nine pages was far more than he had bargained for and he suggested that the law clerk had been too conscientious in trying to make Stephens's arguments seem substantial. But Rutledge said he would undertake to abbreviate the opinion in his own re-draft. The next morning, he reappeared in his clerks' room. A little sheepish, he handed over a revised draft double the length of the original. That is the opinion which appears in volume 337 of the United States Reports.

In retrospect, one can see that the issue presented in *WJR* was, for Rutledge, not altogether new. He had covered what was superficially (but not actually) similar ground before when, seven years earlier, Stephens and Vinson had properly out-voted him in *Rosier*, the case involving repeated applications for release from St. Elizabeth's Hospital.[88] In devoting so much time and thought and craftsmanship to his opinion in *WJR*, Rutledge felt duty bound to the solemn constitutional claims made and rejected; duty bound to his old court and his former colleagues there; duty bound to his new Court, and his new colleagues—the institution and the friendships he was so soon to leave; and, beyond all these, duty bound to the sense of process which

---

88. *See* text accompanying note 15 *supra*.

animated Stephens's massively wrong-headed but infinitely right-hearted decision.

IV.

Rutledge joined the majority of the Supreme Court in one decision which, it now seems widely agreed, falls outside the constitutional pale. That decision was *Korematsu v. United States*,[89] sustaining the 1942 mandate of the government of the United States that Americans of Japanese ancestry leave their west coast homes and report for incarceration in the interior. One may try to deflect criticism from Rutledge by pointing out that Black wrote the Court's opinion, and that Stone, Frankfurter, and Douglas joined him, as did Reed. But all it signifies is the very sobering fact that in this historic instance every one of the major figures on the Court was woefully misguided on an issue of paramount constitutional importance. Moreover, they had no ground for complaint that the issues were not fully joined. Three of the Justices—Roberts, Murphy, and Jackson—had the clarity of vision to recognize the government's trespass on the Constitution for what it was, and to dissent. *Korematsu* illustrated a dictum supplied by Rutledge himself in an essay written in 1944, while *Korematsu* was before the Court (but in which essay he did not mention that case or, indeed, any case by name). In a foreword to *A Symposium on Constitutional Rights in Wartime*, Rutledge wrote, "War is a contradiction of all that democracy implies."[90]

If that dictum needed more case authority after *Korematsu*, further authority was supplied two years later when the Court upheld the death sentence that an allied military tribunal visited on General Yamashita, Chief of Japanese forces in the Phillipines, after the Japanese surrender.[91] Yamashita had been found guilty of multiple atrocities, against American and allied troops, committed by Japanese army units all of whom were nominally, but many not effectively, under Yamashita's eroding command in the Phillipines.

From the judgment and opinion declining to interfere with Yamashita's conviction, Murphy and Rutledge each dissented. Rutledge's dissent was forty pages of overwhelming demonstration that the procedures (if that euphemism may be permitted) followed by the military tribunal were not consonant with American constitutional norms governing civil or military tribunals, or with the norms of international law. In this instance, the power of Rutledge's analysis and conviction was heightened by an unaccustomed eloquence, and so his *Yamashita* opinion ranks as one of the major judicial statements of our time, the

---

89.   323 U.S. 214 (1944).

90.   Rutledge, *A Symposium on Constitutional Rights in Wartime, Foreword*, 29 IOWA L. REV. 379 (1944).

91.   *In re Yamashita*, 327 U.S. 1 (1945).

more so because it asks fundamental questions not only about our own legal order but also about the role our nation and its legal institutions can play in framing a democratic legal order for the transnational community:

More is at stake than General Yamashita's fate. There could be no possible sympathy for him if he is guilty of the atrocities for which his death is sought. But there can be and should be justice administered according to law. In this stage of war's aftermath it is too early for Lincoln's great spirit, best lighted in the Second Inaugural, to have wide hold for the treatment of foes. It is not too early, it is never too early, for the nation steadfastly to follow its great constitutional traditions, none older or more universally protective against unbridled power than due process of law in the trial and punishment of men, that is, of all men, whether citizens, aliens, alien enemies or enemy belligerents. It can become too late.

This long-held attachment marks the great divide between our enemies and ourselves. Theirs was a philosphy of universal force. Ours is one of universal law, albeit imperfectly made flesh of our system and so dwelling among us. Every departure weakens the tradition, whether it touches the high or the low, the powerful or the weak, the triumphant or the conquered. If we need not or cannot be magnanimous, we can keep our own law on the plane from which it has not descended hitherto and to which the defeated foes never rose.

. . . .

We are on strange ground. Precedent is not all-controlling in law. There must be room for growth, since every precedent has an origin. But it is the essence of our tradition for judges, when they stand at the end of the marked way, to go forward with caution keeping sight, so far as they are able, upon the great landmarks left behind and the direction they point ahead. If, as may be hoped, we are now to enter upon a new era of law in the world, it becomes more important than ever before for the nations creating that system to observe their greatest traditions of administering justice, including this one, both in their own judging and in their new creation.[92]

V.

Bob-Lo Excursion Co. v. Michigan,[93] had all the ear-marks of a case fabricated for a moot court argument. Bob-Lo Excursion Company, a Michigan corporation, owned and operated as an amusement park virtually all of Bois Blanc Island, a small island near the mouth of the Detroit River, fifteen miles from Detroit. Bob-Lo also owned and

---

92. *Id.* at 41-43.
93. 333 U.S. 28 (1947).

operated the two excursion steamboats which brought patrons of the amusement park from Detroit directly to the island and back again. These steamboats were the only mode of access to Bois Blanc, notwithstanding that the island happens to be Canadian territory (part of Ontario).

On June 21, 1945, a teacher at Detroit's Commerce High School brought thirteen pupils to Bob-Lo's Detroit dock to embark on a long-planned class outing. Tickets were purchased, the group boarded, and then, just before departure, Bob-Lo's Assistant General Manager Devereaux, assisted by a steward, directed Sarah Elizabeth Ray to leave the boat. Devereaux later testified that, "The defendant adopted the policy of excluding so-called 'zoot-suiters,' the rowdyish, the rough and the boisterous and it also adopted the policy of excluding colored." Sarah Elizabeth Ray had to stay behind because she was black.

Bob-Lo was thereupon prosecuted in the Recorder's Court of Detroit for violation of Section 146 of Michigan's Civil Rights Act, which made it a misdemeanor to deny "full and equal accommodations" in, *inter alia*, "public conveyances on land and water." On conviction, Bob-Lo was sentenced to the minimum statutory punishment—a twenty-five dollar fine. The judgment was affirmed by the Michigan Supreme Court.

From the judgment of affirmance, Bob-Lo, in the fall of 1947, appealed to the United States Supreme Court. Appellant argued that Michigan's civil rights act—a conventional public accommodations statute of the type familiar for decades and infrequently enforced across the northern tier of states—was, as applied to Bob-Lo, a burden on a subject matter committed by the Constitution to the regulatory authority of Congress: namely, "commerce . . . . with foreign nations." This claim might well have been deemed frivolous but for the fact that only a year before the Court, in *Morgan v. Virginia*,[94] had invalidated a Virginia statute requiring racial segregation on common carriers, on the ground that, as applied to Mrs. Morgan who was travelling from Gloucester County, Virginia, to Baltimore, it burdened "commerce . . . . among the several states." The Virginia Jim Crow statute was, of course, the obverse of the Michigan public accommodations statute; but, nonetheless, the ruling in *Morgan* arguably had a strong claim on the Court's attention in *Bob-Lo Excursion Co. v. Michigan*; the reason being that the *Morgan* opinion took as controlling precedent the Court's 1875 decision in *Hall v. DeCuir*[95] invalidating, on burden-on-commerce grounds, the application of a public accommodations statute enacted by Louisiana's reconstruction legislature to a riverboat headed up the Mississippi.

The decision of the Michigan Supreme Court upholding Bob-Lo's

---

94.   328 U.S. 373 (1946).
95.   95 U.S. 485 (1875).

twenty-five dollar fine was affirmed by the United States Supreme
Court by a vote of seven-to-two. Jackson's dissent, in which Vinson
joined, leaned heavily on *Morgan* and *Hall v. DeCuir*:

> The sphere of a state's power has not been thought to expand or
> contract because of the policy embodied in a particular regulation
> . . . . [T]he constitutional principles which have been so apparent
> to the Court that it would not permit local policies to burden na-
> tional commerce, are even more obvious in relation to foreign
> commerce.[96]

Rutledge wrote for the Court in rejecting Bob-Lo's appeal. He
found neither *Morgan* nor *Hall v. DeCuir* a fruitful analogue:

> [Neither] of those decisions is comparable in its facts, whether in
> the degree of localization of the commerce involved; in the attenu-
> ating effects, if any, upon the commerce with foreign nations and
> among the several states likely to be produced by applying the
> state regulation; or in any actual probability of conflicting regula-
> tions by different sovereignties. [Neither] involved so completely
> and locally insulated a segment of foreign or interstate commerce
> . . . . And in [neither] was a complete exclusion from passage
> made . . . . [Moreover,] there is no national interest which over-
> rides the interest of Michigan to forbid the type of discrimination
> practiced here.[97]

Suffusing Rutledge's opinion was a nonconceptual, strongly pragmatic approach to the commerce clause which had found extended expression in *A Declaration of Legal Faith*—a series of lectures in which
Rutledge explored the commerce cases from Marshall's time to the
New Deal.[98] For Rutledge, the Court's development of commerce doctrine was what had chiefly given structure to American federalism, an
oscillation of authority between state and nation, which always recognized the preeminence of national power, but equally understood the
liberating values of state and local initiatives which would not in fact
interfere with or compromise the effectuations of national purposes.

When Rutledge, in *Bob-Lo Excursion Co. v. Michigan*, distinguished *Morgan*, he gave no intimation that *Morgan* was not on its
own facts a proper exposition of the applicable constitutional doctrine.
But one who turns back to volume 328 of the United States Reports
will learn that, although Rutledge agreed with the Court's judgment in
Morgan, he did not agree with Reed's opinion for the Court. Page 386
of volume 328 of the United States Reports discloses, without elaboration, that "Mr. Justice Rutledge concurs in the result."

It is not unreasonable to speculate that Rutledge's laconic concurrence was a constitutional utterance of, ultimately, the first magnitude:
On oral argument, Mrs. Morgan's appeal had been presented by Wil-

---

96.   333 U.S. at 43.
97.   *Id.* at 39-40.
98.   W. RUTLEDGE, A DECLARATION OF LEGAL FAITH (1947).

liam H. Hastie and Thurgood Marshall. Rutledge had asked Hastie whether the principal ground for challenging Virginia's Jim Crow statute was not the commerce clause but rather the equal protection clause. In reply, Hastie had said that he and Mr. Marshall were not making an equal protection argument on Mrs. Morgan's behalf, and then added that he and his co-counsel would return to the Court with a case making that argument in due course.

Rutledge did not live to participate in *Brown v. Board of Education*.[99] But it did so happen that a few days after the regular appellate argument calendar for Rutledge's last Court term was completed, Rutledge served on a special appellate panel which considered—but did not determine—the "separate but equal" questions ultimately resolved in *Brown* and its *sequelae*. On May 2, 1949, Rutledge sat on a three-judge panel reviewing the decision of the California Supreme Court in *Perez v. Sharp*,[100] in which a divided majority had struck down, on various constitutional grounds, California's anti-miscegenation law. The panel on which Rutledge sat was the Harlan Fiske Stone Supreme Moot Court of Columbia Law School. Rutledge prepared to hear the argument with the same care which had marked his preparation for ten years on the Court of Appeals and on the Supreme Court. A law clerk produced the customary bench memorandum complete with a recommended disposition, notwithstanding that Rutledge and his two fellow judges were not, of course, to rule on the momentous issues student counsel were to argue. Those who heard and saw Rutledge that May evening in the handsome Assembly Room at the Bar Association of the City of New York came away from the argument not privy to his views on the merits; but they must have been deeply aware that they had been privileged to hear and see a great judge in action. They would also have sensed that Rutledge was a generous and genuinely humble person, whose first approach to all whom he encountered was the path of acceptance and friendship. They would have seen this in his attitude towards counsel. And they would have seen this in his attitude towards his colleagues—as, for example, his insistence that Chief Judge Loughran of the New York Court of Appeals must preside at a moot court held in his own jurisdiction. The instinctive gesture was vintage Rutledge—an elixir compounded in equal measure of American federalism and American equality.

---

99. 347 U.S. 482. And Hastie, having been named to the Third Circuit by President Truman in 1949, did not have the opportunity to join Marshall in making, in *Brown*, the equal protection argument adumbrated in his colloquy with Rutledge.

In dissents, Rutledge had occasion to speak powerfully and cogently about governmentally ordained classifications which explicitly, or by highly probable implication, drew racial lines. *Compare* Fisher v. Hurst, 333 U.S. 147, 151 (1948), *with* Kotch v. Board of River Port Pilot Comm'rs, 330 U.S. 552, 564 (1947). With respect to gender-based classifications, see Goesaert v. Cleary, 335 U.S. 464, 467 (1948).

100. 32 Cal. 2d 711, 198 P.2d 17 (1948).

VI.

These are the elements which, in combination, yield a proper assessment of Wiley Blount Rutledge. That proper assessment was one made by his fellow dean and fellow judge, Charles E. Clark, when he spoke at the Justice's memorial proceedings. Judge Clark spoke of the Justice's

> sensitivity to moral values which . . . . [became] the very stuff from which came his greatness as a judge and his nobility as a human being . . . . I regard him as one of the most consistent exemplifiers of a way of life, of a belief in morality and character, of any of the Justices who have ever served upon the court. That is certainly high tribute; I make it deliberately because I think it not only amply deserved, but one which history will freely yield.[101]

---

101. *In Memory of Wiley Blount Rutledge*, Proceedings of the Bar and Officers of the Supreme Court of the United States, April 10, 1951, at 30.